SOUTH AFRICAN

WINE

A CELEBRATION

SOUTH AFRICAN

WINE

A CELEBRATION

WENDY TOERIEN

PHOTOGRAPHY BY
SHAEN ADEY AND RYNO

STRUIK

Struik Publishers (Pty) Ltd
(a member of Struik New Holland
Publishing (Pty) Ltd)
Cornelis Struik House
80 McKenzie Street
Cape Town
8001

Reg No.: 54/00965/07

First published in 1999

10 9 8 7 6 5 4 3 2 1

Copyright © in text: Wendy Toerien
Copyright © in photographs: As credited
Copyright © in maps: Struik Image
Library/Jiggs Snaddon

ISBN 1 86872 297 X

PROJECT MANAGER: Linda de Villiers
DESIGNER: Petal Palmer
EDITOR: Gail Jennings
PHOTOGRAPHERS: Ryno and Shaen Adey
STYLIST: Sylvie Hurford
ILLUSTRATOR: Jiggs Snaddon
DESIGN ASSISTANT: Matthew Ibbotson
PROOFREADER: Sean Fraser
INDEXER: Gail Jennings

Reproduction by Hirt & Carter Cape (Pty) Ltd
Printed and bound by Tien Wah Press (Pte) Ltd,
Singapore

Photographic Credits
© ABPL/Roger de la Harpe: pp 72/73;
© Arthur Elliott Collection, Cape Archives:
pp 9, 10, 16; © Cape Archives: pp 13.
© MuseuMAfricA: pp 6, 14/15; © Alain
Proust: cover; © Struik Image Library/Shaen
Adey: pp 7, 8, 11, 12, 17, 18 , 23–40, 41
(bottom), 42/43, 45–48, 50, 52–55, 57
(top), 58, 61, 62, 64–70, 74, 75, 76 (top),
77, 78, 80/81, 82–88, 92–104, 106,
109–112, 115, 116, 118, 119, 121, 122,
136; © Struik Image Library/Ryno: pp 1, 2,
20, 21, 41 (top), 44, 49, 51, 56, 60, 63,
71, 76 (bottom), 79, 89, 90, 105, 108,
113, 114, 117, 120, 124–135, 138–153.

Acknowledgements
The author wishes to thank two gentlemen
of wine, Dave Hughes and the late Simon
Rappoport, for taking a novice wine writer
through her first sips and spits at those early
wine tastings. The photographers and stylist
thank everyone who was involved in this
project for their assistance, in particular
Enoteca Wine Merchants, Banks Shop
and Gift Warehouse.

C O N T E N T S

INTRODUCTION

BEFORE YOU READ ANOTHER WORD, put down this book and pour yourself a glass of wine... By the time you reach the directory – many glasses, and even more wines later – you will not only have read a book but you may have been tempted to start reading wines, too. And next time, you will pour yourself not a glass of wine but a glass of Sauvignon Blanc, or Merlot, or that one estate's particular red blend of Cabernet Sauvignon and Shiraz that presented you with a nosegay of mint, violets, cinnamon and green pepper and a mouthful of juicy blackcurrant fruit, sweet vanilla and spice. And you thought wine was just grape juice with some alcohol added to make hooligans happy?

This book is about Cape wine. For our Cabernet tastes different to that of Bordeaux, our Chardonnays are nothing like white Burgundy, and you will not find a Loire wine among our Chenin Blancs. Our Mediterranean climate, the Table Mountain sandstone and Malmesbury shale soils, the southeast wind and the way the earth's crust pushed up the Cape Folded Mountains millennia ago all create what is known as the terroir, the growing environment that makes the vines ripen their fruit in

their own peculiar ways. The challenge for the wine-maker is to capture that definitive Cape character. And the enjoyment for the wine lover is in weighing up the many attempts.

From the time those first cuttings arrived in the Cape, in the mid-17th century, wine became more than a healer for scurvy-ridden sailors; it became a sign of civilisation and aspiration among the struggling European settlers on the edge of the Dark Continent that was Africa unknown. Wine has been at the heart of South African culture ever since.

Of all drinks that have shared a place with grain alcohol at our tables since ancient times, wine has been regarded as the finest lubricant of social intercourse, probably in no small part due to the complexity and refinement of its provenance and expression. But this does not deter the simplest of palates from its enjoyment, because it is fresh and tasty and jolly fine with food, as well as being slightly alcoholic.

If ever wine has failed, it has been due largely to lack of appreciation. It is worthy of celebration.

ABOVE: WINE IS THE STUFF
OF LEGEND, REGARDED AS THE
NECTAR OF THE GODS AND
VISUALLY REPRESENTED BY
THIS SCENE OF BOUNTY ON
A MARBLE URN OUTSIDE THE
VERGELEGEN MANOR HOUSE.

PREVIOUS PAGE, LEFT: THE
GRACIOUS LIFE AT 18TH-
CENTURY GROOT CONSTANTIA.
HERE JB CLOETE ESQ WINED
AND DINED HIS GUESTS WITH
THE FARM'S WINE — WHILE HE
SIPPED FINE FRENCH CLARET!

PREVIOUS PAGE, RIGHT:
JOY IN THE HARVEST. THIS
CHERUBIC SCENE IS SCULPTED
INTO A WALL AT TWEE JONGE
GEZELLEN, TULBAGH.

LOOKING BACK OVER 350 YEARS OF CAPE WINE

The history of Cape wine is as old as that of Western civilisation at the tip of Africa. The first vine cuttings arrived in the Cape Colony in 1654, just two years after Jan van Riebeeck arrived, seconded by the Dutch East India Company to set up a victualling station for voyagers between Holland and its trading posts in the Dutch East Indies. The cuttings were sourced from France, Germany, Spain and Bohemia (now the divided Czechoslovakia). What they were, nobody knows for sure.

FIRST ARRIVALS

The first vintage, crushed in 1659, is written up as including French and Muscadel grapes and Spanish Hanepoot. Van Riebeeck also referred in his records to 'Spaanse druyfen' (Spanish grape). Hanepoot was later to be identified as Muscat d'Alexandrie, one of the most ancient of vines and thought to hail from the North African city of the same name; it was probably sourced in Spain, which has the largest plantings of this variety in the world. 'Spaanse druyfen' may have been Palomino, Spain's sherry variety, which is one of the Cape's oldest-known grapes. Its traditional local name of White French (or 'Fransdruif'), however, suggests that it was sourced from France. The Muscadel was probably the rather respectable Muscat de Frontignan, which may have come via Spain. And, despite the absence of any specific reference to Chenin Blanc, records indicate that what was known as 'Steen' (and later identified as Chenin Blanc) has been planted here for at least three centuries, which places it squarely among the bundles of vines to have been shipped to the Cape in the 1650s.

More French varieties must have come to our shores from 1688 onwards, with the arrival of the Protestant French Huguenots fleeing Catholic persecution, with families such as the De Villiers and Du Toits noted as having a good knowledge of viticulture. The history of the Huguenots remains an integral part of the Cape winelands today, with champion cellars still carrying names such as L'Ormarins, La Motte, Haute Provence and Mont Rochelle. One of the varieties introduced way back then was most likely Sémillon, given its traditional bias in the areas in which these persecuted French Protestants settled: the Franschhoek Valley and Paarl, with Drakenstein in-between.

Sémillon was one of the varieties ordered by the next commander and governor of the Cape, Simon van der Stel, during his development of the Constantia winelands and the model farm Groot Constantia from around 1690. Besides 'White French' (Palomino) and 'Green Grape' (Sémillon), he also ordered 'Pontac', of which the Cape's current small plantings constitute the world's last-known remaining vines. Writings by early 18th-century visitors speak of the 'lovely red Constantia wine' as well as 'Steenwyn' – Chenin Blanc? – and 'Kristalwyn'.

FORTUNE AND FAME

Van der Stel's Constantia was held up as a model agricultural enterprise for the farming free burghers he had settled in Stellenbosch from 1679, and they were encouraged to grow vines as one of their farming activities. Simon's son, Willem Adriaan van der Stel, shared his father's ambitious interest in viticulture. Succeeding Van der Stel the elder as governor in 1699, Willem Adriaan set about creating his own 'Constantia' at Vergelegen. And he was the one who sallied forth across the Obiqua Mountains to the north of the Paarl/Wellington basin to open up the mountain-ringed Tulbagh Valley, another historic winelands area. At the same time, the farmland of Durbanville was being divided up among settlers.

Although red and white Constantia wine was being exported to Europe by the 1760s, the farms of Groot and Klein Constantia gradually became more run-down until the late 1770s. In 1778 Groot Constantia was bought by the Cloete family, who renovated the Cape Dutch buildings (embellishing them with Baroque-style mouldings and sculpture) and replanted the vineyards. It was the Cloetes who set Cape wine on the road to international fame with the production of sweet wines (Muscadels and Pontacs) to be quaffed by European royalty, including French palates such as Napoleon (exiled on St Helena Island) and King Louis-Phillipe.

WAR AND PESTILENCE

But this success was short-lived, with the growth of a reputable wine industry stunted in part by the British, the Cape Colony's new landlords from 1795 (with a brief four-year interruption when the Dutch temporarily reclaimed their territory in 1802). Initially, though, there was encouragement from the British. Quality controls on winemaking were instituted, for example. An international market was created for Cape wine, first by imposing heavy import duties on French wine (the flow of which had already been curtailed during the Napoleonic Wars) and then by dropping duty on Cape wine to just one-third of that on Portuguese offerings. Add to this the fact that the English had a sweet tooth, and Cape winemakers were on a

THOUGHT TO HAVE BEEN THE OLD SLAVE QUARTERS AT RUSTENBERG, THIS BUILDING IS DATED 1812. IT IS PART OF A WERF THAT WAS, UNUSUALLY, BEHIND THE MANOR HOUSE INSTEAD OF IN FRONT.

THIS DOVECOTE – A COMMON FEATURE OF EARLY CAPE FARMS – CAN BE SEEN JUST INSIDE THE ENTRANCE TO MEERLUST IN STELLENBOSCH. IT IS NOW A NATIONAL MONUMENT, AND THE MISSING CURVED MOULDING ON THE RIGHT WAS RESTORED BY THE MYBURGHS.

winning wicket. But the long-term result of an open, ready market was a drop in overall quality, as vast quantities of cheap wine were shipped off to the motherland. (Ironically, South Africa seems to be facing a very similar situation right now).

The emancipation of the slaves in 1834, a policy aggressively supported by the British, made it that little bit harder for the wealthy farmers who had relied on slave labour to produce their wine. And, a few years later, the British government suddenly raised tariffs on wine imported from the increasingly recalcitrant Cape, whose Afrikaans-speaking

inhabitants had embarked upon their historic Great Trek north to establish states independent of British rule.

A North American fungus, powdery mildew, was next to strike, via the French vineyards, but dusting the vines with sulphur seemed to sort out this little problem. Then, in 1861, the British signed a trade treaty with the French, significantly reducing the trade tariffs on French wine. That pulled the carpet out from under the Cape wine industry's feet. Exports of Cape wine sank from nearly 580 000 litres to about 140 000 litres in three years.

Then the real rot set in. *Phylloxera vastatrix*, an aphid that feeds on the roots and branches of a vine, leaving it vulnerable to rot, had appeared in French vineyards in 1860. It destroyed nearly two-thirds of Europe's vines, then arrived at the Cape 25 years later, despite the Cape Government's ban on importation of possibly infected vine cuttings. Official action included the destruction of damaged plants and the gradual replacement of all vines by grafting them onto American rootstock, which had built up a natural immunity to the insect that had developed in tandem with that country's wild vines.

An already depressed wine industry then had to survive the two turn-of-the-century wars with colonial Britain, waged by the newly independent Afrikaner Boer Republics: the Transvaal and the Orange Free State, north of the Orange River. And, with all the vineyards now regrafted onto new rootstock, a worrying state of over-production came about.

The solution to these circumstances was sought in a co-operative system of wine farming, introduced in 1905. The Cape's first wine co-op was formed in Tulbagh; the Drostdy still exists today, though it is called the Tulbagh Co-op. The co-ops of Helderberg in Stellenbosch, Wellington and Bovlei in Wellington, Overhex in Worcester and Montagu all still exist, too, though some in different guises. While many grape growers, especially those in the marginal viticultural regions, were saved from ruin, the essentially disinterested nature of co-operative winemaking did little to improve the already generally mediocre quality of Cape wine. Still, wine grape production continued to grow, bolstered by the collapse in 1913 of the ostrich-farming industry in the arid Klein Karoo and the Breede River Valley, which saw former grape growers-turned-ostrich farmers pull up their vast tracts of lucerne (used for bird-feed) and revert to vines.

EXPANSION AND CONTROL

A central body for wine farmers was formed in 1918. The 'Ko-operatieve Wijnbouers Vereniging van Zuid-Afrika Beperkt', or the KWV, was to become the Big Brother of the wine industry. Essentially a protectionist body, it undertook to 'direct, control and regulate the sale and disposal by its members of their produce'. With eventually some 95 per cent of the Cape's wine-grape growers signed up, the KWV proceeded to successfully negotiate better wine prices with merchants. Its power over the wine industry was entrenched in 1924 with the Wine and Spirit Control Act, passed by the government of the Union of South Africa. The Act empowered the KWV to set a minimum price for wine delivered by its members for distilling purposes; hardly an incentive to vinify fine table wines.

But then the taste of the time was mainly for brandy and sweet fortified wine – Hanepoot, Jerepigo and Muscadel – for which there was ample historic precedence and a ready source. Hence the proliferation of varieties not recognised for their fine-wine attributes, from Raisin Blanc to Hanepoot (Muscat d'Alexandrie) and Colombard. Port had long been a successful Cape export, and had been lapped up by the British since the 1800s.

It was, in fact, an independent wholesale wine merchant, Stellenbosch Farmers Winery (SFW), that played an important role in educating the Cape palate. Ironically, its founder was an American, William Charles Winshaw. A trained doctor, Winshaw advocated the health merits of natural wine. From making his own wine on his farm Oude Libertas – the site of the current SFW cellars just outside Stellenbosch – he set out in 1935 to convert the masses. The white wine La Gratitude and its red stablemate Chateau Libertas were born; they are both blends that have survived for more than 50 years as standard-bearers of consistent quality and examples of popular, appealing every-day drinking wine.

A WOOD CARVING ON A BARREL IN KWV'S CATHEDRAL CELLAR. IT DEPICTS THE GREEK GOD OF WINE, DIONYSUS (THE ROMANS CALLED HIM BACCHUS) – OR IS IT SOME DUTCH GENTLEMAN IMBIBER FROM THE CAPE OF GOOD HOPE?

RESEARCH AND DEVELOPMENT

Not that others were not working behind the scenes to improve Cape wine. Viticulture and oenology were part of the Department of Agriculture's curriculum at Stellenbosch University (then still Victoria College) by 1917, which is where leading local viticulturist Prof Abraham Perold conducted the research that led to his creating South Africa's first *Vitis vinifera* hybrid in 1925. His crossing of Pinot Noir and Cinsaut (then called Hermitage) gave us Pinotage, although it was to take another 20-odd years and the insight of successor Prof Chris Theron to nurture Perold's forgotten plants into vines for distribution among grape growers. In 1926 the university linked up with Elsenburg Agricultural College to form a joint training institution, which counted viticulture and viniculture among the courses offered.

But, despite the application of the viticulturists, wine merchants and assorted individualists – from artist Georg Canitz of Muratie, who bottled the first Pinot Noir in 1927, to Johann Graue at Nederburg, who in the late 1930s recognised Chenin Blanc's potential as a classic white wine – the Cape wine industry was to remain pedestrian. And with no little assistance from the KWV, which, in 1940, sought and received government sanction to establish a minimum price for 'good' wine, destined for the table. All transactions between producer and merchant had to be approved by the KWV. And no one could produce wine without a permit from the KWV. This stifling control was further extended in 1957 with the introduction of the quota system, which limited the number of vines that could be grown by a farmer in one of the demarcated districts approved by the KWV. In protecting the existence of wine-grape growers, the KWV – which, in effect, was now the industry – was rewarding mediocrity, and even guaranteeing to take in any distilling wine crop that could not be sold to a merchant and paying the farmer a minimum price upfront.

The 1950s were not all about control, however. There was development, too, in the establishment in 1955 of the Agricultural Research Council's Viticultural and Oenological Research Institute at Nietvoorbij, just outside Stellenbosch. And success – in the form of Lieberstein, SFW's semi-sweet table wine made from Chenin Blanc, released in 1959 and becoming, after five years, the world's biggest-selling bottled wine at 31-million litres. This era also saw some world firsts in winemaking

A RELIC OF THE PAST. THIS LARGE, OLD OAK VAT IN THE VERGENOEGD CELLAR SHOWS THE CRAFTER'S TOUCH IN ITS DECORATIVE BRASS HANDLE – TODAY YOU'LL FIND STEEL TANKS WITH HINGED PORTALS.

techniques, most importantly the development of equipment such as special stainless-steel tanks and various methods to allow for cold fermentation, which revolutionised the production of quality white wine in South Africa and in the world's other hot-climate wine-growing regions. The research was begun by the KWV, which advised against it, and continued by the Graues of Nederburg in Paarl and the Krones of Twee Jonge Gezellen in Tulbagh. Cold fermentation also enabled winemakers to explore white wines of a slightly finer, drier style than the ubiquitous semi-sweet known as Stein. By the '50s, the 'braaivleis, rugby, sunny skies and Chevrolet' brigade had added Premier Grand Cru to its list of lifestyle necessities. This crisp, dry-white style of blended wine made famous the Bellingham label and its squat bottle – it was then-owner Bernard Podlashuk who initiated the style that was to become synonymous with South African white-wine drinking habits over the next 20 years.

THE BUSTLING VILLAGE GREEN IN STELLENBOSCH, KNOWN AS DIE BRAAK, IN THE 1860S. THE TRAPBALIES (FOR FOOT STOMPING) ARE BEING CLEANED AND THE WINE WAGONS ARE HEADING FOR TABLE BAY.

TAKING THE HORSE TO WATER

A watershed decade dawned for Cape wine in 1970. The wine-route concept was introduced by three stubborn Stellenbosch wine farmers who were determined to open up the world of Cape wine to the South African public. Frans Malan of Simonsig, Niel Joubert of Spier and Spatz Sperling of Delheim established the Stellenbosch Wine Route in 1971 after the first two discovered something similar on a visit to Burgundy. Other wine areas soon followed suit.

These vintners were assisted in their endeavours by the Wine of Origin (WO) legislation, introduced in 1973, that divided the Cape winelands into official regions and districts, in turn containing wards (for example the Simonsberg ward in the Stellenbosch district of the Coastal Region). It was a rudimentary form of the French appellation system, based more on geographic boundaries than strict viticultural considerations. The French system would have taken into account hegemony of wine style as a result of similarity in terroir, encompassing the soils and microclimates of specific areas. The WO was more of a consumer guarantee that what the producer

claimed on the label was true of the contents of the bottle than that it was a sound viticultural division of the winelands. It also involved a new, laborious system of checks and balances, administered by the still all-powerful KWV.

But it worked for vintners with a sense of pride, and gave the serious winemakers striving to produce top-quality wine an opportunity to tell the public as much. And it did ensure that nothing untoward was foisted on a market that was, in world terms, still somewhat unsophisticated. South Africans were at last becoming true wine lovers, with the necessary curiosity and courage to explore new tastes, new styles and new varieties – a realm beyond the ubiquitous Premier Grand Cru whites and the enduring red blends such as Tassenberg and Chateau Libertas. Thus Cabernet Sauvignon, Shiraz and Pinotage became the red varieties of note, with the whites mainly represented by Crouchen Blanc (what was known here as Cape Riesling, Paarl Riesling or just plain Riesling), Colombard and Chenin Blanc.

Hand-in-hand with the Wine of Origin system came the principle of a wine estate, with vintners committing themselves to bottling wine from grapes grown and vinified on their property. The name of the estate was offered as a guarantee of quality or, at least, integrity.

So, too, did the Wine of Origin seal, popularly known as the 'bus ticket', which certified the wine as true to its origin, vintage and variety, as stipulated on the label. The gold-backed version, denoting a Wine of Origin Superior, was instituted in 1982. It was a seal of quality as judged by the government-instituted Wine and Spirit Board – through which all wine must be passed before being sold to the public – and was the only official quality grading until its abolition in 1990. But it did its job, providing invaluable guidance to a wine-loving public becoming increasingly inundated with new varieties and styles of wines.

A new, official certification and identification sticker on the capsule of a bottle has now replaced the bus ticket. The WO still exists, however, and has been expanded to

encompass a wider area such as 'WO Western Cape', giving producers the freedom to buy in grapes from whereever they wish and blend it into one wine (the equivalent of the French *vin de pays*).

Something was certainly needed to help the public cope with this new richness of choice, so in 1980 the Cape Wine Academy (CWA) was formed, an educational body run under the auspices of SFW. What was a rather unnecessary duplication with the KWV's wine and spirits courses was finally ended in 1992 with a merging of the two, leaving the more advanced and internationally recognised CWA as the sole official wine and spirits education body in South Africa. The challenge to keep up was also met by the winemakers themselves, in the formation in 1983 of the Cape Independent Winemakers' Guild (CIWG). Founded by self-taught winemaker Billy Hofmeyr of Welgemeend, the CIWG sought to – and still does – advance the quality of Cape wine by sharing skills and developing, through workshops, the knowledge, capabilities and horizons of its member winemakers. By way of the annual CIWG wine auction, guild members are encouraged to produce small batches of top-quality experimental wine and given the opportunity to test it on the discerning wine lover.

MAKING IT BACK TO THE GARDEN

The '90s heralded the age of freedom. The KWV finally abolished the quota system in 1992, giving progressive wine farmers carte blanche to explore new areas for wine production. This long-awaited release from stricture was also granted to one man, the long-time political prisoner Nelson Mandela, just a year later. It saw South Africa, and with it the Cape wine industry, welcomed back into the playground of world economics. After years of isolation, which had its not unexpectedly stifling effect on growth and progress, South Africa became the flavour of the month in the UK, which is traditionally the wine world's most important and discerning market. Exports soared, from fewer than one million cases of wine in 1990 to over 11 million in 1996.

The Cape wine scene has blossomed in the past decade. With much of the early entrepreneurial spirit in Cape winemaking found among immigrant winemakers – the Graues, Backs, Podlashuks, Pongráczes, Laszlos, Brözels and Sperlings of the wine world – it is perhaps not surprising that it is knowledgeable overseas investment that has rejuvenated wine farms, both new and historic. Some, whether far-sighted or foolishly brave, preceded the '90s boom, such as the Müllers of Buitenverwachting and German banker Hans

Schreiber of Neethlingshof and Stellenzicht. But they were soon followed by Burgundian *négociant* Paul Bouchard, who joined Peter Finlayson in the Hemel-en-Aarde Valley, while brother Walter Finlayson went into partnership with Californian wine mogul Donald Hess at Glen Carlou in Paarl. The talented Californian couple viticulturist Phil Freese and winemaker Zelma Long have teamed up with Michael and Jill Back of Backsberg in a joint Cape venture to create wines under the label Simunye. The famous Cognac combination of Alain and Anne Huchon-Cointreau has put Morgenhof on the map, the Moueix family of Château Pétrus fame has linked up with Savanha Wines in Simondium and a scion of the Bordeaux royal family of De Rothschilds has joined the Ruperts of Rembrandt at R & de R Fredricksburg just down the road. The Swiss Bührer clan is ensconced at Saxenburg and is linking up with its French estate to produce Afro-French blends. Italian Count Riccardo Agusta is piecing together historic wine properties such as Haute Provence and La Provence in Franschhoek. The list goes on and on.

Not that local money is being left behind. Big corporates are behind the renovation of historic properties such as Vergelegen, Boschendal and Steenberg. Maverick banker Christo Wiese has lit a cracker beneath Lanzerac, while coal magnate Graham Beck chose Robertson as the place in which to build his winery and make his mark on the wine industry. Businessman Harold Johnson has rebuilt Zevenwacht. And neuro-surgeons, doctors, quantity surveyors, construction engineers, opera singers, advertising people and business people are living their dreams by investing money and passion in small but sophisticated new cellars, all producing top-quality wines.

Cape winemakers are also benefiting from the expertise of colleagues of the ilk of Australian Robin Day of Pernod Ricard, Frenchman Paul Pontallier of Château Margaux and Burgundian Martin Prieur,

who consult for local cellars. Cape cellars such as Rustenberg and Longridge have also lured young talent from other New World wine countries such as Australia and New Zealand, and there is a steady flow of mostly French student winemakers to the Cape vineyards each vintage.

THE FUTURE IS IN THE VINE

Thus has history brought the Cape wine industry to a point, nearly 350 years after the first vines were planted at the southern tip of Africa, where it is faced with perhaps its best chance of proving itself a world player. With the once-all-powerful KWV becoming an independent wine and spirit company in 1998 and offering to hand over its regulatory and management role, the industry has the chance to take control of its own destiny. While the temporary Wine Industry Trust runs affairs (with logistical help from the KWV), a project dubbed 'Vision 2020' is in the starting blocks. As the Australians did a decade ago, local government, academia, merchants and producers are working together to determine how the Cape wine industry should be run.

The foundation is being laid by going back to grass roots by accurately identifying what is in the vineyards and then selecting the best varieties and sites to produce the quality that will meet future market requirements. Since the early days of the 18th century, nature and individuals have shown the Cape capable of producing great wines. And with independent, quality-driven merchants replacing the old protectionist producer/ wholesaler monopolies, co-operatives being run as businesses and viticulture earning the respect it deserves, there is a chance to do it right on grand scale.

A DETAIL OF A PAINTING HANGING IN THE ENTRANCE TO THE MURATIE CELLAR AND TASTING ROOM, WHERE THE AMBIENCE OF THE 'OLDEN DAYS' HAS BEEN MAINTAINED.

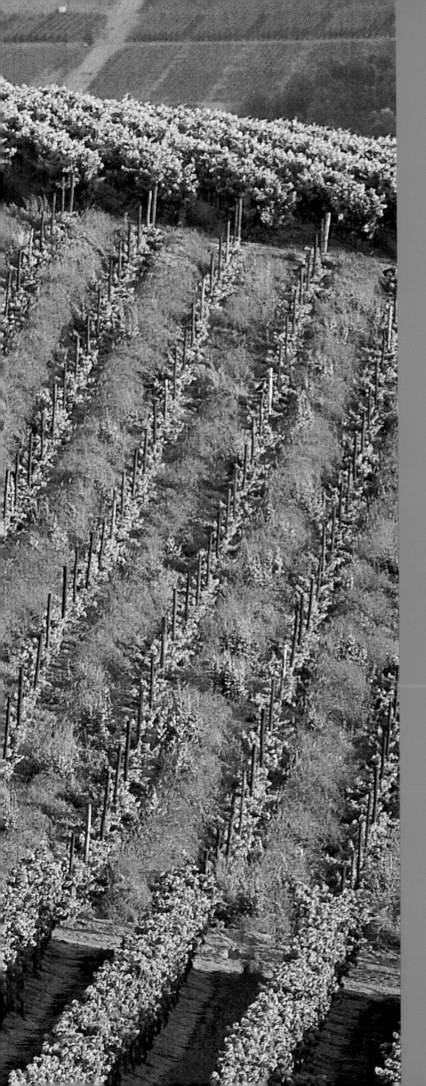

THE STARS

RATING THE WORTH OF A WINE GRAPE cannot but be controversial. Variables abound, from clones to climate, soils to cellar techniques. Yet a fairly standard list of the so-called noble (or classic) varieties has been arrived at, based on a few fundamental character attributes: the strength to retain its distinctive personality wherever it is planted; the complexity to develop, be it through the influence of wood or simply time in the bottle; longevity; versatility of style; and, ultimately, the proven ability to produce wines of widely acknowledged greatness.

Most of the noble varieties are here: in the Cape and in this chapter. Some inclusions may be unexpected, for example Sémillon and Weisser Riesling, but they deserve a place if only because the potential is there, though it may as yet be recognised by just a few. Others may not be noble in international circles but are true Cape classics: Muscat de Frontignan (Muscadel to us) and Pinotage. One or two have become synonymous with South African wine, such as Cinsaut. Tinta Barocca is a specialist variety with an unexpected versatility, a back-room boy only now sharing some of the spotlight.

Whether current, future or fading – through no fault of their own, like Weisser Riesling – each is a star in the firmament of Cape wine.

WHITE

Chardonnay, Chenin Blanc, Muscat de Frontignan, Sauvignon Blanc, Sémillon, Weisser Riesling

RED

Cabernet Sauvignon, Cabernet Franc, Cinsaut, Merlot, Pinotage, Pinot Noir, Shiraz, Tinta Barocca.

CLASSIC WHITE VARIETIES

CHARDONNAY

Probably the most popular white wine in the world, Chardonnay plays queen to Cabernet Sauvignon's king. It is loved by wine drinkers and winemakers alike, for many reasons, but perhaps mostly because it combines versatility with classicism.

It is easy to grow, which is why it has become one of the most widespread varieties in the world: from the cold Champagne region to the hot Cape hinterland, from England to Chile to Bulgaria. It does well in most soil types and is a fairly vigorous grower, ripening early in the season. The fruit yield is consistently generous and achieves high sugars.

Its versatility is evident in its range of styles. As a major component of Champagne – which accounts for as much as a third of the total plantings of Chardonnay in France – it provides elegance and structure. Perhaps its most famous expression is found in Burgundy, where an exalted position has led to worldwide reference in broad generic terms: white Burgundy can mean only Chardonnay. Here the variety's response to oak-barrel fermentation and maturation is a benchmark for most New World Chardonnays. And further north, in Chablis, the same grape has produced another holy grail: talk about Chablis and you will be referring to Chardonnay, primarily as an unoaked wine.

This multitude of permutations makes it difficult to pinpoint the definitive flavour profile of the grape. It can be quite a neutral wine if made as an unembellished dry white. What it always has, however, is natural body, a weightiness in the mouth. Unwooded Cape Chardonnays can charm with a lemony freshness on top of that body. Clonal characteristics are particularly recognisable in Chardonnay, for example, the tropical fruit in one clone and the nuttiness in another.

As easy as it is to make a 'nice' Chardonnay, this variety needs wood to show its real depth of character. The naturally lemon-yellow white wine then assumes the lustre of burnished gold.

Wood turns simple lemon or lime aromas and flavours into a marmalade mélange, natural smoothness into creaminess and nuttiness into buttered toast. It imparts vanillins, infuses with spice (cloves, cinnamon) and carries the flavours and textures of caramel, toffee and butterscotch. Wood can make a ripe, fruity young wine last a good few years, becoming honeyed with age. The variety is newer to local winemakers than other classics such as Weisser Riesling and even Sauvignon Blanc. In fact, its introduction in the early 1980s, pioneered by Sydney Back at Backsberg, was even further delayed by a case of mistaken identity. What was thought to be Chardonnay vine stock turned out to be

THE ORIGINAL HAMILTON RUSSELL WINE-PRODUCTION CELLAR WITH ITS DISTINCTIVE CYPRESS TREES.

Auxerrois, known as Auxerrois Blanc at home in Alsace where Chardonnay has been mooted as one of its relatives.

Chardonnay is very much a grape unto itself, though it was long thought to be of the Pinot family (probably because of its proliferation in Burgundy in partnership with Pinot Noir, with which it shares a near-identical leaf shape). White Muscat is generally accepted as its ancestor – one of the Chardonnay clones actually shows distinct Muscat overtones.

Chardonnay is one of the 'big six' in the Cape, one of the noble varieties upon which the fine-wine industry hopes to build a secure and lasting future in the world wine market.

Today it accounts for what may seem like a meagre five per cent of *Vitis vinifera* plantings, but the increase has been steady over recent years.

Chardonnay's swings in style and quality are only now beginning to settle down, as winemakers become more adept at drawing out the best of this responsive, malleable grape. As the vines mature and as subtlety replaces the heavy hand of inexperience with wood, Chardonnay is showing yet another side of its multi-faceted personality: longevity. For this is a wine that has remarkable bottle-ageing potential, but only if the balance between its many parts is right: full-ripe grapes, lively acid and delicate, smooth oak.

For wine lovers, Chardonnay's versatility offers a variety of styles without necessarily compromising quality. And winemakers have found a workhorse with a fine pedigree, able to add body to their blends, make mediocre wine to please most palates or try to achieve greatness. Teamed with anything from Sauvignon Blanc (Jordan in Stellenbosch) to Weisser Riesling (Twee Jonge Gezellen in Tulbagh) to Colombard (a blend synonymous with the Robertson region), Chardonnay is also an equal partner in the Cape's Cap Classiques. Witness the benchmark bubblies under leading labels such as Villiera Tradition, Pierre Jourdan, Krone Borealis, Pongrácz, JC Le Roux and Graham Beck. And it is Graham Beck that has reached for the

stars with a traditional Blanc de Blanc. A pure Chardonnay Cap Classique, it has taken the production of this top echelon of Champagne-style wine (established by local luminaries such as Cabrière's Pierre Jourdan and The Bergkelder's JC Le Roux Chardonnay MCC) to new heights.

Within this 'serious' category you will find two predominant styles. The elegant wines emphasise the typical lemony freshness, with delicate oak flavours lending just a hint of creaminess and toastiness. Cool-climate wines such as Hamilton Russell, Bouchard Finlayson, Buitenverwachting and the Neil Ellis wines as well as Rustenberg's Brampton, Saxenburg's Private Collection and Mulderbosch are made in this style. New cellar Laibach is also one to try.

The blockbusters combine ripe citrus fruit flavours with a rich butteriness and strong wood. Glen Carlou is an example par excellence. Vergelegen's Reserve and standard bottling does it, as do Stellenzicht and Laborie.

In-between lies a variety of wines exhibiting varying degrees of fruitiness and toastiness. Like De Wetshof, Louisvale is a Chardonnay specialist with several styles to study and enjoy. Thelema, Dieu Donné and Simonsig are always the epitome of balance, while Hartenberg and Hoopenburg are quietly making their mark, and unassuming Eikendal seldom disappoints. Constantia Uitsig has emerged as a newcomer of interest. The list is endless, and satisfaction lies in the pleasure of exploration.

WINEMAKER'S COMMENT
Gyles Webb, Thelema: 'My aim is a full-bodied, full-flavoured wine ... that makes a statement.'

WINE WRITER'S COMMENT
Hugh Johnson, English author, on White Burgundy: 'Half-smoked aromas and flavours, rich and sappy, dry without exception, but fat with flavour, either soft and succulent, hard and strong – the greatest still dry-white wine ...'

FOOD RECOMMENDATION
Full-bodied: dishes with cream, cheese or nutty sauces; veal, poultry, pork, rabbit; meaty fish; perlemoen. Medium-bodied: Parma ham, smoked salmon, paté, terrines; creamy cheeses.

THE TASTING ROOM AT THE GRAHAM BECK WINERY IN ROBERTSON IS AS SLEEK AND SOPHISTICATED AS THE BOTTLE-FERMENTED BUBBLIES PRODUCED THERE.

CHENIN BLANC

A grape variety that is steeped in history, Chenin Blanc is a French aristocrat that became a Cape

workhorse. Its origins can be traced back to the 9th-century Anjou-Touraine area of the Loire, where it still holds court today. Although Chenin Blanc has lost support in its homeland, it has been conquering New World vineyards; South Africa is one of its strongest power bases, with nearly a third of the country's more than 100 000 hectares of vineyard planted to Chenin – three times as much as in France.

Chenin is inextricably bound up with the making and drinking of wine in the Cape. It is highly probable that the variety was represented in those first few bundles of vine cuttings shipped out by Jan van Riebeeck in 1655. What was known as 'Steen' thrived, coping admirably with the heat, the wind and the most common vine pests, and providing generously at harvest time. As such, it became all things to all people, not least one of the stalwarts of the distilling wine industry as a base for early South Africans' beloved brandy. Co-operative cellars formed in the first half of this century paid their members for fruit on the basis of alcohol content. It was the reliable, heavy-bearing Chenin that came through for grape growers looking for big crops.

Ironically, these growers did not realise that they were working with a noble variety. To them it was simply Steen. When bottled as the ubiquitous semi-sweet table wines of the time, Steen often became confused with the semi-sweet style of wine generically referred to as 'Stein' (which was not necessarily made from Steen). Amid all this confusion came a revolution: Stellenbosch Farmers Winery's Lieberstein, a semi-sweet blend of Steen and Clairette Blanche launched in 1959, is credited with changing South Africans' drinking habits, wooing traditional beer and brandy drinkers

and establishing wine as an everyday drink. Its phenomenal appeal resulted in it becoming the world's biggest-selling single brand of wine (with sales of 31-million litres in 1964), and grape growers were soon frantically replacing everything with this wildly successful variety – identified a year later as classic Chenin Blanc.

Although Chenin's versatility has largely stripped it of nobility in the eyes of South Africans, class will out. While nowhere in the world has it been able to produce what its does in the Loire, this Cinderella grape of the Cape is beginning to emerge from her scullery with special attention from a host of new suitors.

Made as an easy-drinking dry or slightly sweet wine, Chenin can be wonderfully fresh and fruity, with the youthful fermentation character that often comes across as pure guava. It can hail from anywhere: Haute Provence in Franschhoek, Boland Wine Cellar in Paarl, Helderberg Winery in Stellenbosch, Bon Courage in Robertson. Best enjoyed in the year of their vintage, these wines are equally pleasing to the pocket.

Chenin is one of the major varieties in the typical South African semi-sweet, such as Nederburg Stein. It is the backbone of most Late Harvests, such as Delheim Spatzendreck, while Special Late Harvests – from big brands like Zonnebloem to estate wines such as Simonsig Franciskaner and popular co-operative wines typified by Mamreweg – also rely on Chenin Blanc.

Put Chenin in a barrel, however, and an entirely different wine emerges: serious, surprisingly full-bodied and reminiscent of Chardonnay but more delicate. A new movement among Cape winemakers is to explore the potential of Chenin if treated as a noble variety, in an attempt to uncover some of the richness of character achieved in the Loire. This has resulted in the resurrection of old, mature bush vines, severe pruning to cut down on yield, riper picking and partial barrel fermentation or maturation, or both. Walter Finlayson of Glen Carlou in Paarl first wooded a Chenin Blanc in 1994 as a one-off commemorative wine, and it intrigued wine writers and wine lovers alike.

ABOVE: THIS DARK-GREEN CHENIN BLANC LEAF SHOWS POORLY DEFINED LOBES; THE LEAVES CAN SOMETIMES HAVE THREE DEEPLY INDENTED LOBES.

OPPOSITE: MORGENHOF'S UNDERGROUND BARREL-MATURATION CELLAR-IN-THE-ROUND WAS INSPIRED BY THAT OF CHÂTEAU LAFITE-ROTHSCHILD IN BORDEAUX.

Encouragement from international Masters of Wine (lamenting the loss of charming Cape Chenin into innocuous blends), local wine critic Michael Fridjhon and *Wine* magazine (SA) saw others follow suit. Leading the pack are renowned cellars such as Villiera, Mulderbosch, Fairview, Morgenhof, Hartenberg and Simonsvlei. A wooded Chenin has become the speciality of restaurateur-turned-wine grower Ken Forrester at Scholtzenhof in Stellenbosch, and it is the sole wine produced under the Blue White label for Cape Wine Master Irina von Holdt. New names include Haute Provence, Laibach, Savanha and Beaumont. And L'Avenir gratified those appealing for a benchmark Chenin Blanc that was not necessarily wooded by producing an award-winning wine in 1997: unwooded, yet rich and ripe and recognisably Chenin, with a racy acidity and sugar to match.

Chenin, by virtue of sheer quantity, remains integral to big-volume Cape blends, from box wines to best-selling bubblies such as Grand Mousseux (one of South Africa's most popular carbonated sparkling wines). In fact, Chenin was the grape from which the Cape's first commercial bottle-fermented sparkling wine was made: Simonsig's 1971 Kaapse Vonkel (now a traditional Chardonnay Pinot Noir combination). But with increasingly discerning tastebuds out there, particularly those who turned branded wines such as Graca and Craighall into top sellers, Chenin is losing ground as a common blending wine to varieties such as Sauvignon Blanc, Chardonnay and Sémillon, which are capable of achieving greater distinctiveness, smoothness and body with minimal effort.

Chenin has probably achieved its most noble form in the Cape in that most noble of wines, the naturally sweet dessert wine, for which the apt colloquial term Noble Late Harvest was coined. The variety's greatest weakness has proved to be perhaps its greatest strength in warmer climes: severe susceptibility to botrytis. Historically the benchmark of local botrytised wines, Nederburg's

A DECORATIVE SIGNPOST AT MORGENHOF REFLECTS ATTENTION TO DETAIL BY OWNERS ALAIN AND ANNE HUCHON, SCIONS OF THE COINTREAU FAMILY OF COGNAC.

ABOVE: THE TASTING ROOM AT LIEVLAND, PIONEER OF THE ELEGANT, SAUTERNES STYLE OF NOBLE LATE HARVEST.

Edelkeur (introduced in 1969 and available only at the annual Nederburg Auction since 1975) is pure Chenin, as is the consistently fine and always affordable Fleur du Cap Noble Late Harvest. Lievland also counts on Chenin to deliver botrytised grapes.

WINEMAKER'S COMMENT
Jeff Grier, Villiera: 'It's a wonderful variety: more versatile than Sauvignon Blanc and an easier blender. It can be made dry and lively; in a Late Harvest style; or picked early for sparkling wine. It can be enjoyed young, but gains complexity with age.'

WINE WRITER'S COMMENT
Michael Fridjhon, SA wine importer: 'Some Cape Chenin Blanc has real Old World charm: a muscularity of structure, firm natural acidity, several quite distinctive fruit characters, a light citrus style, a more tropical style, still quite taut – midway between grapefruit and pineapple – a robust, almost terpene character, a ripe melon fruit, more spanspek than green melon, a smoked almond flavour, in part derived from oak, but also showing full-ripe fruit and fragrance.'

FOOD RECOMMENDATION
Dry, lightly wooded: creamy fish dishes; vegetable bakes, vegetarian grain dishes. Sweetish: warm fruit desserts or tarts, flans, sweet pastries.

MUSCAT DE FRONTIGNAN

The leader of the pack when it comes to the vast Muscat family of grapes, this variety somehow sounds more superior by its standard French tag of Muscat Blanc à Petits Grains. This title describes the variety in its purest form: a white grape with small berries. Muscat de Frontignan (so-renamed after one of its earliest home sites in France), can, however, produce grapes with a skin colour varying from pink to reddish brown, which is why in the Cape we have white Muscadel and red Muscadel, both made from exactly the same variety.

Muscat de Frontignan is regarded as the finest incarnation of Muscat and, typically, is a shy bearer. This is probably why the lesser Muscat d'Alexandrie, or Hanepoot, has far outstripped it in general popularity; the Cape is no less a predictable slave to quantity above quality, despite the fact that it is Muscat de Frontignan that is responsible for our finest fortified sweet dessert wines. Muscat de Frontignan was probably among the first cuttings to arrive in the Cape in the 17th century, which explains the quality of the sweet Constantia wines that achieved international fame for Cape wine. It is, ironically, because of its synonymity with Muscadel that it is in danger of losing its superior connotation in the common perception; we have given the very generalist name Muscadel to a particularly fine specimen of a particular grape that makes a very specific style of wine.

Cape Muscadel is made only from the Muscat de Frontignan grape, with white Muscadel from the white-skinned variety and red Muscadel from the darker skinned type. Suited as it is to warmer climates, De Frontignan does best in the drier, less fertile regions of the Breede River Valley and as far inland as the banks of the Orange River. Here it clocks up high sugar and acid counts, the all-important balance that makes for a full-sweet wine that is fresh rather than cloying, yet richly flavoured. All the fragrant, musky, grapey aromas and flavours of the variety are extracted during fermentation. This fermentation is then arrested by the addition of neutral grape spirit, leaving a full-flavoured wine with plenty of unfermented sugar (anything between 100 and 200 g/l) and an alcohol of between 16,5 and 18 per cent by volume.

BELOW: BOUND BY THE LANGEBERG RANGE LIES THE BREEDE RIVER VALLEY, WHERE NUY PRODUCES ITS AWARD-WINNING MUSCADELS FROM MUSCAT DE FRONTIGNAN.

As it comes from the same variety, there is little difference between white and red Muscadel, other than colour; white Muscadel has shades of burnished gold, while the red has curious translucent hues of coral, copper and mahogany. Red Muscadels seem to offer just a little more of everything: Muscat aromas and flavours, character, concentration and consistency of quality. Yet it was a white Muscadel from Nuy in Robertson that joined the elite group of wines to earn the South African *Wine* magazine's highest accolade of five stars. The winemaker, Wilhelm Linde, had a decade earlier won the 1988 Diners Club Winemaker of the Year award, when Muscadel was the category judged. Neighbouring Robertson co-operative Rooiberg has taken its cue from Nuy as far as quality and reliability are concerned. In fact, the entire Breede River Valley is a font of fine Muscadel, from Du Toitskloof Co-op to De Wet, Bon Courage to Bakenskop, McGregor to Montagu.

And it is not all sweet, highly alcoholic stuff; winemakers are offering some variations on the theme. De Wetshof recently produced a Muscat de Frontignan Blanc, which is fresh and fruity with an alcohol of only 15 per cent (the new minimum allowed for fortified wines). As a partner to its Edelkeur, Nederburg introduced Eminence, a natural, sweet dessert wine made entirely of Muscat de Frontignan and reserved for sale at the annual Nederburg Auction.

EARLY-SUMMER SPRAYING IN THE BREEDE RIVER VALLEY PROTECTS VINES AGAINST DOWNY MILDEW, WHICH CAN CAUSE THE YOUNG BERRIES TO SHRIVEL AND DROP OFF.

WINEMAKER'S COMMENT
Philip Jordaan, Du Toitskloof: 'Wine is for drinking; that's why I like my Muscadels, although rich and sweet, to still be light and delicate, as much an aperitif as a dessert wine.'

WINE WRITER'S COMMENT
David Biggs, SA columnist: 'Some winemakers claim that there is no difference at all in the flavours of the two varieties [Red Muscadel and White Muscadel] and that, if you taste them blindfolded, you will not be able to discern which is which. Others disagree ... And who cares whether you can or not? It's a marvellous way to get a winter party swinging along with some lively discussion.'

FOOD RECOMMENDATION
Snoek; deep-fried cheese (Camembert, Brie) with fruit sauces, aged blue cheese, ripe Roquefort; chocolate desserts.

LEFT: KLEIN CONSTANTIA, HISTORICALLY ONE OF THE GREAT ESTATES OF THE CAPE, IS STILL AMONG THE REGION'S TOP CELLARS AFTER ARCHITECTURALLY SENSITIVE AND VITICULTURALLY SCIENTIFIC RESTORATION BY THE JOOSTE FAMILY.

BELOW: A SIGNPOST IN DELHEIM'S LIVING LIBRARY OF WINE VARIETIES, WHERE WINE LOVERS AND VITICULTURISTS ARE ABLE TO STUDY THE VINES OF EACH VARIETY ON THE FARM.

SAUVIGNON BLANC

Although not one of the world's great grapes, Sauvignon Blanc is regarded as a classic variety – if only just. It is certainly one of the most fashionable, particularly in the New World. New Zealand, led by a winery named Cloudy Bay, put the variety on the map in recent years, producing strongly scented, full-bodied wines that could be recognised a mile away in blind tastings.

But Sauvignon Blanc earned its stripes in France, where it has been grown for centuries. The Loire is its home, where wines under the Sancerre and Pouilly-Fumé appellation established the variety's reputation for a racy white wine with the distinctive aroma and fruity flavour of gooseberries and a greenness best described as grassy. This pungency can make for a 'love-it or hate-it' kind of a wine, perhaps the reason behind its tenuous grip on star status. Yet the variety is full of surprises. It responds to different terroirs and treatments with a remarkable versatility that deserves greater appreciation than it is often afforded.

The first surprise is that it is not new to the Cape. Inherited from the French, it was widely planted back in the 1700s. But inferior plant material led to poor crops and it became quite scarce until the 1980s,

ABOVE: VERGELEGEN'S PUBLIC
GARDENS HAVE CAMPHOR
TREES DATING BACK A
CENTURY OR MORE TO THE
EARLY DAYS OF WINEMAKING
ON THIS HISTORIC PROPERTY.

OPPOSITE: THE FRENCH-
DESIGNED OCTAGONAL CELLAR
AT VERGELEGEN WAS SUNK
INTO A HILLTOP ON THE SLOPES
OF THE HOTTENTOTS HOLLAND
MOUNTAINS TO MAKE IT
LESS OBTRUSIVE.

when it was rediscovered by increasingly sophisticated wine growers. Since then it has steadily gained ground, becoming the only other white – together with Chardonnay – among the 'big six' varieties identified as of paramount importance in establishing the Cape as a serious wine region. It also matches Chardonnay on total vineyard space: nearly five per cent.

A fine Sauvignon Blanc is not easy to grow or to make. It produces the goods in cool areas, which is why it occupies the high ground in our warm Cape vineyards.

Sauvignon Blanc is marked by high acid, which gives it its trademark crispness and raciness – sometimes to a fault when the fruit is picked slightly unripe and made into some of the run-of-the-mill wines that occupy a place among the 200 or so labels in South Africa. But the acid rises and falls with alarming alacrity, much as the wine's concentration and character continuously change in the bottle. The grape needs attention in the vineyard, particularly when it comes to controlling the leaf canopy during ripening, and is attracting technical expertise in the cellar. Like other progressive New World winemakers and a new generation of European vintners, South Africans are experimenting. Techniques such as reductive handling to limit exposure to oxygen and the addition of ascorbic acid are among the attempts to draw out the elusive character of this wine, which is sometimes described as 'nervous'.

Cape Sauvignon can be superb, and often its source is surprising. Cool-climate Constantia is tops (Nicky Versfeld is doing for Steenberg what he did at Welmoed, when he made this co-op in Stellenbosch one of the best-kept secrets as a Sauvignon producer of note – it still is). The high-lying slopes of Stellenbosch also produce some stunners. Further along the foothills of the Helderberg mountains (an area renowned for reds) are the scintillating Sauvignons of Eikendal and Vergelegen.

On the opposite regional boundary with Paarl, Villiera has balanced its less-than-perfect terrain

with bush vines, and has produced a wine that won Jeff Grier the 1997 Diners Club Winemaker of the Year award. Bloemendal and Nitida have established Durbanville as Sauvignon territory.

The fact that Neil Ellis's consistently capped Groenekloof Sauvignon came from Darling in the Swartland hinterland has long been an open secret – it has not taken long for others to realise that the mists of the West Coast shroud these inland vineyards in suitable Sauvignon coolth.

Even the small Cederberg cellar among the red rocks behind the Olifants River Valley comes up with an authentic, fresh, grassy Sauvignon. As for the 1998 Fleermuisklip Sauvignon Blanc ... well, that sure shook 'em up! It is made by Lutzville Co-op, also in the Olifants River Valley. And back to the coast, where the Walker Bay cellars of Bouchard Finlayson and Hamilton Russell have firm fans. Consultant winemaker Bartho Eksteen (who put Wildekrans Sauvignon Blanc on the map) is bottling his own version, sourced from 'snowline' vineyards in Villiersdorp between the Overberg and Worcester regions.

Acidity is the secret behind Sauvignon's success as a sparkling wine. If you like your bubbles especially tingly, try JC Le Roux Brut Sauvignon Blanc, Papillon Brut from Van Loveren or Eikendal's C'est si Blanc non-vintage Brut.

The grape's thin skin and compact bunching makes it quite susceptible to noble rot, which opens up another door to the variety's complex personality. Renowned in France for its seamless blending ability with Sémillon to produce the delectable Sauternes natural sweet dessert wines, Sauvignon Blanc is also one of the handful of white varieties used for the Cape's highly rated botrytised Noble Late Harvests.

It's worth noting that some Sauvignons have astonished with their bottle-ageing potential. A Klein Constantia 1986 was the first white to earn a full-house, five-star rating in *Wine*. This places it in rarefied company – just seven five-star wines have been found in five years of monthly category tastings. Klein Constantia repeated the style – boosted by just a suggestion of botrytis – in 1987.

Sauvignon's blending capability has also been tested locally in recent years, notably with Chardonnay. The results have been received with mixed feelings, due in part to Sauvignon Blanc's dominant varietal character. Generally, these blends do neither variety any favours, but in the hands of experts they just seem to gel. Jordan Chameleon is one such gem, while Weltevrede gets it consistently right with its popular Privé du Bois (which sports some subtle oaking).

Efforts with wood maturation have been successful. Californian mover and shaker Robert Mondavi pioneered this style in the 1970s, cheekily coining the term Fumé Blanc to draw on the reputation of the world-famous Loire Pouilly-Fumé (despite the fact that the latter is unwooded!) The few local examples, called Blanc Fumé, are perennially popular. The ubiquitous L'Ormarins made it fashionable, and serious Sauvignon Blanc cellars such as Villiera and Jordan hit the high notes. But those who love the unbridled brilliance of a fine unwooded Sauvignon Blanc, though not necessarily purists, tend to regard wooding as an injustice.

WINEMAKER'S COMMENT
Mike Dobrovic, Mulderbosch: 'There are very few wines that can be described as mouthwatering. The range of flavours on good Sauvignons can vary from the grassy, green pepper and goose-berry to the light, fruity apple and pear, with a magnificent array of tropical aromas. A good Sauvignon will show a balance of almost all these things ... dammit, I'm getting thirsty.'

WINE WRITER'S COMMENT
Dave Hughes, SA writer: 'Sauvignons that appeal to me have nettle, capsicum and peppery noses. Big alcohols and a slight sweetness are best but, above all, they must be clean, rich and racy.'

FOOD RECOMMENDATION
Thai and Chinese food; light fish dishes and, trout, shellfish, seafood salads; light asparagus and tomato dishes; chicken pie; cuts through oil and garlic (pasta with pesto).

CONSTANTIA'S SOUTHEAST-FACING SLOPES OVERLOOKING FALSE BAY PROVIDE ONE OF THE BEST SITES IN SOUTH AFRICA FOR THE LONG, SLOW RIPENING REQUIRED FOR FULL-FLAVOURED GRAPES.

SÉMILLON

Sémillon once dominated South African vineyards – to the tune of more than 90 per cent in the 1820s. Its prevalence was most aptly reflected in its colloquial name, 'Wyndruif' (wine grape), which was to become 'Groendruif' (green grape) until a decade ago, by virtue of its unusually bright green foliage. The decline of Sémillon in the Cape has been nothing short of shocking – it now takes up less than one per cent of total vineyard surface – which is largely due, one suspects, to sheer ignorance of this noble variety's identity and provenance. Today there are still doubts about the true pedigree of some vines, grafted from descendants of some of the

first *Vitis vinifera* cuttings to be sent to Jan van Riebeeck in the mid-17th century. But while plantings may be meagre, the number of converts intent on making the most of grand old vines and brand-new clones is on the rise.

Sémillon (pronounced Semi-yon) is a native of Bordeaux, where is stands second in line behind France's most widespread variety Ugni Blanc (Trebbiano). A strong vine, Sémillon rewards the grower with a generosity of fruit that, sadly, is mostly turned into a lake of bland white wine. That this variety is indeed capable of greatness has been left to the makers of those stunning sweet wines from Sauternes and Barsac to prove, while attentive vintners in the Pessac-Léognan denomination of Graves produce seamless dry white blends of Sémillon and Sauvignon Blanc.

Australia has also done its bit towards shining up the tarnished image of this variety. Sémillon could quite possibly have been among the first cuttings acquired by New South Wales governor Captain Arthur Phillip on a stopover at the Cape in the 1780s. The rich, toasty, lively Hunter Valley Rieslings that are touted as world-class wines are in fact Sémillon, made in a way that exhibits the variety's remarkable ability to mature.

The Cape has not been much different. Those few remaining vineyards, primarily in the Paarl and Franschhoek districts, have been a source of some very ordinary white wine, but where the winemaker has applied himself, nobility has shone through. Hilko Hegewisch's special bottlings of Boschendal Jean le Long were a '90s breakthrough for barrel-fermented Sémillon in South Africa. Both Eikehof and Fairview have nurtured the tiny yields from vines planted by the winemakers' grandfathers into lovely, fat wines balanced by a lemony freshness and the enriching power of oak. This has encouraged them, and inspired others, to replant with Australian and French clones.

A new Australian clone is responsible for this lively lemon flavour, and Klein Constantia's latest unwooded version illustrates how fullness can be achieved from fruit alone. (This wine's selection for sale on the prestigious annual

Cape Independent Winemakers Guild Auction shows what cachet Sémillon now has.) Haute Provence in Franschhoek is also a member of the no-barrel brigade. But oak, and often sweet American wood, seems to bring out the best in the Sémillons from several new Franschhoek cellars – Stony Brook, Boekenhoutskloof, Landau du Val and Rickety Bridge – as it does in the star-studded Stellenzicht Reserve and the new Hartenberg, both Stellenbosch cellars.

Winemakers, often those at large co-operative wineries such as Simonsvlei, have also become aware of Sémillon's blending potential, though more have opted for controversial Chardonnay than for traditional Sauvignon Blanc, perhaps because a lot of South African Sémillon already has strong grassy overtones. Sémillon's natural fatness tones down the acidity found in many Cape whites, adding body and texture to balance the crispness and freshness of Sauvignon or complementing the limey, butteriness of an oaked Chardonnay.

Sémillon has done a turn as a Sauternes-style dessert wine in the Cape, in the hands of genius winemaker André van Rensburg, who while at Stellenzicht used it on its own and in tandem with Sauvignon Blanc.

WINEMAKER'S COMMENT
Charles Back, Fairview: 'It's probably my favourite: full-bodied, but straightforward and honest.'

WINE WRITER'S COMMENT
Angela Lloyd, SA writer: 'Fashioned dry, it produces softly textured, languid wines with beguiling lanolin, beeswax and sweet lemon purity, developing nutty richness with age. Sweet Sémillon achieves the nonpareil in seductive drinking.'

FOOD RECOMMENDATION
Fish (prawns, mussels), chicken, spicy pork; dishes with delicately creamed or spiced sauces; waterblommetjie bredie; goat's or cream cheese; any dish for which a Sauvignon Blanc is too light and sharp and a Chardonnay too heavy.

RIESLING (WEISSER OR RHINE)
Hooray for Riesling, the only variety from Germany among the French phalanx that makes up the internationally acknowledged category of classics. Sadly, however, its star does not shine brightly at the Cape.

To what is its nobility ascribed? Of all the classic white varieties, it is perhaps the most notable for its longevity, developing extraordinary complexity in the bottle over many years and maintaining that plateau of peak performance for many more. And, like Cabernet, it retains its distinctive character almost everywhere it goes – a taster's dream.

Another give-away of its nobility may be the tendency, in many countries, to appropriate the name Riesling for far lesser varieties. What was that about the 'sincerest form of flattery'? South

CHOOSE A SWEET DESSERT WINE MADE FROM WEISSER RIESLING FROM THE STAR-STUDDED WINELIST OF THE LORD NEETHLING RESTAURANT, NEETHLINGSHOF.

Africa is a perfect example: what was, in fact, an arbitrary French variety called Crouchen Blanc became known as Cape Riesling.

The real Riesling's origins are undeniably German, with records of its first cultivation going back to the 15th century. From there it has spread far and wide across the winemaking world – except in France, where tight appellation control restricted a foothold everywhere but in Alsace. It is a recent addition to the varietal line-up in the Cape, first tested in the 1960s and established 10 years later. But it barely drew enough support to make one per cent of total plantings, and is now inexorably losing ground.

Weisser Riesling, as it is commonly known in the Cape, is a cool-climate grape, hence its distribution in mainly the Coastal Region, where high-lying, breeze-blown slopes are reserved for its cultivation. Despite this, it ripens relatively early in the season compared with most other varieties, nevertheless achieving the high sugars and acids desirable for a wine that is to last. Yet it is naturally on the shy-bearing side, unlike in its homeland.

It is a strong vine and shakes off most plagues, but because of its compact bunch it does fall prey to noble rot, particularly in warmer, more humid conditions like ours. This can be a nuisance for winemakers, most of whom plant Weisser to make a drier style of wine as a varietal or for blending, but it is not unwelcome to the dessert wine specialists. Of all our wines, Noble Late Harvests are considered potential world-beaters. And though Nederburg sticks to Chenin for its renowned Edelkeur, and Sauternes stylists are looking at that region's more classic combination of Sémillon and Sauvignon Blanc, the Cape Noble Late Harvests made from Weisser still seem to have the edge on the rest.

Take Neethlingshof, for example. Its Weisser has been a class winner at the Top 100 Sydney International Wine Show; six consecutive vintages from the early '90s were local national show winners. Recently, sister estate Stellenzicht started making its mark, also with a Weisser Riesling Noble Late Harvest (which consistently seems to outperform the Neethlingshof Sauvignon Blanc NLH and Stellenzicht's

BACKING UP BEHIND THE MANOR HOUSE, THE VINEYARDS OF NEETHLINGSHOF – ON THE BOTTELARY HILLS FACING FALSE BAY – ARE CONSIDERED AMONG THE TOP TERROIRS IN THE CAPE.

The compact bunch of the Weisser Riesling is an ideal breeding ground for the noble rot fungus.

Sémillon alternative). Lievland, though attempting to follow the more elegant Sauternes style of botrytised wines, also relies on Weisser Riesling as one of the sources for its stunning dessert wines. As does Buitenverwachting for its Noblesse.

Yet the Cape's finest Rieslings are not all sweetish. Simonsig in Stellenbosch continues to make a top dry Weisser Riesling, with all the richness, fullness, honey and spice this variety can deliver. Most of the other good Rieslings, though sometimes less robust, benefit from a little residual sugar. Groot Constantia, Klein Constantia, Hartenberg, Kaapzicht, Neethlingshof, Jordan and Zonnebloem all know what they are doing with this variety. Also look out for newer names Laibach and Morgenhof.

Kaapzicht and the cool-climate Constantia wines have proved Weisser Riesling's ability to age well, but at Buitenverwachting winemaker Hermann Kirschbaum has opted for a style intended to appeal as a young, fresh wine with a suitably low alcohol.

WINEMAKER'S COMMENT
Hermann Kirschbaum, Buitenverwachting:
'I like a slight botrytis character in a Riesling; I don't like too much terpene.'

WINE WRITER'S COMMENT
Jancis Robinson, UK author: 'It is (potentially) the world's greatest white-wine grape because, like Cabernet Sauvignon, it is a wonderfully transparent medium for communicating the characteristics of place. Like Cabernet, it is also capable of evolving in the bottle for decades (unlike most Chardonnay), and (again, unlike Chardonnay) it is truly appetising.'

FOOD RECOMMENDATION
Dry: lightly spiced or curried dishes; stir-fries.
Sweeter: pork, chicken, delicate meats with fruit sauces; pecan pie and apple tarts/desserts.

CLASSIC RED VARIETIES

CABERNET SAUVIGNON

Cabernet is king! Long live the king! Amid oft-expressed claims to preferences for the more rarefied red wines – such as Pinot Noir or Shiraz – by well-travelled and sophisticated South African wine drinkers, good old Cabernet Sauvignon still comes through for most people. Cabernet is the most commonly grown red variety in the Cape right now, nudging the five per cent mark in a wine-growing country that still has less than 20 per cent of its viticultural land under red vines.

Cabernet is synonymous with France's finest. An integral ingredient of many great clarets, it gained a strong foothold in the Médoc and Graves in the late 1700s, where it was identified – and sometimes still is known – as Vidure, in reference to its hard wood.

The grape's inbred nobility is perhaps most evident in the vine's naturally low yield, achieved after a prolonged ripening period, which is ideal for optimum phenological development of the fruit. Virus problems in Cape vineyards have taken this to uneconomic extremes, however, but the cleaning-up and propagation of virus-free old clones have helped, as has the importation of new material from France, Germany and California. Besides producing bigger crops and ripening by as much as three weeks earlier, these 'new' clones have also spawned a generation of richer, riper, fruitier Cape Cabernets.

The different flavours attributed to clonal variance expresses itself in 'new-clone' Cabernet by way of a fleshy texture and a rich fruitiness, reminiscent of blackcurrant, or cassis, and ripe plum. A full-bodied Cabernet can also proffer aromas and taste associations of liquorice, chocolate and grassiness. A distinct mintiness or menthol characteristic can be a dead ringer for a new-clone Cabernet. Wines from older clones seem to be more herbaceous, with a green-pepper character, sometimes ascribed to slightly unripe grapes (which may result in more pronounced tannin).

Cabernet Sauvignon that has been matured in wood assumes even greater complexity. It is made for lengthy maturation, with the sheer guts and natural fruit density and acid to thrive.

The grape's exact arrival in the Cape is undocumented, but by the 1920s it had already laid claim to its exalted position as one of the top-quality local red varieties. It grew well in warm areas, on low-lying alluvial soil, but when it found its way onto good soils, with a high clay content that retained moisture during the hot, dry, summer ripening period, it exposed its easy fruit and rich resources of tannin and fruit acid. On cooler sites, which granted it a long, slow development period, it rewarded further with an even greater concentration of fruit and the enduring structure that a wine needs to attain the veneration of great age.

Cabernet plantings are widespread and on the increase, boosted by a leading position in the so-called 'big six' important varieties that growers are being encouraged to plant.

Of all the varieties, Cape winemakers have probably proved most adept at Cabernet, allowing single cellars to build enviable track records which, in turn, have enabled the wine lover to enjoy the security of consistent quality. Among the most familiar names: Meerlust, Rustenberg, Backsberg, Vergenoegd, Alto, Le Bonheur, Allesverloren, Blaauwklippen, Delheim and Nederburg.

But now it is the turn of the new generation. Armed with better plant material than in the '70s and '80s, new clones, small, new-oak barrels and the privileged position of drawing from both a long local tradition and progressive international techniques, they are turning out Cabernets that combine power with easy charm: Saxenburg, Plaisir de Merle, Neil Ellis, Morgenhof, Jordan, Warwick and De Trafford. Beyers Truter's Beyerskloof has been given a five-star rating by the rather serious UK wine publication *Decanter*, high praise indeed from critics not prone to handing out bouquets for local efforts.

If winemakers are going to spend any money at all on very expensive French-oak barriques, then Cabernet Sauvignon will probably head the list of deserving recipients. But where fruit is still given higher ranking than wood, the following are the wines to seek out, as much for their drinking pleasure as for their kind prices: Helderberg, Swartland, Bovlei and Vlottenburg.

THE FAURE FAMILY FARM OF VERGENOEGD, WHERE CONSISTENTLY FINE CABERNET SAUVIGNON IS THE RESULT OF TRADITIONAL WINEMAKING TECHNIQUES AND MODERN VITICULTURAL PHILOSOPHIES.

The Cape's sure success with Cabernet soon gave rise to consideration of the potential to make the type of blend that gave Bordeaux its star status. In the early 1980s this classic tradition of combining Cabernet Sauvignon with Merlot and Cabernet Franc resulted in what is still loosely referred to as 'Bordeaux-style' red blends. Although the presence of Cabernet, renowned for its structure and strength of flavour, is difficult to hide, it shares a grassiness with Cabernet Franc and a rich chocolaty character with Merlot that can confuse individually. Together, they make magic.

It is tough to choose a top 10 of these classic blends, given vintage variations, but it is a start to explore the treasures from Cape cellars that concentrate on Cabernet and have a reputation for consistency of quality. Try Buitenverwachting Christine, Grangehurst Cabernet Sauvignon Merlot, Groot Constantia Gouverneurs' Reserve, Kanonkop Paul Sauer, Meerlust Rubicon, Overgaauw Tria Corda, Rozendal, Thelema Cabernet Sauvignon Merlot, Warwick Trilogy and Welgemeend Estate Reserve.

THE RUSTIC CHARM OF THE MEERLUST TASTING ROOM, WHERE THE WALLS ARE LINED WITH MEMORIES OF GIORGIO DALLA CIA'S WINEMAKING ACHIEVEMENTS AND MYBURGH FAMILY MEMORABILIA.

Backing them up are wines such as Backsberg Babylonstoren, Claridge Red Wellington, Delheim Grand Reserve, Glen Carlou Grande Classique, Klein Constantia Marlbrook, Le Bonheur Prima, Lievland DVB, Neil Ellis Cabernet Sauvignon Merlot, Simonsig Tiara, Veenwouden Classic, Vergenoegd Reserve and Villiera Cru Monro.

While there was never any doubt as to Cabernet's merits as a varietal wine, it has long proved its worth as the base for what some still regard as the truly traditional Cape blend. Cinsaut was an early partner, most famously in well-loved Chateau Libertas.

Rust-en-Vrede supports the cause of Shiraz to accompany Cabernet, as winemakers look to possibly establishing a traditional Cape red blend – as do Uitkyk, Saxenburg, Hartenberg, Alto and Zandvliet. The same goes for partnerships with Pinotage by cellars such as Simonsig and Clos Malverne.

But it is now Merlot that is proving to be the most successful mate for Cabernet. Two Cape champions prove the point: Jeremy Walker's Grangehurst was the first red to rate five stars in *Wine*, and Thelema's Cabernet Sauvignon Merlot earned its maker Gyles Webb the 1997 Diners Club Winemaker of the Year award as best Bordeaux-style blend.

WINEMAKER'S COMMENT
Nico van der Merwe, Saxenburg: 'I like Cabernets full bodied, rich smooth and complex, and this starts in the vineyard. No tricks in the cellar: no fancy filtration, no fining, no cold stabilisation; the best treatment is no treatment.'

WINE WRITER'S COMMENT
Michael Broadbent, Christie's wine director, on Cabernet-dominated Château Margaux: 'The bouquet is extraordinary – rich, singed creosote, cedary, intense, lovely; rich, silky, elegant, long flavour, very dry finish.'

FOOD RECOMMENDATION
Beef – roasted, casseroles, grilled, marinated or heavily sauced; stews; kidneys; venison.

CABERNET FRANC

You may be forgiven for brushing aside Cabernet Franc as little more than Cabernet Sauvignon's 'country cousin'. But you would be making a mistake. And you may miss out on one or two exciting new wines in the Cape that are set to prove that this variety is more than just the odd winemaker's personal pet.

It came to the Cape just a couple of decades ago, introduced by top winemakers looking to emulate the classic reds of Bordeaux, in which Cabernet Franc shares the limelight with Cabernet Sauvignon and Merlot. In fact, until the late 1970s, Cabernet Franc was more widely planted than Cabernet Sauvignon in France, where it was first recorded in the late 18th century. Together with Merlot, it has become synonymous with many of the great wines of Pomerol and St-Emilion, where it is also known as Bouchet.

It has been slower to take off in South Africa. Relegated by most winemakers to a supporting role to Cabernet Sauvignon and Merlot, it seldom makes up more than 20 per cent of their flagship blends. But its contribution is significant. Besides adding richness of colour, it has a distinctive spiciness and attractive herbaceousness, which often causes it to be confused with Cabernet Sauvignon. But it is probably its softness – of tannin, acid and extract – without the loss of the typically Cabernet flavour and structure that most charms local winemakers, especially those seeking to ameliorate the hard, masculine character of Cape Merlot (curiously different to the luscious femininity that makes French Merlot great).

Despite the current proliferation of top-quality Bordeaux-style red blends in South Africa since the first pioneering attempts by Billy Hofmeyr of Welgemeend, the Van Veldens of Overgaauw and Giorgio Dalla Cia of Meerlust at the start of the '80s, few have concentrated on Cabernet Franc as a varietal wine. Many of our finest red blends count Cabernet Franc as an essential ingredient, no matter how small: Klein Constantia Marlbrook, Kanonkop Paul Sauer, Vergenoegd Reserve, Glen Carlou Grande Classique, Meerlust Rubicon, Warwick Trilogy, Welgemeend Estate Reserve and Lievland DVB.

Yet it took a woman to recognise the hidden charms of Cabernet Franc in the Cape.

Norma Ratcliffe of Warwick has become synonymous with the variety. She first planted it in the early '80s as an ingredient for her Bordeaux-style blend Trilogy and introduced a varietal Cabernet Franc in 1988. Her 1994 is one of just a handful of South African wines to have earned a five-star rating in *Wine*.

Besides Warwick, Bellingham and Landskroon have been the most consistent producers of a varietal Cabernet Franc. Several star winemakers have been led to bottle a one-off, whether it be

LEFT: THE RICH GARNET OF A FINE CABERNET FRANC HAS VISUAL APPEAL IN A CLEAR, NON-COLOURED GLASS.

BELOW: NORMA RATCLIFFE OF WARWICK, ONE OF THE CAPE'S FIRST WOMAN WINEMAKERS AND SELF-TAUGHT, BUCKED THE TREND BY CONCENTRATING ON CABERNET FRANC AS A VARIETAL WINE RATHER THAN A MERE BLENDING COMPONENT.

FROM THE VINEYARDS OF VERDUN, A VIEW ACROSS PRIME STELLENBOSCH VITICULTURAL LAND TOWARDS THE HELDERBERG. THE HOTTENTOTS HOLLAND MOUNTAINS AND THE ATLANTIC OCEAN ARE IN THE DISTANCE.

due to a particularly fine Cabernet Franc crop or some wine left over from their flagship red blend. All have been good wines: Walter and David Finlayson's 1994 Glen Carlou, André van Rensburg's Stellenzicht 1995 and a wine made in 1990 by Etienne le Riche from some Cabernet Franc left over from the famous Rustenberg Gold.

Others have come out with blends dominated by Cabernet Franc: Avontuur and Overgaauw have blended it with Pinotage, while Fairview and Wildekrans have combined it with Merlot.

Welgemeend's easy-drinking Soopjeshoogte, also made by a woman (Louise Hofmeyr), has a lot of Cabernet Franc in it too.

As vines mature and winemakers become more adventurous, Cabernet Franc may yet come into its own – much as it has done on the slopes of the Helderberg in Stellenbosch, where Chris Keet has been quietly nurturing the new vines of Cordoba. Working towards a premium red blend of the three classic Bordeaux varieties, he came up against a Cabernet Franc of such

outstanding quality that it muscled its way into a predominant position in his maiden Cordoba Crescendo.

WINEMAKER'S COMMENT
Charles Hopkins, Bellingham: 'It's an expression of my personality, I think; I always support the underdog. And, in world terms, Cabernet Franc is perceived as inferior to Cabernet Sauvignon. But it's simply shyer and softer, especially when made with a full-fruit character rather than in the leafy, green way. It may not have the length of Cabernet Sauvignon, but it has a lovely middle palate, meaty and chewy.'

WINE WRITER'S COMMENT
David Biggs, SA writer: 'I like the earthy aromas with rich, plum-pudding flavours.'

FOOD RECOMMENDATION
Red meat dishes that are lighter and spicier; pork, gammon, ham, veal; braaied meaty fish.

CINSAUT

Cinsaut's star is waning in the Cape. Sadly so, for it has the potential to deliver the soft and fruity reds many wine lovers look for in their daily tipple. Plantings have dropped by two thirds in the past two decades, bringing what was then the most widely planted red variety to today's mere four per cent of South Africa's total vineyard.

Its origins are noble: Hermitage in the Rhône, source of the world's most stunning Shirazes. But Cinsaut, called 'Cinsault' by the French, never quite recovered from a 19th-century phylloxera epidemic.

It is now a Jack-of-all-trades in Languedoc-Roussillon, France's largest wine-producing region, and it crossed the Mediterranean to North Africa. Cinsaut arrived in South Africa in the 1850s – introducing itself as Hermitage. It ended up playing an important role: as parent, with Pinot Noir, to the all-new, cross-named Pinotage in 1925. With its ability to cope with a hot climate, it was welcomed in the irrigated areas of the Orange and Olifants rivers. Cinsaut grown in these conditions is typically thin and watery, and is used to make popular, sweet Rosé wines. But if the vines are trained as bush or goblet vines and cultivated in cooler coastal areas (and heavily pruned), Cinsaut can produce quite a full-bodied wine, remarkable for its soft tannins and acids and with a distinctive sweetness, even though the wine is technically dry.

It has proved a useful softener for Cabernet Sauvignon and even Shiraz, although Merlot has since cracked the nod as a more pedigreed partner. Tassenberg, South Africa's biggest-selling red by the mid-'80s, started life as a Pinotage Cinsaut blend. It still contains Cinsaut, though now in a mélange with Tinta Barocca, Carignan and some Cabernet Sauvignon. One step up in quality and image, though as much a Cape tradition, Chateau Libertas also counts Cinsaut as one of its ingredients.

Cinsaut has been given a new lustre in modern blends with Merlot and Shiraz by Vergenoegd and Landskroon respectively, and Nelson's Creek and Somerbosch have combined it with Cabernet Sauvignon. Innovative Charles Back of Fairview landed up with a gold medal at the 1996 International Wine & Spirit Competition in London for his maiden '95 blend with Zinfandel.

The Cinsaut used is always well made, from carefully tended vines. And the results – soft, fruity wines with an immediate drinkability – show the enormous virtues of this grape as a blending component.

Those same virtues make do for a varietal wine, no more admirably so than in the Cinsaut from Windmeul, a Paarl co-operative. A pure

CAPE CINSAUT MAY SURPRISE WITH ITS DEPTH OF COLOUR AND FLAVOUR.

Cinsaut is a new addition to its tiny own-label range, as it is at Landskroon. Both Wellington and Wamakersvallei co-operative wineries also set aside some Cinsaut for bottling, where they're consistently well-priced, charming wines.

Though not an acknowledged port variety, Cinsaut has done duty as such in many local cellars – mostly co-operatives that wish only to produce a Ruby-style port with the high level of sweetness many South African palates prefer.

WINEMAKER'S COMMENT
Hein Koegelenberg, Windmeul: 'A new clone is allowing us to make Cinsauts with better colour and richer fruit flavours. Fermenting it slightly cold to start off with, plus adding some wood chips, has got rid of that burning character and complemented the flavours with vanilla. It'll never be a Cabernet or Merlot, but it's a good early-drinking wine.'

WINE WRITER'S COMMENT
David Biggs, SA columnist: 'Probably the only reason why Cinsaut is not popular among winemakers is that it is too easy to turn into good wine and can therefore not be sold for high prices. Have you ever tasted a bad Cinsaut?'

FOOD RECOMMENDATION
Red meat stir-fries; pasta with meat sauces; heavy soups (French onion, ham and pea); beef Stroganoff; pizza; corned beef.

THE CENTURY-OLD VATS IN THE VERGENOEGD CELLAR ARE STILL USED TO STORE RED WINE SUCH AS CINSAUT BEFORE BOTTLING.

ABOVE: MERLOT'S THIN-
SKINNED BERRY MAKES IT
SUSCEPTIBLE TO BOTRYTRIS,
WHICH IS NOT WELCOMED
BY WINEMAKERS.

OPPOSITE: NOW GERMAN-
OWNED AND PRODUCING
CLASSIC REDS INCLUDING
A CHAMPION MERLOT,
BUITENVERWACHTING HAS
VINDICATED 17TH-CENTURY
CAPE GOVERNOR SIMON VAN
DER STEL'S CHOICE OF
CONSTANTIA AS A PRIME
WINE-GROWING AREA.

MERLOT

Though a noble variety, it is relatively new, both here and in its homeland, France. It is most closely associated with the rich, powerful but luscious wines of St-Emilion and Pomerol, where it was quite widely planted in the late 18th century. Its fame as a truly great wine was probably single-handedly established by Château Pétrus in Pomerol, a rare and great 100 per cent Merlot Bordeaux. But it is Merlot's seamless union with Cabernet Sauvignon that has made it the third most populous red variety in France.

Although introduced to the Cape as early as 1910, it was only at the start of the 1980s, when winemakers set about making Bordeaux-style red blends, that Merlot took off. The recipe of 65 per cent Cabernet Sauvignon, 25 per cent Merlot and 10 per cent Cabernet Franc was known by rote by students of wine. Some winemakers still stick to it, with minor variations, most notably Giorgio Dalla Cia for his Meerlust Rubicon and Louise Hofmeyr of Welgemeend, but the recipe was adapted to suit individual sites and styles. The use of Cabernet Sauvignon and Merlot in equal quantities has become more commonplace, which produces wines in a dense, New World style (more robust than the elegant classics that that fine balance with Cabernet Franc seems to achieve).

Top winemakers such as Gyles Webb of Thelema and Jeremy Walker of Grangehurst have made pure Cabernet Merlot blends famous.

All the characteristics that make Merlot so masterfully complementary to Cabernet Sauvignon mark it as a great solo act too. It is the feminine counterpoint to Cabernet's masculinity, filling out its partner's almost aromatic herbaceousness and firm, austere structure with fleshy fruit, soft acids, silky tannins and accessible drinkability. Little wonder it has sidled up to Chardonnay in the fashion stakes.

The grape's popularity also has something to do with its greater productivity and earlier ripening than Cabernet Sauvignon. Merlot does best in cooler conditions and medium-potential soil; excessive warmth (and overly fertile soil) results in bunch rot and a drop in acid.

Overgaauw bottled the first commercially available Merlot in 1982, and Braam van Velden and Chris Joubert are still making one of the Cape's most memorable Merlots as well as putting together a selection called DC Classic for the exclusive Cape Independent Winemakers Guild Auction each year.

Jean Daneel produced a Diners Club award-winning Merlot at Buitenverwachting in 1991 and is now establishing Morgenhof Merlot as one of the top exponents of this variety. Other names to watch are Eikendal, Avontuur, Jordan, Hartenberg, De Trafford, Veenwouden, Saxenburg, Lanzerac and Vergelegen, as well as Fleur du Cap for pure drinkability. Several top-notch cellars with flagship Cabernet Merlot blends inevitably offer a Merlot almost equal in stature: Grangehurst, Yonder Hill and Warwick.

Merlot is one of the four 'big six' varieties in South Africa. Plantings have climbed dramatically in recent years, currently taking up about two per cent of total vineyard space.

Cape Merlots seem to be a little more tannic, concentrated and powerful than the French models. While this does not make them quite as accessible as they could be, it is still advisable not to cellar them for as long as Cabernet.

WINEMAKER'S COMMENT
Jean Daneel, Morgenhof: 'Merlot shouldn't be made too heavy, otherwise it loses its fruit. The challenge is to extract enough of its character, while keeping it soft and easy on the palate.'

WINE WRITER'S COMMENT
Fiona Morrison, UK Master of Wine: 'My ideal is exotic and voluptuous; dark in colour with the look of old velvet, shining and rich. A bouquet of truffle, dark cherry and violets.'

FOOD RECOMMENDATION
Red meat; duck, ostrich; stews; foie gras.

PINOTAGE

Where Chenin is the Cape's Cinderella variety, Pinotage is the prince. On it is pinned all the hopes and aspirations of this wine-producing country, which is fashionable on the international market but has yet to cross that threshold of acknowledgement as a long-term world player. If this cannot be achieved by making wines that have the beating of a Bordeaux or a Burgundy, then at least let the Cape make its mark with something uniquely, distinctively its own. The challenge is the Cape's alone, for despite a recent interest in the variety in New Zealand, the few wines bottled there and in Zimbabwe have been mediocre. And little has come of the meagre plantings in the United States.

Developed by viticulturist Prof Abraham Perold in 1925, Pinotage is the result of a cross between Pinot Noir and Cinsaut (then known as 'Hermitage'). Pinot Noir, a tricky, cool-climate customer, was a newcomer to Cape vineyards. It was struggling to find the right terroir, but promised a noble elegance of colour, fragrance and flavour. By matchmaking it with the established, adaptable Cinsaut with its ready yields, Prof Perold hoped to breed a strapping, blue-blooded youth.

Pinotage is exactly that. As a vine, it is strong and easy to grow. The fruit ripens early, achieving high sugars quite easily. It produces yields of moderate size, with trellising and pruning increasing and decreasing the crop respectively; this pleases the grower intent on quantity and the winemaker focused on quality. A young, good-quality Pinotage is a ruby red, assuming a blue-black density with a royal purple rim when grown and vinified with grand intentions.

The wine boasts the truly distinctive sweetness of red berry fruit (sometimes reminiscent of Pinot Noir's boiled-sweets aroma) with a characteristic banana-like aroma and flavour. This is perhaps most prevalent in a straightforward, unwooded or lightly wooded Pinotage. In its full-ripe, highly extracted, generously wooded robes, it takes on all the richness and complexity (supported by a firm acid and tannin structure) of a fine claret.

In its unwooded version, Simonsig has shown just how fruity and flavoursome Pinotage can be when treated seriously; the wine has an inherent structure that allows years of bottle-age. Eersterivier, Swartland, Rooiberg and Vlottenburg, all long-time co-operative Pinotage producers, seldom fail to feature the fresh, fruity, juiciness of the grape. Other traditional Pinotage producers, such as Jacobsdal and Kaapzicht, have honed the vigour and astringency of their erstwhile powerhouses down to a full-fruited, complex elegance, without losing that all-important structure.

The young Turks, however, are matching the old guard in producing heavyweights from new vines: look at Grangehurst and L'Avenir, and the latest ventures by Hamilton Russell (Southern Right). The new cachet of Pinotage has lured several winemakers renowned for their red-wine making ability into trying their hand at it: Warwick's Norma Ratcliffe and Charles Hopkins of Bellingham. These are fully extracted wines, with a density of colour and flavour to carry the weight of new wood and secure the reputation of the variety as one of the Cape's very own members of the modern international nobility.

Then, of course, there is Kanonkop, the undisputed Prince of Princes: bush vines produce lower yields and greater concentration, and these great blockbuster wines are high in acid and alcohol, rich in plummy fruit and banana sweetness and firm on tannin and oak. At the end of 1997, leading American wine publication *Wine Spectator* published its annual Top 100 wines: alongside the likes of Mondavi Chardonnay, Château d'Yquem, Château Lafite-Rothschild and Cloudy Bay Sauvignon Blanc stood the 1995 Kanonkop Pinotage. Say no more.

In 1996 Beyers Truter was instrumental in the formation of the SA Pinotage Producers' Association. This was a long-awaited initiative to establish Cape Pinotage benchmarks,

ABOVE: THE DENSE INKY COLOUR AND CRIMSON EDGE OF THIS PINOTAGE PROMISES A YOUTHFUL BLOCKBUSTER OF A WINE.

OPPOSITE: A MISTY MORNING AT SIMONSIG DURING THE STELLENBOSCH SUMMER HELPS THE MALAN BROTHERS GROW TOP-QUALITY GRAPES FOR THEIR RICH, FRUITY PINOTAGE.

AN OAK BARREL IS CHARRED
TO MEET A WINEMAKER'S
REQUIREMENTS FOR A SPECIFIC
DEGREE OF TOASTING, WHICH
INFLUENCES THE STYLE OF
THE WINE TO BE MADE.

quality guidelines and international marketing expertise, at a time when Pinotage was finally becoming known to palates worldwide.

After a slow start – it took more than 20 years to reach a handful of farmers' vineyards after that first successful cross – Pinotage first achieved prominence in 1959 when it surprised everyone by winning the Cape Young Wine Show. The wine was made by Pieter Morkel of Bellevue; he was a grape supplier to Stellenbosch Farmers Winery (SFW) and, with Senator Paul Sauer of Kanonkop,

the first to plant Pinotage. SFW bottled the first commercially available Pinotage, in 1961, under the Lanzerac label; this label was to become synonymous with the variety and establish it as one of the Cape's most popular wines.

But, as tastes became more sophisticated and winemakers started concentrating on international classic varieties such as Shiraz and Merlot, Pinotage lost favour. Often heavy and astringent, with a marked acetone character sometimes likened to nail varnish and paint, its share of total vineyard space declined from just under three per cent in 1981 to less than one per cent in 1990. The turn-around was again aided by international input, this time positive. Veteran UK wine critic Michael Broadbent wrote that Pinotage deserved serious attention and that it had a place in the world of wine. Urged to make their mark internationally with a distinctive wine, the Cape's winemakers started dusting off their existing Pinotage vines and ordering new material.

Now plantings are well over three per cent and climbing, with a shortage of plant material the main obstacle to meeting market requirements.

And winemakers really did dust off their vines: the lower yields of the older plants, grown as a bush rather than trellised, are producing fruit of enormous intensity.

The 'bush vine versus trellis' discussion is matched only by the 'French oak versus American oak' debate. Some believe that the distinctive vanilla character of American oak is tailor-made to enhance the variety's typical sweetness of fruit. Too sweet, say others, preferring the classic wood char and oak spice of French barrels to add a claret-like complexity and elegant austerity to an already fruit-rich wine.

Pinotage is one of the 'big six', and also has a role to play in the search for an 'authentic' Cape red blend. A groundbreaking combination of Pinotage and Cabernet Sauvignon by Johan Malan of Simonsig in 1994 wowed wine lovers and critics alike, and has earned a place at the top of this venerated cellar's range of red wines under the Frans Malan Reserve label. Besides

producing two award-winning varietal wines, Clos Malverne puts Pinotage together with Cabernet and Merlot in its highly rated Auret blend. Stellenbosch red-wine specialist Overgaauw quirkily combines Pinotage with Cabernet Franc for an easy-drinking red, which has proved remarkably long lasting.

Pinotage also pops up in Delheim's Rosé, Villiera's Tradition Carte Rouge and La Cotte port. Laborie has used Pinotage to produce a unique version of the Pineau des Charentes-style eau-de-vie. Pineau de Laborie is wine from a single Pinotage vineyard blended with pot-distilled Pinotage and matured in oak.

WINEMAKER'S COMMENT
Johan Malan, Simonsig: 'There's more beautiful fruit and substance in a good Pinotage than I've ever tasted in a Penfold's Grange.'

WINE WRITER'S COMMENT
Sue van Wyk, Cape Wine Master: 'Pinotage is like an old friend: a wine that comforts and cheers me and a joy to have on hand.'

FOOD RECOMMENDATION
Full-bodied: game dishes; roasts; gammon, ham. Medium-bodied, spicy: boerewors; ostrich; sauced meat pastas. Fruity: lamb curries.

STEPS DOWN FROM THE HAMILTON RUSSELL CELLAR LEAD YOU TO THE TASTING ROOM IN A QUAINT CAPE COTTAGE WHERE YOU CAN TASTE SOUTHERN RIGHT PINOTAGE.

ABOVE: ART AND ARTISANSHIP CONVERGE IN A STAINED GLASS WINDOW IN THE MURATIE TASTING ROOM, ILLUSTRATING THE MONASTIC INFLUENCE ON THE HISTORY OF WINEMAKING.

RIGHT: THE MELCK FAMILY, WHOSE 18TH- AND 19TH-CENTURY FOREBEARS OWNED MURATIE FOR OVER A CENTURY, REGAINED OWNERSHIP OF THIS ROMANTIC STELLENBOSCH ESTATE IN THE 1980S.

PINOT NOIR

Unpredictable in the vineyard, difficult in the cellar, Pinot Noir is nevertheless able to make one of the world's great red wines.

Pinot Noir is as venerable in age as it is in reputation. It was described as far back as the first century AD and is thought to be one of the first cultivated offspring of the wild vine. This strong, ancient lineage may explain the vine's uncommon capriciousness; its streak of wildness shows in its inability to settle down anywhere, including its home territory. The Côte d'Or (or 'slope of gold') in Burgundy is where Pinot Noir became firmly ensconced in the 15th century, and it proved to be one of the most prolific mutators, spawning a host of variations, both red and white.

Georg Canitz grew Pinot Noir on Muratie in Stellenbosch in the 1920s. But by the time Prof Abraham Perold decided to cross it with Cinsaut to develop the Pinotage grape, it was already making life difficult for growers.

This did not deter winemaker Peter Finlayson, when in the 1980s he laid the groundwork for the international success of Hamilton Russell's red

Burgundian speciality, then moved next door to establish his own vineyards with Burgundian *négociant* Paul Bouchard of Bouchard Aîne & Fils.

The success of Pinot Noir in these cool, southern vineyards of Walker Bay emulates the achievements of other New World winemakers, in chilly Oregon and on carefully selected cool sites of Western Australia.

Pinot Noir is like a ballerina. Fine-tuned and *en pointe*, it has a rare fluidity, a delicacy, a beguiling beauty that belies an underlying power and structural strength responsible for an unexpected ability to age with grace.

Ripeness of fruit and tannin is the ultimate achievement of the grape grower. This is particularly pertinent to Pinot Noir, which can turn lean and mean if not pampered by warm sun, cool nights, conscientious canopy management and a gentle touch in the cellar.

As with Chardonnay, Burgundy has always been the benchmark for Cape Pinot Noir. Achieving this self-set goal was not made easier by the predominance of the Swiss BK5 clone, intended for sparkling-wine production

and certainly not for fine red Burgundy. With the arrival in the 1980s of the genuine article in the forms of the PN113 and PN115 clones, wine styles changed from the typically organic, rather austere and slightly browning wines to a more fruit-full, rich and robust Pinot redolent of raspberries and underpinned by spicy new oak. Two long-time Pinot producers to have embraced this change are Meerlust and Muratie.

Led by Haute Cabrière (winemaker Achim von Arnim arrived at Pinot Noir via his specialisation in Méthode Cap Classique sparkling wine), this wave of new wines includes examples from such varying vineyards as cool-climate Klein Constantia; De Trafford, Hoopenburg and Neil Ellis in Stellenbosch; Glen Carlou in Paarl; and two other Walker Bay wineries, WhaleHaven and Goedvertrouw.

This variety has the unequivocal support of most of the committed Cap Classique cellars. While pure Chardonnay cuvées are counted among the top Champagnes, the classic combination with Pinot Noir has a charm all of its own. The Pinot provides a delicate fruitiness and fullness that smoothes and softens the structure and austerity of the Chardonnay. It is also the source of that incandescent partridge-eye pink that marks many of the Grande Marque's Brut Rosé Champagnes.

A couple of local wineries have made still-wine blends of Chardonnay and Pinot Noir, notably Boschendal, Haute Cabrière and Zevenwacht.

WINEMAKER'S COMMENT
Peter Finlayson, Bouchard Finlayson: 'I make wine to suit my palate, which is how the French do it. And I try to make a wine that will keep for at least five years. Pinot Noir is very fragile: I see myself simply as a caretaker of the product.'

WINE WRITER'S COMMENT
Michael Fridjhon, SA wine importer: 'You expect to find a little raspberry and a whiff of something organic, euphemistically called "farmyard" but actually more like hoenderhok (chicken run).'

FOOD RECOMMENDATION
Light meat dishes; chicken, ham, veal, Coq-au-Vin; anything with a mushroom sauce or filling (from risotto to omelette).

SHIRAZ
Unsung Shiraz, underrated and understated. In the Cape, that is, because elsewhere the variety is capable of some of the most powerful red wines in the world. We may not produce benchmarks to give the Rhône a rev, or the smooth and spicy, ripe and fruity gulpable reds that saw Australia conquer the international market, but Cape Shiraz offers wine lovers unplumbed depths of pleasure.

Shiraz (or Syrah, the French synonym) is one of the most ancient varieties. It is Middle Eastern in origin, but whether it hails from Shiraz in Persia (now Iran) or was shipped out from Egypt via Syracuse in Italy is not known. It is certain, however, that the variety was established in the Rhône by the time of the Roman Empire.

Shiraz flourishes on the 'roasted slopes' of the Côte-Rôtie and the south-facing aspects of the hills of Hermitage, and it produces the big, black wines that combine spiciness and silkiness, weight and finesse – and seem to get better and better with age.

Shiraz is a 'hot' wine: it loves warmth, and needs it to achieve full ripeness. It also does best on medium- to low-potential soil, as illustrated by its response to the struggle in the granite soils of rock-based Hermitage. Poor soils contain its naturally rather vigorous growth, thereby improving the quality and intensity of the fruit. No wonder it warmed to conditions in Australia, where it landed in the early 19th century and is now the second most planted variety there (accounting for nearly half of all red-wine vines). And no wonder it does well in the Cape.

Shiraz has always stopped short of achieving star status here. Local winemakers struggled with something colloquially called 'Shiraz disease', which affected the bark and killed off the vine.

PICTURE-BOOK PERFECT, THE 18TH-CENTURY ZEVENWACHT MANOR HOUSE HAS BEEN CONVERTED INTO A RESTAURANT SPECIALISING IN CAPE CUISINE.

But now there is some talent waiting in the
wings. Stellenzicht gave the Aussies a run for
their money in a bi-nations taste-off involving an
international panel of judges in 1995; the then-
winemaker André van Rensburg was placed third
with his 1994 Syrah, beating the famous Penfolds
Grange. Saxenburg is another new '90s cellar
making serious Shiraz, while a rejuvenated
Hartenberg has revamped its perennially sturdy
Shiraz into something even more sophisticated.
Recent vintages of the very fine Lievland, mean-
while, show a greater density, with long-time

winemaker Abé Beukes now working at the West
Coast cellar called Darling, where his touch is
already evident in its fruity, spicy Shiraz.

While Shiraz has done well in Stellenbosch
and Paarl, it has also shown its mettle in the
rather harsh, high-potential red-wine country
of the West Coast. Maverick vintner Charles
Back of Fairview is set to repeat his success with
Shiraz in the new Spice Route Wine Company's
vineyard venture near Malmesbury. And the large
Swartland co-operative winery often surprises
with a spicy, juicy Shiraz.

Shirazes from old-timers such as Van Loveren have these elements in very drinkable guise.

The range of Shiraz styles in the Cape is evidence of this grape's generous bounty. Its response to wood extends the range of flavours even further, with some winemakers enhancing its soft sweetness with the vanillins imparted by American oak; others believe in classic French oak to balance its rich fruit and savoury spiciness. Some combine the two, as is the case in that classic Cape Shiraz Rust-en-Vrede.

The Rust-en-Vrede cellar is at the nub of discussions around what constitutes a true Cape red blend. With Cabernet Sauvignon widely regarded as the first-choice ingredient, votes swing from Merlot to Pinotage to Shiraz as the most desirable match. There are some fine examples of Cabernet Shiraz blends: Rust-en-Vrede, Uitkyk and Saxenburg.

Cape Shiraz, one of the 'big six', is moving away from its old-style 'pong' (variously described as 'farmyardy', 'sweaty saddles' or 'leathery') towards a wine that combines red-berry fruit intensity with a spicy pepperiness and an inherent sweetness. Some still pick up the pong, but it has assumed the more acceptable overtones of gaminess and smokiness – in extremes, burnt rubber and tarriness. Highly desirable, believe it or not.

WINEMAKER'S COMMENT
Abé Beukes, Darling Cellars: 'Shiraz must struggle a little for water, which naturally curbs its vigorous growth, so one doesn't need to prune too heavily.'

WINE WRITER'S COMMENT
Angela Lloyd, SA writer: 'Seductive Shiraz – who could resist a wine with the dense, heady piquancy of wild herbs and bushes carried on a warm breeze? Just a whiff of that smoky, peppery fragrance fires the senses.'

FOOD RECOMMENDATION
Red meat dishes with sweet and spicy overtones; venison, oxtail, ostrich; bredies; goulash.

The variety has succeeded in Franschhoek and Robertson, too. In these once traditionally white-wine regions, Jacques Borman of La Motte has been producing consistently fine, forceful, fruit-rich wines, while Zandvliet Shiraz is evolving from a traditional, savoury, elegant wine into something that's still lean but has more fruit.

This development reflects the challenge of Shiraz: to combine the typical Rhône spiciness and pepperiness with the full-ripe fruit achieved by the Aussies. The first wines from new names such as Slaley and JP Bredell and the new-look

ABOVE: TINTA BAROCCA IS
BIG IN THE LITTLE KAROO,
WHERE VARIETAL WINES AND
PORT ARE MADE FROM IT.

RIGHT: KWV'S LOFTY
CATHEDRAL CELLAR HAS GIVEN
ITS NAME TO A RANGE OF
THIS NOW-PRIVATE COMPANY'S
WINES THAT RATE AMONG THE
CAPE'S BEST. THEY ARE,
UNFORTUNATELY, AVAILABLE
ONLY IN OVERSEAS WINE SHOPS.

TINTA BAROCCA

Essentially a port variety, Tinta Barocca is more readily recognised in South Africa than its sometimes classier companions in the port world, because it has appeared on the labels of several varietal red wines. And it was a slow but steady decline in the port market during the second half of this century that had local growers looking for alternatives for their Tinta Barocca, by far the most widely planted and quite highly rated port-wine grape in the Cape.

The variety was brought into the country in the mid-1900s. Even in Portugal, Tinta Barocca has been around for only a century – a short time in European terms.

Its merits as a port grape commended it as a varietal wine. Besides adapting well to local conditions, where it grows its typically long bunches with loosely packed berries, Tinta Barocca has a particularly rich red colour. It is less harsh and tannic than other port varieties, which adds accessibility, although it does remain an earthy, robust sort of a character.

This comes through in some of the Cape's few varietal Tinta Baroccas. Rust-en-Vrede in Stellenbosch, a red-wine estate of note, has long had a loyal following for its Tinta. A change of style from the old-fashioned gravelly, powerful wines of the early '80s to a mouthful of ripe berry fruit and soft oak vanillins has kept pace with taste trends. Die Krans, one of the champion port cellars, has also resurrected a varietal Tinta, full of berry fruit and spicy sweetness. Allesverloren is a paler wine, but still plummy, and Swartland's unwooded version highlights the fruitiness that Tinta can deliver. Goue Vallei still offers a reminiscent rusticity.

The more noble Touriga Nacional and Touriga Francesa are being introduced on a small scale, but all our world-class ports, such as the Vintages and Vintage Reserves from Boplaas, Die Krans and JP Bredell, are predominantly Tinta Barocca. And much of the KWV's finest includes Tinta Barocca, a lot sourced from Anton Bredell's farm in Faure. Landskroon, Vergenoegd and

Allesverloren – the traditional port cellars – still rely on Tinta Barocca. So, too, does Theo Rudman, in his exclusive Rudman's ports (made to his specifications by Stefan Smit, whose own Louiesenhof Perroquet port is also Tinta Barocca).

Tinta Barocca is, after all, on the list of the six varieties considered the best for port production in Portugal. And, with this variety firmly in their back pocket, Cape port makers are asserting themselves as contenders to be reckoned with.

WINEMAKER'S COMMENT

Boets Nel, Die Krans: 'Prunes, plums, some coffee, sometimes a pepperiness. Also an earthiness reminiscent of Italian Chianti. It has a good tannin structure, but we don't wood it because it's intended as a good-value dry red.'

WINE WRITER'S COMMENT

Tony Mossop, Cape Wine Master: 'Port is a cocktail, and while Touriga Nacional gives wonderful colour, tannin and chocolaty, pruney fruit, Tinta also brings colour and fruit, plus much-needed sugar to the party. Old Tinta Barocca vines can make damn good port, though, and for easy-drinking Ruby, it will always have a place in South Africa.'

FOOD RECOMMENDATION

Casual meat dishes with fruity or spicy flavours; braais.

THE
CHORUS LINE

BY NO STRETCH OF THE IMAGINATION CAN these be considered among the great grapes of the world of wine. But the regional classicism, for example, of Gewürztraminer in Germany and Alsace has rubbed off in many of the wine-producing regions, including the Cape. Similarly with Touriga Nacional, one of the world's several top port varieties. But besides that, Muscat d'Alexandrie (Hanepoot), Bukettraube, Colombard and Gewürztraminer are examples of lesser varieties that are somehow woven into the fabric of recent wine history in the Cape.

PREVIOUS PAGES: THE
CONSTANTIABERG FOOTHILLS
OFFER SLOPES WITH DIFFERENT
ASPECTS, PROVIDING WINE
ESTATES SUCH AS KLEIN
CONSTANTIA WITH A VARIETY
OF TERROIRS FOR TOP-QUALITY
WHITES AND REDS.

They are familiar and loved, and among the most recognisable names on labels. They are in the background, yes, but they offer a comfortable, pleasing alternative to the stars with their strong, assertive characters.

And there are plenty, particularly the port varieties, that may not shine individually but together make magic. Many of these varieties, and some new recruits such as Viognier and Petit Verdot, show the promise of becoming perhaps not regular performers in their own right but back-up artists that may make the lead look that much better – or simply help to raise the general level of wine quality in South Africa.

WHITE
Bukettraube, Colombard, Crouchen Blanc, Gewürztraminer, Fernão Pires, Furmint, Hárslevelü, Kerner, Muscat d'Alexandrie, Pinot Blanc, Pinot Gris, Sylvaner, Viognier

RED
Barbera, Gamay, Malbec, Petit Verdot, Pinot Meunier, Pontac, Ruby Cabernet, Souzão, Tinta Francisca, Tinta Roriz, Touriga Nacional, Zinfandel

WHITE VARIETIES

BUKETTRAUBE

BELOW: DESPITE ITS EASY
ADAPTABILITY, BUKETTRAUBE IS
NOT WIDESPREAD; THE CAPE IS
ONE OF THE WORLD'S FEW
WINE REGIONS TO BOTTLE
VARIETAL WINES.

Believe it or not, but South Africa is one of the few wine-producing countries in the world that bothers to bottle varietal Bukettraube. It was imported in the late 1960s, without much being known about its origins, though it is probably the same as Bouquettraube in Alsace. The German and French prefixes both mean 'bouquet'.

Bukettraube shares an aromatic character with another, more regal Alsatian grape, Gewürztraminer, which the individualistic Parkers of Altydgedacht successfully exploit in a blend of the two varieties in their lovely, spicy, semi-sweet Chatelaine.

Although Bukettraube is less popular than Gewürztraminer, it still commands plenty of loyalty among fans of its essentially grapey character with hints of sweet/spicy Muscat. Most Bukettraubes are semi-sweet, with Du Toitskloof and Goue Vallei the pick of the bunch.

Besides Altydgedacht, the places to go for varietal Bukettraube are the co-operative cellars, mainly in Stellenbosch and Paarl, which source some of their grapes from farmers in cooler, coastal climes.

Bukettraube matures easily, producing generous sugar and acid. This, together with its aromatic charm, is put to good use in blends. It also makes for a fairly successful Special Late Harvest sweet wine – try this one and the semi-sweet varietal version from Koelenhof co-op.

WINEMAKER'S COMMENT
Oliver Parker, Altydgedacht: 'I blend it with a dry Gewürztraminer to make the most of its floral character .... They complement each other nicely.'

WINE WRITER'S COMMENT
Allan Mullins, Cape Wine Master: 'The most that varietal wines made from Bukettraube have to commend them is a vague sort of a tropical fruit-salad flavour and a bit of grapiness ... best to drink them as lunchtime wines, well chilled and with lots of ice!'

FOOD RECOMMENDATION
Salads with lightly spiced flavours; smoked cold meats; ice cream.

AS THE SCREW TURNS, THESE FRESHLY HARVESTED GRAPES ARE GUIDED INTO THE CRUSHER AT VLOTTENBURG.

COLOMBARD

What South Africa did for Chenin Blanc in the 1960s, California did for Colombard in the '70s and '80s. But at least the Cape picked a classic to turn into its most planted variety! Whereas Chenin is acknowledged as a noble variety, capable of producing some of the world's most highly rated still wines, Colombard's main claim to fame lies in its contribution to fine Cognac. Yet even here it has been superseded by Ugni Blanc in recent decades. Originating in the southwest of France, it remains simply a crisp, fruity, dry and off-dry wine of modest quality.

It is as such that it has become established in the Cape, though it was initially introduced as a variety for the production of rebate brandy, based on its showing in Cognac. Thus it found its way into the hot hinterland, where it grows, often under irrigation, in the Orange River and Olifants River areas. It is also widespread in the Klein Karoo. Similarly big in the Breede River Valley, it was at Robertson Co-op that it first found favour, in the 1950s, as a variety that made passably good table wine.

Colombard is still one of the country's most widely planted varieties. A vigorous vine, it does well in hot climes. Its high natural acidity, which comes to the fore in warmer areas, gives life to white blends and is used to good effect with Chenin Blanc, which can often lose acid in similar conditions.

An aromatic, floral fragrance recommends it for palate-pleasing *vin de table*. Swartland and Villiersdorp wineries have pleasant Colombards, but the Breede River Valley has particularly good examples. Try cellars such as Nuy, Goedverwacht and Robertson for dry wines and Nuy, McGregor, Van Loveren and Weltevrede for off-drys.

Some winemakers in the area, including Springfield's Abrie Bruwer and Van Loveren's Wynand Retief, have tried blending it with Chardonnay, which to many palates is a far more harmonious marriage than the more fashionable Sauvignon Blanc Chardonnay combination.

While the distillers of the Charentes largely dismissed Colombard, some of the explorative Cape estate winemakers who are committed to producing a new generation of local potstill brandy to equal Cognac have selected Colombard as their grape of choice. Carel Nel of Boplaas and Roger Jörgensen of Claridge are among them. In Worcester, little-known Louwshoek-Voorsorg cellar produces a rare local version of a fortified Pineau des Charentes from Colombard, called Nektar de Provision.

WINEMAKER'S COMMENT
Danie Marais, McGregor: 'Although I like Chenin Blanc, I like to make fruity wines, for easy drinking. That's one of the charms of Colombard.'

WINE WRITER'S COMMENT
Phyllis Hands, SA author and educator: 'This is one of our less expensive white wines that not only smells good but tastes good, too. You don't have the disappointment of a good nose and a rather watery palate.'

FOOD RECOMMENDATION
Salads; light fish dishes; delicate terrines.

CROUCHEN BLANC (CAPE RIESLING)
This is a grape undergoing something of an identity crisis, which is the story of its long life. Among the first varieties to arrive in local vineyards a few centuries ago, it was then thought to be the German Rhine or Weisser Riesling. At some stage – probably when the real Riesling popped up – the error was discovered. But the Riesling tag remained – misleading, perhaps intentionally so – and the Cape adopted the grape as its own, calling it Cape or South African Riesling. On many labels it was simply varietally identified as Riesling, and Nederburg claimed the name Paarl Riesling for its white wine, with which it became synonymous.

The Australians were drawn into the confusion, importing cuttings from the Cape and first calling it Clare Riesling and then Sémillon. It was Down Under, in the 1970s, that a French ampelographer finally cottoned onto this variety's true origin and identity: Crouchen Blanc, a humble grape from southwest France and now almost non-existent there. Noble Rhine Riesling, a wine of great character mysteriously losing support among local wine lovers, had been done no favour by being linked, however subliminally, to this very ordinary white wine.

Yet this same ordinary wine had become a traditional favourite among South Africans, and grape growers planted it in increasing quantities in the '70s and '80s.

Crouchen Blanc is fussy, preferring a cool climate and not overly rich soils. Fertile soils make the berry prey to downy and powdery mildew and sour rot; a soft, thin skin does not help either.

The wine is at its finest when young, crisp and dry, though some residual sugar can add charm. High acidity can be a problem, but if gently handled, Cape Crouchen can be seductively soft, gently fruity and aromatic, with overtones of grass, hay and herbs.

The variety finds its best expression from cellars such as Nederburg (which has stunned with its bottle-ageing potential), Boschendal, Van Loveren, De Wet and Neethlingshof.

OPPOSITE TOP: THE ELANDSKLOOF AND WITZEN-BERG RANGES FLANK THE VINEYARDS AND WHEAT FIELDS AT RIEBEEK KASTEEL.

OPPOSITE BELOW: THE COLOMBARD VINE IS A GROWER THAT DOES WELL IN HOT CLIMES.

BELOW: THE COLOUR OF A COLOMBARD WINE CAN VARY BETWEEN A BRIGHT, PALE-STRAW YELLOW TO A VERY PALE GOLD, OFTEN WITH A HINT OF GREEN DENOTING YOUTH.

Theuniskraal in Tulbagh is perhaps the 'Riesling' many long-time wine drinkers hold most dear to their hearts, after that of Nederburg.

WINEMAKER'S COMMENT
André Bruwer, Bon Courage: 'I have a soft spot for Cape Riesling. I make it [unusually] off-dry.'

WINE WRITER'S COMMENT
Michael Fridjhon, SA wine importer: 'A couple of these wines develop a lovely, soft, round, flowery mid-palate after five or six years in the bottle.'

FOOD RECOMMENDATION
Light, green salads.

GEWÜRZTRAMINER
Of Italian parentage, this variety was officially so named in the 1970s in its traditional home territory of Alsace. Its former name of Traminer Aromatico was perhaps more apt, for it produces wines that are notably aromatic rather than spicy (the German word for spice is 'Gewürz').

It has become one of the great grapes of Alsace. For all the sweetly pretty promise of its appearance – blushing pink berries, peachy coloured liquid, a perfumed floral fragrance – Alsace Gewürz is classically dry on the palate. And it has a fair whack of alcohol. Gewürztraminer has a low, erratic yield, and in South Africa it can ripen too quickly to develop flavour, but if left beyond mid-season it loses acid. Cool areas with fertile, clayey soil to retain moisture suit it best, which is why you find Constantia and Elgin wines capturing the aromatic freshness of Gewürz; those from warmer Stellenbosch, Paarl and Robertson are often sweeter, though De Wetshof in Robertson has cocked a snook at this theory with a bone-dry, rose-petal wine.

Generally, the Cape-style Gewürztraminer is far more delicate than that of Alsace, often with relatively low alcohols. Styles do vary, though, with the light Buitenverwachting leading the dry contingent, followed by fine wines from Fairview and Altydgedacht. Paul Cluver in Elgin and Groot Constantia are good examples of an off-dry, as are Weltevrede, Neethlingshof and Villiera. Some residual sugar adds flavour and weight, while the dry wines risk carrying a vestige of bitterness.

GREEN FOLIAGE PROTECTS THE GRAPES AGAINST THE HOT SUMMER SUN IN THE VALLEY OF TULBAGH, ENCIRCLED BY THE GROOT WINTERHOEK AND WITZENBERG RANGES.

The Cape does rather well with its late-harvest sweet Gewürz. Vlottenburg is jolly fine, but even finer is Bon Courage, which won winemaker André Bruwer the coveted Diners Club Winemaker of the Year award when this variety was the category judged in 1985. Not too shabby for a grape that holds an increasingly tenuous grip on a share of local vineyards. The aroma and flavour profile includes the fragrant scents of rose petals and incense, with a touch of spice and a hint of honey on a mouthful of tropical fruit.

WINEMAKER'S COMMENT
Nicolaas Rust, Weltevrede: 'Mature vines make a big difference: ours are between 15 and 20 years old. And I leave the juice on the skins overnight after pressing and add juice from a second pressing of the almost dry skins to get as much flavour into the wine as possible.'

WINE WRITER'S COMMENT
Malcolm Gluck, English columnist, on Van Loveren Special Late Harvest Gewürztraminer: 'The most hedonistic of delights, for it reeks of rose petals, tastes of mango and peach with a sort of nutty undertone (a fat, greasy nut like macadamia) and, yes, it is sweet, but it drips with flavour.'

FOOD RECOMMENDATION
Smoked cold meats; aged Cheddar or pungent cheeses; mild curries (if wine is sweeter); Thai and Indonesian dishes.

STORM CLOUDS GATHER OVER THE CONSTANTIABERG IN SUMMER, BRINGING COOLTH TO THE VINEYARDS OF BUITENVERWACHTING IN THE LEE OF THE MOUNTAIN.

FERNÃO PIRES

South Africa is one of the few countries outside Portugal where this aromatic white variety is cultivated as a wine grape. Upon finding its way to the Cape sometime during the second half of this century, it quickly found its niche in the dry, arid areas of Worcester and Robertson, being quite a productive plant and ripening early in the season.

Here, it seemed to charm several winemakers sufficiently to bill it as a one-man show. In 1982 Van Loveren was the first to bottle a varietal Fernão; co-operative wineries Nuy, Bergsig,

Merwida and Die Krans in the Klein Karoo soon followed. While Fernão Pires in Portugal is distinguished by an aroma and flavour that is pure peppercorns, the early versions of the local wines had more of a herby, wildflower character with a hint of Muscat. Initially made dry and quite alcoholic, the wines have evolved, and most winemakers have settled for a far more appealing, slightly sweet style. It still has its Muscat character, but some lemony, citrous fruit is coming through.

Of the current wines being bottled, the Nuy is close to capturing the pepperiness of the

Portuguese Fernão. The off-dry Van Loveren and Swartland are more fruity and fresh, while De Wet Co-op in Worcester has a slightly sweet wine that develops an unexpected richness in the bottle.

For the rest, small crops in areas as diverse as Stellenbosch and the Olifants River Valley contribute towards easy-drinking blends, such as the off-dry Delheim Grandesse and the Vredendal Piquant. And it is used to add a touch of spice to co-op sparklers, from Klawer's Demi-Sec to both dry and semi-sweet bubblies at Vredendal.

WINEMAKER'S COMMENT
Bussell Retief, Van Loveren: 'It's almost like a Chenin, with a firm acidity. But it's slightly more full and round – the alcohol can climb quite high – and sometimes you get a bit of spiciness.'

WINE WRITER'S COMMENT
Allan Mullins, Cape Wine Master: Van Loveren's Fernão is 'a delicious off-dry wine with just a hint of Muscat honey on the nose.'

FOOD RECOMMENDATION
Delicately spicy foods; a peppery salad.

FURMINT

Say 'Furmint' and many will look uninterested; say 'Tokay' and at least those who relish noble rot wines will register recognition. Around since at least the 13th century, Furmint is the Hungarian variety that dominates that country's world-famous sweet dessert wines, with Hárslevelü as its partner. Much like Sauvignon Blanc and Sémillon in Sauternes, Furmint is the tart, pungent partner balanced by Hárslevelü's soft, full-bodied character.

Hárslevelü and Furmint were introduced in South Africa at roughly the same time, about 20 years ago, though strangely have never performed together; Hárslevelü settled mainly in the then-relative backwaters of Robertson and Worcester, while Furmint wandered indiscriminately through the Cape's winelands, popping up in Stellenbosch, Malmesbury and Worcester.

In the early 1980s, two family wine farms – the Lategans' Bergsig in Worcester and the Pecks' Oude Nektar in Stellenbosch – were among the first to bottle Furmint on its own. Like the hefty Hungarian dry whites, it was quite a heavyweight – substantial, with firm alcohol and acid and a distinctive flavour of apples.

But Furmint gradually lost favour, with no varietal example surviving today. Scraps of vineyard remain, however, and their crops go towards all-purpose white blends, such as Delheim's best-selling Heerenwijn.

HÁRSLEVELÜ

This was one of the unusual varieties tested by South African viticultural researchers during the 1970s, but it has not made much of an impression on local winemakers (despite the fact that it has left its mark in the famous, smoothly sweet Tokay dessert wines and produced some pungent sweet and spicy varietal wines in its homeland).

Rather, it was as a dry white that it gained credence here. Adaptable to low-lying, sandy, gravelly ground with clay sub-soils, Hárslevelü is a vigorous grower, and careful pruning and trellising are needed to achieve the characteristic pungency and flavour extract that makes this rarity worthwhile. Although a handful of wineries in Robertson, Malmesbury, Franschhoek and Tulbagh flirted with this exotic for a couple of vintages, only two endured: Van Loveren and Lemberg. Van Loveren was first in the bottle, launching it together with its equally unusual Fernão Pires in 1982. A crisp, dry wine with a pineappley palate, it was later developed into something more substantial, marked by a hint of herbs and honey.

At Lemberg, then-owner and winemaker Janey Muller devoted all her attention to it and her Sauvignon Blanc, and the varietal wine has been available since 1984. She coaxed a rare richness and character out of these large, thick-skinned grapes. This dry white is still a pleasant mouthful, high in alcohol but low on acid.

WINEMAKER'S COMMENT
Bussell Retief, Van Loveren: 'It produces a much lighter wine than the Fernão, softer, fruitier, more like Colombard. We make it off-dry. But we won't be making it anymore; the name is just too complicated for everyday wine drinkers.'

WINE WRITER'S COMMENT
Hugh Johnson, English author, on the variety's Tokay sweet wines: 'Pure succulence.'

FOOD RECOMMENDATION
Mild curries; fresh fruit desserts.

BURGUNDIAN VINEYARD
PRACTICES AT BOUCHARD
FINLAYSON IN THE HEMEL-
EN-AARDE VALLEY INCLUDE
PLANTING VINES CLOSE
TOGETHER – JUST OVER ONE
METRE APART – WITH EVERY
SIXTH ROW MISSING TO
ACCOMMODATE A TRACTOR
FOR SPRAYING.

KERNER

This wine made a relatively recent crossing to the Cape from the German wine-training institute Weinsberg. Some say it is named for the 19th-century poet and physician Justinus Kerner; others that it has far more practical connotations – the grape has a faint taste of the pip or 'kernel', which gives the wine a tannic, almost nutty bite, more typical in a white that has been wooded.

Another oddity is its ancestry. Sired by the regal Riesling, its other parent is a red grape, Trollinger – perhaps the source of its tannic trait? Trollinger, a variety common in Germany, is actually an Italian table grape called Schiava Grossa or Black Hamburg.

Kerner was one of the better-quality varieties among the rather rag-tag bunch brought into South Africa in the 1970s, and for a time it did take off as a bottled wine.

The first attempts to make a varietal Kerner were mostly dry, which emphasised the grape's steely character and brought out related peppery, smoky, leafy and appley aromas and flavours. But it was found that a spot of residual sugar softened the wine's inherently robust nature.

There was quite a selection of Kerners in the 1980s, reflecting the wide-ranging presence of the variety on both premium cool-vineyard sites and the warmer winelands of Robertson and Worcester. But contrary to its continuing cachet in Germany, Kerner has more or less died in the Cape. Today you will find Kerner only in the odd white blend, for example the rather fine Bouchard Finlayson Blanc de Mer.

MUSCAT D'ALEXANDRIE

This venerable ancient has become the Cape's everyday old 'Hanepoot'. Depending on which rural or urban legend you believe, this vine of African origin (graced with the name of the exotic Egyptian city of Alexandria) has been bastardised by either the Boers or the British.

Apparently, all the Queen's men were so taken with the succulent sweet grapes that they snacked on in-between fighting the Afrikaners at the turn of the century that they nicknamed them 'honeypot' (which in the local vernacular became 'hanepoot'). Another version is that the three-stalked bunches of grapes are shaped like a rooster's foot, hence the Afrikaans translation 'hanepoot'. The more bawdy version will have it that 'hanepoot' is in fact a corruption, whether accidental or polite, of the Dutch 'hanekloot' or cock's testicles, which the large, egg-shaped berries are said to resemble.

Born under the hot African sky, Muscat d'Alexandrie warmed to conditions in the Cape, where it is thought to have been the 'Spaanse druyfen' ('Spanish grapes') referred to by Van Riebeeck in the 17th century. It was only in the 1920s that viticultural research proved that the humble Hanepoot and the Muscat d'Alexandrie (planted in an arc around the Mediterranean) were one and the same.

Its proliferation in the Mediterranean, and here, was surprising, given its overall weakness as a vine, being susceptible to most diseases and preferring deep, moisture-retaining soils. As a natural wine it is soft and sweet, with low acid and a simple, perfumed Muscat flavour. But its charm in dry places was unveiled when the combination of high sugars and a concentrated sweetness – resulting from the natural dehydration as it begins to raisin – combined to produce a rich, honeyed liquid.

Muscat d'Alexandrie is one of two major Muscat varieties – the other being Muscat de Frontignan – that have given rise to the reputation of Robertson, Worcester and the Klein Karoo as the home of Muscadel and Hanepoot Jerepigo. It is fourth on the list of most-planted wine grapes in South Africa, despite being the lesser of the two varieties. It is used mostly for Jerepigo, which is often branded as Hanepoot Jerepigo or Soet (Sweet) Hanepoot, or simply Hanepoot. Those wines labelled as just Jerepigo are often made from other grape varieties.

Our Hanepoots are in the same league as Portugal's Moscatel de Setúbal and Italy's Moscato di Pantelleria, though not half as famous. Similar methods of stopping fermentation of the grape juice by adding natural spirit are used.

Most of the co-operatives in the Breede River Valley and beyond, as well as those in the west, produce outstanding examples of Hanepoot Jerepigo. Some are rich and sweet, marked by honey and raisin flavours, such as Calitzdorp Golden Jerepigo, Douglas Soet Hanepoot and Mooiuitsig Soet Hanepoot; these are the wines for lovers of real 'stickies'. Most classic Hanepoots are fresh and delicate but still full-flavoured: Du Toitskloof Hanepoot Jerepigo, Rooiberg Hanepoot, Domein Doornkraal Hanepoot, Fleermuisklip Hanepoot and Bergsig Soet Hanepoot.

Many goodies are cropping up in fine-wine country, too, such as the Hanepoots from Vlottenburg and Koelenhof in Stellenbosch, and the Boland Hanepoot in Paarl, a 1998 gold medallist at the annual Veritas national wine judging (as was the Hanepoot from Swartland, also in 1998).

A handful of Cape cellars have garnered the tropical-fruit sweetness of Muscat d'Alexandrie for a semi-sweet blended

MUSCAT D'ALEXANDRIE, WHETHER DRY OR SWEET, IS ONE OF THE FEW WINES TO ACTUALLY SMELL AND TASTE DISTINCTLY OF GRAPES.

white wine: Koelenhof's Koelenheimer, Haute Provence's Angel's Tears, Nelson's Marguerite, and Stellenzicht's Fragrance. But it is at the Eersterivier Cellar in Stellenbosch that students of wine are presented with an interesting study in comparisons: its traditional Hanepoot Jerepigo alongside its Muscat d'Alexandrie, a perfumed yet firm, bone-dry surprise.

WINEMAKER'S COMMENT
Philip Jordaan, Du Toitskloof: 'I like to make my Hanepoot Jerepigo full-sweet and full-flavoured. With the minimum level of fortification now officially lower, one gets less of a distinctive spirity character, which makes the wine much softer and more drinkable. I leave my wine on the skins overnight during fermentation, to extract

that lovely fruity, pineappley flavour. Older [50-year-old] bush vines of the old, long-berry clone still produce the best Hanepoot.'

WINE WRITER'S COMMENT
David Biggs, SA columnist: 'I believe it captures the very soul of the South African winelands: juicy and sweet, with the aroma of sun-warmed honey. My late father, who was not a wine drinker at all, used to say he would drink any kind of wine, as long as he was allowed to add a splash of Hanepoot.'

FOOD RECOMMENDATION
Dry: spicy, light white meat such as chicken or fish. Sweet: mild curries; mild, creamy cheeses.

THE HEAT OF THE KLEIN KAROO HAS FORCED SOME GROWERS IN CALITZDORP TO TRAIN THE VINES ACROSS WIRES BETWEEN THE ROWS TO GIVE THE FRUIT EXTRA SHADE.

A RESTORED ROW OF CAPE
DUTCH OUTBUILDINGS ON
L'ORMARINS ESTATE IN
FRANSCHHOEK. THE ORIGINAL
OLD CELLAR, STILL IN PARTIAL
USE, IS AT THE FAR END.

PINOT BLANC

A mutation of the noble red Pinot Noir, Pinot Blanc is a white variety that has been readily confused with Chardonnay the world over. This is no doubt due to the fact that it hailed from the Côte d'Or before establishing itself in Alsace in the mid-16th century, and its relatively neutral flavour and easy productivity did not do much to distinguish it from simply vinified and unwooded Chardonnay. What is labelled Pinot Blanc in Australia is, in fact, often Chardonnay.

The first varietal Pinot Blancs only started coming through in South Africa in the early 1990s, and mostly from warmer areas such as Paarl and Robertson. South African Pinot Blancs have received quite serious treatment. Both Landskroon and Van Loveren have wooded their Pinot Blancs, balancing racy acidity with soft, sweet vanilla and coming up with Chardonnay-like butteriness and toastiness on top of a fundamentally firm mouthful. These wines could age, too, developing honeyed tones. Sometimes

you will find a definite musky, spicy Muscat fragrance lurking there, very much à la Alsace.

In 1997, Hartenberg bottled a wood-fermented Pinot Blanc under its new Montagne label (kept for unusual additions to its regular range), and a full-bodied, slightly spicy, firmly fruited wine appeared. Nederburg's Pinot Blanc, first introduced at the 1996 Nederburg Auction as the Private Bin D250, was also barrel-fermented, but in American oak for a change.

WINEMAKER'S COMMENT
Paul de Villiers, Landskroon: 'We've tried a lot of things with this wine, fermenting in small wood, with wood chips. The barrel-fermented produces a nice wine: full-bodied, quite high alcohol, with an almost Chardonnay-like citrus character.'

WINE WRITER'S COMMENT
Roger Voss, UK author: 'This produces some of the most readily drinkable wines in Alsace.'

FOOD RECOMMENDATION
Light meat or fish dishes with mild curried or creamed sauces. Aged: spicy or honeyed food; anything you would normally match with a mature Rhine Riesling.

PINOT GRIS
This is another scion of Pinot Noir but, like Pinot Blanc, it is a white variety. You may not think so, however, when looking at the bluish-pink hue of the grape skins; could this have given rise to the reference to grey ('gris') in its name? Or was it the generally indeterminate nature of the fruit and its wine, which is low in acid and light in flavour? Perhaps its early place in the medieval vineyards of the robed Cistercian monks inspired the Hungarian reference to it as Szürkebarat, which means 'grey monk'.

If left on the vine in northerly regions such as Alsace and Hungary, it does develop flavour, which together with the sweetness of late-harvested grapes results in some fine dessert wines known as Tokay. But a propensity to lose acid if left on the vine too long in warmer climes forces growers to pick early and sacrifice flavour. The result? Rather grey wines.

Cape wines are somewhere in-between. Pinot Gris arrived here in the 1970s, with the promise of disease resistance, good yields and wines with deep colour and body. This, plus its neutrality, recommended it as a fine blending wine and as a base for bubbly. The first varietal wine came from L'Ormarins in Franschhoek in the mid-1980s.

Different areas and winemakers' preferences produced different styles. Some liked the fat, oily, full-bodied wines with high alcohols (sometimes wooded). Later, the wines became more delicate and fresher, with a slightly spicy, earthy character.

The Cape's few remaining Pinot Gris wines are typically simple, soft and faintly fruity: Fairview, L'Ormarins, Louiesenhof and Stellenzicht.

WINEMAKER'S COMMENT
Wrensch Roux, L'Ormarins: 'I leave it on the lees for a bit, and it comes out with a delicate floral fragrance and just a hint of earthiness.'

WINE WRITER'S COMMENT
Roger Voss, UK author: 'I am generally torn between a good Tokay [Pinot Gris] and a good Riesling.'

FOOD RECOMMENDATION
Salads: green, noodle or rice.

THE PRIVATE HOME OF L'ORMARINS OWNER ANTONIJ RUPERT IS OFF-LIMITS TO VISITORS — BUT ITS EARLY 19TH-CENTURY NEO-CLASSICAL GABLE IS WORTH A PEEK THROUGH THE DRIVEWAY GATE.

SYLVANER

SYLVANER, THE PALEST OF YELLOW IN YOUTH, CAN TURN POSITIVELY GOLDEN AS IT AGES.

Sylvaner 'belongs' to Overgaauw. Not because – as is popularly but erroneously believed – this historic Stellenbosch estate has been the only winery to vinify the grape as a varietal wine, but because cellarmaster Braam van Velden's nearly nine hectares is practically all there is left of the 20 hectares planted in the early 1970s.

Sylvaner's introduction to the Cape was influenced by the then-strong German tradition of winemaking in South Africa, with Geisenheim-trained guru Günter Brözel at the helm. He bottled a few vintages of Sylvaner for Nederburg, until lack of demand led to its demise. And although Overgaauw's first wine labelled as Sylvaner came out in 1971, it was subsequently identified as Müller-Thurgau, of which Sylvaner is a parent. In fact, there is confusion about Sylvaner, which is generally accepted as having originated along the banks of the Danube, but also mooted as coming from Austria.

Whatever the case, Overgaauw Sylvaner has definitely been the real thing since 1978, when new plantings were established, and regrafted in 1989. The wine, traditionally made dry, is now a more approachable off-dry, with some sweetness to balance its naturally high acidity.

Although made to be enjoyed in its youth, Overgaauw Sylvaner has shown delightful development in the bottle. A vintage such as the 1982, with its creamy, citrus and honey flavours, has emulated the ageing potential of some of the Alsace Sylvaners (the only other region where the variety is not spelt Silvaner).

In 1997 Overgaauw stepped out with a Sylvaner Sémillon blend, balancing the Sylvaner's acidity with some Sémillon fatness and oak vanillins, emphasising its spiciness.

WINEMAKER'S COMMENT

Braam van Velden, Overgaauw: 'My father [David van Velden] was looking for something that ripened earlier than Chenin. We planted in 1963 and have been going ever since. Sylvaner is a consumer-friendly wine and people would be disappointed if we didn't make it. We're conserving an endangered species.'

WINE WRITER'S COMMENT

Dave Hughes, SA writer: 'Fruit salad nose of peach, mango and spice, balanced with rich, grapey flavours. Almost frivolous in its youth, sincere and satisfying as it ages and distinctly elegant but very comforting in full maturity.'

FOOD RECOMMENDATIONS

Quiche; chicken salad.

VIOGNIER

The origins of Viognier are unsure, but Roman Emperor Probus is said to have introduced it to France towards the end of the 3rd century.

Viognier (pronounced Vioni-yay) is isolated to just a few appellations in France, and has a minuscule yield of around 20 hectolitres a hectare. That winemakers have persevered with it is evidence of its greatness; that it has come to the Cape at all says something for the fortitude and tenacity of our winemakers.

What is all the fuss about? Viognier is lauded for its intensity of perfume, both in aroma and flavour; it confounds with its ever-present promise of sweetness, despite being made technically dry. It is a rare combination of fullness and finesse; it is fat without being flabby.

Although it is one of the great white wines of the world, Viognier has also found its way into the famous Côte-Rôtie Shirazes.

The exciting thing about the Cape's fledgling Viognier is that it is proving even more full-bodied than many of the Rhône proponents. Fairview first planted Viognier in the mid-1990s, finding the upper reaches of its Paarl Rock

vineyards (decomposed granite on a clay sub-strata) most favourable for this lover of hot, dry conditions. The soils are well drained and ideal for a drought-resistant variety that does not like getting its feet wet, and the vine has behaved in the requisite shy way, giving just two tons a hectare at this infant stage.

Winemaker Charles Back and his Rhône ranger Anthony de Jager went the whole hog, picking full-ripe grapes, pressing whole bunches, fermenting in barrel, working the lees for four months and maturing in second-fill French oak. The result, bottled in time for a connoisseur's Christmas 1998, is vintage Viognier: high in alcohol, with the recognisable ripe apricot and dried peach aromas, perfumed and mouthfilling. A grape to watch.

WINEMAKER'S COMMENT

Anthony de Jager, Fairview: 'It's quite a heavyweight, rich, high alcohol, but with gorgeous fruit, very distinctive, strong – apricot and peach, but more of a dried peach. People will either like it or hate it. I'm very excited by this wine – we're getting some of the typical Rhône character here.'

WINE WRITER'S COMMENT

Remington Norman, UK author: 'It is one of the more unusual and enigmatic great white varieties – unusual because of its seductively opulent character of apricots, blossom and dried fruit; enigmatic in its determination not to surrender its charms in less than ideal growing conditions. As winemakers tame this capricious variety – or more likely, the converse – expect great things!'

FOOD RECOMMENDATION

Creamy fish soups (Lobster bisque); mild, coconut-milk curries.

OPPOSITE: THE COMPACT GROUP OF CELLAR BUILDINGS AT OVERGAAUW, WHERE THE VICTORIAN TASTING ROOM IS A RARITY AMONG THE MORE COMMON MODERN OR CAPE DUTCH STYLES.

BELOW: FAIRVIEW HAS BOTTLED THE CAPE'S FIRST VARIETAL VIOGNIER, WHICH HAS TAKEN WELL TO THE RHÔNE-LIKE CONDITIONS OF SOME HOT, DRY SITES IN PAARL.

RED VARIETIES

BARBERA

With Italy never playing a significant role in the Cape winemaking industry, Italian grapes were never much considered. So this 13th-century peasant from Piedmont – Italy's most common red-wine grape and also popular in California – found only one supporter in the Cape: Ralph Parker, third-generation owner of the historic Altydgedacht in Durbanville, was persuaded to plant some in the early 1900s. It was only in 1981 that wine lovers became aware of it, when the crop from this single hectare was bottled in a 50/50 blend with Shiraz. It was called Tintoretto.

The wine was established as a regular member of the small Altydgedacht range in 1986 by grandson Oliver Parker, the current winemaker. By this time, the octogenarian vines were barely producing a crop, but the Parkers decided to replace them with new plantings; the maiden vintage of the Cape's only varietal Barbera appeared in 1992.

Although most suited to poor, calcareous soils, the variety does fairly well on loamy soils and can produce characterful wines in cool areas.

The approach at Altydgedacht is highly individual. The wine is robust, and high in alcohol and acid – the latter is prized in Barbera overseas, where its role in a blend is to give some power and zing. The wine's almost purple colour, as well as its dry finish, resembles that of the highly rated examples from northwest Italy. Its profile has changed, though, with the first vintage showing a herby dryness and recent vintages delivering more fruity richness, though still with that typical brambly finish.

The Parkers may have some company soon: the equally individualistic Gyles Webb of Thelema has put Barbera on his shopping list.

FIVE GENERATIONS OF PARKERS HAVE FARMED AT ALTYDGEDACHT IN DURBANVILLE; THEY STEADFASTLY STICK TO TRADITIONAL WINEMAKING TECHNIQUES IN THEIR CELLAR, WHICH DATES BACK TO 1710.

Oliver Parker, Altydgedacht: 'It has a wildness about it that I thought would be well matched by the robustness of American oak barrels, a bit like Pinotage. And it seems to have worked out. It's a strong wine, sort of rustic.'

WINE WRITER'S COMMENT
Dave Hughes, SA writer: 'A most unusual but most attractive wine: herbal nose, yet good brambly and ripe blackberry flavours and firmness in the mouth, with lots of vanilla from a couple of years in American oak. Reasonably robust.'

FOOD RECOMMENDATION
Italian fare: antipasti; pasta with tomato-based sauces; Parma ham.

GAMAY NOIR

Synonymous with the fresh, fruity wines of Beaujolais, the Gamay Noir (or plain old Gamay) grape is a native of Burgundy from around the 14th century. But it is the very antithesis of the refined Pinot Noir, producing a joyful, juicy wine, much loved by even the most serious connoisseur and well recommended as a starting point for those new to the juice of the grape. In fact, it can be as close to grape juice as you can get, give or take 10 per cent or so of alcohol.

As the pundits will point out, however, there is Gamay and there is Gamay, even within the Beaujolais genre.

The Cape produces a little of both, though the Nouveau fruit-juice style, usually unwooded and somewhat derogatorily described as 'bubblegum wine', has been popularised by the annual Paarl Nouveau Wine Festival.

True-blue Gamay is produced by the traditional carbonic maceration method: whole bunches, sealed in with carbon-dioxide, undergo an automatic fermentation within each berry. At the same time, normal fermentation of juice from the bottom layer of berries, crushed by the weight of the whole bunches, takes place.

Fairview leads the pack, with the latest offerings leaning more towards the full, fruity, spicy style of a benchmark Beaujolais.

Gamay was introduced in the 1920s, but never made serious inroads in Cape vineyards with the more prolific and consistent Cinsaut as an alternative for fruity, easy-drinking reds, and the number of varietal Gamays has been dropping.

It is a grape noted for its high acidity, and should be balanced by the luscious sweet fruit typical of the variety. Grape tannins are usually low and many Beaujolais wines are unwooded. They are not meant to last long, although the finer proponents have bucked the trend with the development of a silky smoothness with time. But some of the best Beaujolais is oaked and full of fruit, tannin and intensity, the choice of connoisseurs. Verdun in Stellenbosch, famous for its then-unusual varietal Gamay back in the 1970s and early '80s, recently resurrected the grape, and winemaker Marius Lategan has treated it to some sweet, spicy American oak à la Burgundy.

The Côte d'Or winemakers blend controlled amounts of Gamay into their Pinot Noir, and the variety is used for blending elsewhere in France. Cape winemakers, however, have experimented with slightly more unorthodox combinations. Charles Back of Fairview has snuck it into everything from Shiraz to Cabernet Sauvignon, invariably coming up with a quaffable wine. His pure Gamay dry Rosé was a local novelty when introduced in 1993 – it now includes Cinsaut and Cabernet Franc. Vlottenburg Co-op has impressed with a Reserve wood-matured blend of Shiraz and Gamay, and Rhebokskloof has used it in a dry red with Merlot, Cabernet

THE USUALLY LIGHT-BODIED, EASY-DRINKING GAMAY NOIR IS GIVEN SOME EXTRA BODY FROM BARREL TREATMENT AT VERDUN.

Sauvignon and Cinsaut, but is now wooding it to produce a savoury wine with typical astringency yet soft tannins.

WINEMAKER'S COMMENT
Charles Back, Fairview: 'We had this piece of land on the lower part of the farm with sandy soil and low potential. We knew it would produce grapes with low acid. We chose Gamay Noir. We had a gap for an easy-drinking light wine, and our Gamay Noir has slotted into that gap.'

WINE WRITER'S COMMENT
Allan Mullins, Cape Wine Master: 'The wines are pleasant, fruity and enjoyable drinking. For South Africans, Nouveau wines have come to stay.'

FOOD RECOMMENDATION
Cold meats; light pasta dishes; smoked meats; spicy sausage dishes; pork; mild Malay curries.

MALBEC
Malbec is one of the traditional, if less renowned varieties upon which the Bordelaise (who call it Cot) have built their reputation for fine clarets. Despite a problem with berry set, Malbec is a fairly heavy bearer; this, together with its low acidity and soft fruitiness, was probably responsible for its initial popularity in France. But it is falling out of favour there, though it still forms the backbone of the Argentinean wine industry, however, and is a popular partner to Merlot in Chile.

Colour and bouquet were Malbec's main contributions to reds in the Cape, where it arrived in the 1920s and was planted mostly in Paarl and nearby parts of Stellenbosch (it thrived in the rich soils and warm climate). But difficulties in obtaining the right plant material have been a drawback to winemakers pleased with the potential of Malbec as a varietal wine.

LOOKING ACROSS VERDUN'S VINEYARDS TOWARDS STELLENBOSCH MOUNTAIN AND THE HELDERBERG; THESE SLOPES PRODUCE SOME OF THE CAPE'S FINEST RED WINES.

The crop can also be inconsistent, lacking concentration if too heavy, and the vine requires a fair bit of work in the vineyard.

In the early 1990s Backsberg produced the first bottled Malbec on the market, followed by Fairview and, more recently, Stellenzicht. All are made as young, fruity, easy-drinking wines, though with some elegance and delicate wooding.

It is this same softness that commends it for blending. Not surprisingly, Bordeaux-style classicist Welgemeend has Malbec in its vineyards, combining it with the other traditional Médoc varieties in its second-label Douelle. As does Mulderbosch in its Faithful Hound red blend. Malbec helps to make up Fairview's accessible Tower Red, while Backsberg is exploring a mix with Cabernet. Small Franschhoek winery Rickety Bridge has planted Malbec for its limited quantities of a new claret called Paulina's Reserve.

WINEMAKER'S COMMENT
Hardy Loubser, Backsberg: 'It's a terribly inconsistent variety, bearing well one year and then producing hardly anything the next. We get a medium-bodied wine, but with the typical Malbec characters of cherry and spice, particularly since we've replaced older vats with small used-oak barrels. It's a lighter style wine, a good alternative to Cinsaut, but with more intensity and flavour – I add a little Cabernet, just to beef it up!

WINE WRITER'S COMMENT
Richard Neill, UK writer: 'Malbec [in Argentina] comes with New World succulence and power, sensual elegance or in a leathery, inimitable Latin style.'

FOOD RECOMMENDATION
Light stews and bredies.

Welgemeend in Stellenbosch was the first to plant Petit Verdot, in the 1970s, as part of the varietal mix for what was to be the Cape's first and still one of its finest Bordeaux-style reds, simply called Welgemeend Estate Wine. In vintages when Petit Verdot does not come up to scratch, the variety is used in Welgemeend's second-label Douelle, an unusual catch-all combination of Malbec, Merlot, Cabernet Sauvignon and Cabernet Franc.

Glen Carlou in Paarl is also using its Petit Verdot in a blend; its more accessible, earlier-drinking Les Trois takes in the Cabernet Sauvignon, Merlot and Cabernet Franc not reserved for the grand blend Grande Classique. Simonsig in Stellenbosch has planted a viable quantity of Petit Verdot, intended for its flag-ship red blend, Tiara, and the revamp of old Stellenbosch wine farm Verdun includes the introduction of some Petit Verdot. Champion red-wine maker Gyles Webb is also planning to plant Petit Verdot on Thelema.

It is a difficult grape, slow to ripen and an erratic cropper. It is thick skinned, almost black in colour, and ripens late in the season, sometimes struggling to reach full-ripeness in northern climes. But its difficulty in the vineyard is outweighed by the substance and what some have described as the 'seasoning' that just a dash of Petit Verdot adds to a red blend.

PETIT VERDOT

This is a classy variety that has crept into Cape vineyards with the promise of adding a subtle new dimension to our Bordeaux-style blends. It comes with a fine reputation from the Médoc, where it was once superior to Cabernet Sauvignon and probably preceded it as an established vine in the 1700s.

It is a variety that has it all: colour, tannin, alcohol, fruit acid, flavour. To a blend it brings all this, plus a characteristic spicy, peppery piquancy, reminiscent of Shiraz – and it is for blending that it is most sought-after, increasingly so in the Cape as winemakers seek to intensify and extend the life of their quality reds.

PINOT MEUNIER

Pinot Meunier is one of Champagne's best-kept secrets, which is probably why it has taken until now for Cape Cap Classique specialists to catch on. Believe it or not, but it outstrips by far both its more famous partners, Pinot Noir and Chardonnay, in the French vineyards.

A member of the Pinot family headed by the ancient Pinot Noir, Pinot Meunier is easy to spot in the vineyard. The upper leaf reflects white when it catches the light, primarily because it is covered in a fine, felt-like down, like cottonwool (or flour, hence the reference to a miller, 'Meunier' in French and 'Müller' in German, where it is known as Müllerrebe).

This hardy, rangy vine produces small, compact bunches with tiny, thick-skinned berries of an almost mahogany red. Pinot Meunier is more productive than Pinot Noir and ripens early and easily. One tough cookie, this, but with charm to spare. The wine is full and fresh, offering even more fruit than Pinot Noir, plus a distinctive aromatic, spicy sort of flavour that enhances the characteristic fruitiness of Pinot Noir. Pinot Meunier reaches maturity quite quickly, making austere, aristocratic Champagnes that are much more accessible: the reason behind Pinot Meunier's unassailable position in many of the non-vintage Champagnes of the great houses.

No need, therefore, to explain Johan Malan of Simonsig's motivation in planting the Cape's first commercial amount of Pinot Meunier in 1994 for future bottlings of his classic Kaapse Vonkel bottle-fermented bubbly.

PONTAC

The name has a resonance, a ring of import to it – you may even be forgiven for thinking it somehow port related. Well, it is not. Sketchy information on origin places it firmly in France, with links to the De Pontac family (an important grape-growing dynasty in the Médoc from the mid-16th to mid-17th century).

Some of the literary works of that era report that Europeans were enjoying a rich, red French wine called Pontac, said to hail from a region of the province of Béarn in southwest France, where you will find a little village called Pontacq. Later records show the arrival in 1772 of the good ship *De Hoop* in the Netherlands. On board was some Pontac, produced in the Cape and probably planted here by the French Huguenots.

Today, Pontac is regarded as essentially a Cape variety. Pontac, red Muscadel and white Muscadel are the three varieties listed as the ingredients for the famous sweet wines of Constantia enjoyed by kings and queens of late 18th-century European courts. And Constantia is where you will find the re-emergence of Pontac plantings today, in an attempt by modern wineries to re-create those historic wines.

'Attempt' is the key word, because Pontac has proved pernickety. Vine health is a problem; the vines are easily infected, resulting in poor yields. Ripening early to mid-season, a Pontac vineyard may provide a beautiful sight with its unseasonal autumnal hues, but there will be a winemaker with head in hands, lamenting an unripe grape crop that is dehydrated and turning to raisin. This forced ripening drives the natural sugars up as high as 40° Balling, resulting in a potential alcohol level of portly proportions – probably what seduced those languid royals centuries ago.

Both Klein Constantia and Groot Constantia are working with Pontac, primarily for the production of a natural sweet wine, a red to match Klein Constantia's already internationally acclaimed Vin de Constance. But nothing has yet been made available commercially.

ABOVE: THE PRESERVATION OF PERNICKETY PONTAC IS NOT AIDED BY ITS GENERALLY FRAGILE CONSTITUTION.

BELOW LEFT: THE SOFT, FLOURY, DOWNY COVERING THAT DISTINGUISHES THE LEAF OF THE PINOT MEUNIER GRAPE, A NEW ADDITION TO SIMONSIG'S VARIETAL MIX.

The grape is no more accommodating in the cellar than in the vineyard. Though highly desirable for a red wine as a rule, Pontac's richness of colour – it is one of just two red varieties that actually has red flesh – translates, unfortunately, into a trail of red juice stains on cellar equipment, hands and clothes. And its extreme fleshiness causes blockages in the crusher and screw press, which is when the old-fashioned basket press comes into its own.

Enter Hartenberg, the only Cape cellar to bottle a varietal dry-red Pontac from its two-and-a-half hectares of vines, some dating back nearly 60 years. And it is proof of the grape's potential, recognised by viticulturists, for top-quality wine. Marked by deep, dense colour, it has a nose that is perfumed and spicy, with sweet, berried fruit; a palate that is full-bodied, mature, with firm tannins; and a lifespan of a good few years. These were the characteristics that encouraged Blaauwklippen to pop it into its port, made primarily from another atypical port variety, Zinfandel.

WINEMAKER'S COMMENT
Carl Schultz, Hartenberg: 'Pontac can make really good red, if one treats it well: planting it on high-potential soils and giving it plenty of time in small, new French-oak barrels. We're not producing it only for its novelty value; it has historical significance and I'd like to see it become more established.'

WINE WRITER'S COMMENT
John Platter, SA writer: 'The |Hartenberg Pontac| highlights the variety's slight wildness, combining a spicy, leafy herbaceousness with sweet, ripe fruit. It has great intensity of flavour and can be wonderfully chewy, yet it has a dryness that makes it almost classic.'

FOOD RECOMMENDATION
Venison or oxtail; red meat roasts and stews.

RUBY CABERNET
Local wine growers went borrowing from Uncle Sam when they started planting Ruby Cabernet in the Cape in the early '80s. It is a cross between the noble Cabernet Sauvignon and Carignan, one of the world's most productive varieties, and was bred at the University of California, Davis, around 1950, by Prof HP Olmo. The result is a wine with the deep colour of Carignan and the aroma of Cabernet.

Ruby Cabernet is a star among the big-volume producers in the warmer regions: co-operative cellars in the northern Cape regions of the Olifants River, Orange River and the Breede River Valley around Worcester. Lack of pretension was a redemption here. All that these wine technicians were looking for was an economical blending component to fill out their otherwise insipid reds. Ruby Cabernet fitted the bill.

A vigorous grower, wind-resistant and practically disease free, it behaves like any healthy hybrid. And it is equally misleading: a crimson colour translates into just the faintest of grassy aromas and a fresh, fruity and crisp taste. It benefits from a quick dunk in a barrel.

Large plantings of the variety for blending purposes, a '90s red-wine shortage and an export boom for Cape wine have combined to see Ruby Cabernet appear on several labels as a varietal wine.

If picked ripe and well made, with the emphasis on fruit rather than on tannin, Cape Ruby Cabernets have shown that they can be surprisingly pleasing, easy-drinking red wines, such as those from Berg & Brook, Fairseat, Oude Wellington, Douglas and Goudini. It has also shown itself capable of impressing wine judges: the Vredendal Cabaret, a blend with Cabernet Franc, was voted the overall champion wine at the annual SA National Young Wine Show in 1994.

WINEMAKER'S COMMENT
Pou le Roux, Douglas Winery: 'A very pleasant, easy-drinking, soft wine with strong berry-like character.'

WINE WRITER'S COMMENT
Dick Davidson, Cape Wine Master: 'It is a red wine acceptable to the entire spectrum of wine drinkers. It is not pretentious, yet is always worthy of being served. It is fruity without being simple, with enough tannins to tingle the tastebuds. Most of all, it is affordable.'

FOOD RECOMMENDATION
Casual meals; pastas and braais; chilled with cold meats.

THE VINES OF KLAWER CO-OPERATIVE MEMBERS ALONG THE OLIFANTS RIVER; THE RED ROCKS OF THE FLAT-TOPPED GIFBERG RANGE FORM A DRAMATIC BACKDROP.

SOUZÃO

It is not a great port grape, but at least it is a good one. Souzão was on the ship that brought that party of very important port varieties to South Africa in the second half of this century.

Colour is Souzão's speciality – the grape itself has red juice, just like Pontac. Unfortunately, the Cape's older plantings seemed to lose their colour (as did the Pontac), but new material has solved this hiccup.

Souzão is less shy-bearing than some rather more highly rated port varieties – the almost reclusive Touriga Nacional being a prime example. And it has pleasantly surprised local growers with its crisp acids – quite unlike its performance in Portugal. So, overall, there is much to recommend it, which is why practically all the top port producers in South Africa have some Souzão tucked away: from the Calitzdorp clan – Boplaas and Die Krans – to Landskroon in Paarl, Allesverloren in the Swartland and Overgaauw and Muratie in Stellenbosch.

Among the stars in the Cape port repertoire, Anton Bredell is perhaps most liberal with it, dividing his JP Bredell Cape Vintage Reserve equally between Souzão and the enduring Tinta Barocca. He also supplies both in large quantities to the KWV for its ports. Bredell's own blend deserved its recent five-star rating in *Wine* magazine, an accolade as rare as hen's teeth. And it actually found favour with Charles Symington of that famous family of port shippers. So, despite a character that has been described as coarse, there is something to be said for Souzão in the right hands.

TINTA FRANCISCA

This variety is in the top echelon of grapes for port making in the Douro, though it is not as highly rated as Touriga Francesa, with which it is easily confused. Like Touriga Francesa, its wines are sweet-smelling, delicate. It is the sister act to brother Barocca, much like Francesa is to Nacional in the Touriga family, adding aroma and finesse to a port.

Tinta Francisca accompanied Tintas Barocca and Roriz to South Africa around the mid-20th century. Long-time port producers such as Allesverloren, Overgaauw and Muratie still have Tinta Francisca vines in production, but it is not widespread, despite being a vigorous grower and generous bearer, probably because it rots easily. Like Tinta Barocca, it was thought to be somehow related to Pinot Noir, but in fact both look far more like Cabernet Franc in Cape vineyards, with loosely shaped, ragged leaves.

TINTA RORIZ

Tinta Roriz, considered one of the leading port varieties in the hard country of the Douro, is in fact Spanish nobility: Tempranillo by another name. It does not belong to the Tinta family.

Of course, as Tempranillo it is best known for the perfumed, powerful red wines of Rioja, from where it did a quick border hop into northern Portugal more than a century ago. It came to the Cape in the company of other port stalwarts such as Tinta Barocca and Souzão about 50 years ago.

It loves the heat, so settled here quite happily, bearing thick-skinned grapes that ferment into richly coloured wines. Like Souzão, it is also low in acidity and is less tannic in the Cape than in Portugal, where its wines have been described as plummy, almost jammy. It can be quite soft here, too. Allesverloren in the Swartland is sufficiently impressed with it to be planting more, as is Die Krans in Calitzdorp and Landskroon in Paarl. Both traditionalist Muratie and newcomer Glen Carlou rely on Roriz to make up their blends.

TOURIGA NACIONAL

This is the Cabernet Sauvignon of port wine. It used to be the major ingredient in the reds from the Dão region in Portugal from at least the mid-19th century. The vine's characteristically small yields have tempered its popularity for all but port, which is probably why South African port-wine makers waited until less than a decade ago to acknowledge its invaluable contribution to premium port.

It was tested here in the 1940s and '50s, but it was only at the start of the '90s that it emerged in the finer ports, with vintners such as Braam van Velden and Chris Joubert of Overgaauw in Stellenbosch and the kings of Calitzdorp – the Nels of Boplaas and Die Krans – paving the way for their less adventurous pals. New vineyards such as Glen Carlou have therefore been able to make their entrances with Touriga Nacional in their line-ups. It is increasingly insinuating its way into most Cape ports of note.

What this vigorous grower lacks in quantity it makes up in the concentration of fruit and tannin that its small, densely packed berries provide. What is especially heartwarming to Cape wine growers is that it likes heat. The wines it makes are powerful, but beautifully balanced. The colour is a dense, almost black purple and the aroma is typically mulberry fruit. It is strong enough to handle fortification with consummate ease, marrying happily with the spirit. And it is built for barrel maturation, as it is complex and characterful enough to absorb all the vanilla and spice an oak barrel has to offer.

Overgaauw has recently tried Touriga Nacional as an unfortified, wooded red wine, blending it with Merlot and some Malbec. The varietal mulberry fruit and spiciness are there, but there is no getting away from a recognisable port character, which perhaps illustrates this variety's inherent suitability for its chosen specialisation. Touriga Nacional, above all other port varieties, can produce a true Vintage port that can take – in fact, requires – time in the bottle.

ZINFANDEL

Zinfandel was to the Californians what Cinsaut was to the Cape: common. It found its way to the brave new world in the mid-1800s, and everyone assumed it came from Hungary, probably because it had been adopted by Hungarian Agoston Haraszthy, one of the founding fathers of the American wine industry. But relatives, if not siblings, have been traced to Italy and the former Yugoslavia, where Primitivo and Plavac Mali are the spitting image of Zinfandel.

'Zin', as the buzzy Californians now call 'their' most widely planted and rather popular red variety, came to South Africa only in the 1970s. It found a home in the vineyards of Stellenbosch at Kleine Zalze, Hartenberg and Blaauwklippen. Here it led a Cinderella-like existence. Initially found good only as a loyal servant helping to invigorate blends, its soft and fruity nature soon won the hearts of the men in the cellar.

When nurtured in the vineyards, picked at full ripeness, allowed extended skin maceration and given careful maturation in American oak (sometimes even French barriques), Zinfandel blooms. It is ripe and sweet with plummy berry flavours, yet a latent wildness can emerge, resulting in distinctive brambly, spicy and peppery overtones. In fact, it can be quite tart and jammy, with some extraordinarily high natural-alcohol levels.

The variety's versatility, which led to its workhorse reputation in California, has also now emerged in the Cape. While the Hartenbergs and Blaauwklippens are traditionally rather well-bred, albeit fairly rich, Fairview's Charles Back has recently brought some in-your-face debutantes to the ball: thick, tarry, textured and extracted wines with almost port-like properties and alcohols to match. And he has blended it with the Cape's own 'commoner', Cinsaut, to make a cheeky wine aptly nicknamed 'Sin-sin'. Hartenberg's latest vintages are also bringing out the fruitiness of the variety, realising a softer, less strongly savoury and more accessible wine.

So what is it about Zinfandel that has kept it out of the vineyards – barring Australia? Its very responsiveness. Winemakers struggle with heavy bearing, slow ripening and attacks of fruit-fly, which lead to botrytis (not desirable in a red).

These difficulties account for Zinfandel's continuously tenuous grip on the hearts of the Cape's vintners. But Blaauwklippen endures, even maintaining its Zinfandel's pre-eminent position in its port.

As for wine drinkers? Something rich, wild, a little untameable and always unpredictable does not make for a lasting relationship. But for those looking for a distinctive, unusual flavour in a red, Zinfandel is where you will find it.

WINEMAKER'S COMMENT
Carl Schultz, Hartenberg: 'I've tried to temper the wildness and make it a little softer, more medium bodied, fruity and accessible, though still with the Zinfandel character. It is a food wine.'

WINE WRITER'S COMMENT
Angela Lloyd, SA writer: '[It produces] a welcome style of quality red wine that is definitely, clearly not Cabernet.'

FOOD RECOMMENDATION
Venison; ostrich; rich cheeses.

A BOTTLE-AGED ZINFANDEL ASSUMES RUSTIC, GARNET HUES WITHOUT LOSING THAT SLIGHTLY WILD, BRAMBLY CHARACTER.

THE BIT PLAYERS

SOME HAVE STORIES TO TELL, such as Auxerrois. Others just hang out, popping up now and then as an interesting varietal wine or in a supporting role to the main act, such as Morio Muscat. And Clairette Blanche, Schönburger and Malvasia Rei? Well, they still play the odd part but will probably never make it to the big time. A few, for example Roobernet and Nebbiolo, however, seem set to audition for the chorus line. Of all of them, Grenache is the one most likely to hit centre stage in the new millennium, with Mouvèdre waiting in the wings.

ABOVE: TRAPPINGS OF THE GRACIOUS LIFE ASSOCIATED WITH WINE — A LUXURIOUSLY DECORATIVE URN OUTSIDE THE VERGELEGEN MANOR HOUSE

WHITE

Auxerrois, Chenel, Clairette Blanche, Emerald Riesling, Malvasia Rei, Morio Muscat, Muscat Ottonel, Schönburger, Therona

RED

Carignan, Cornifesto, Grenache, Mouvèdre, Muscat de Hambourg, Nebbiolo, Roobernet, Sangiovese, Touriga Francesa

WHITE VARIETIES

AUXERROIS

A cause of anxiety and embarrassment to local winemakers, Auxerrois arrived at the Cape under false pretenses. Impatient with the industry bureaucracy that held up approval of new, imported plant material, a few progressive wine growers resorted to 'smuggling' in some cuttings of what they thought was Chardonnay, newly fashionable in the early 1980s thanks to the Australians and Californians. The faux pas came to light and the bubble burst with a bang in 1986 with no less than a 'Presidential Commission of Enquiry into Chardonnay'.

Shocked farmers reacted by ripping up their Auxerrois-masquerading-as-Chardonnay as quickly as they had planted it, replacing it with the real thing, now more speedily sanctioned. The Chardonnay 'scam' was long spoken of in hushed terms, (though the quantities involved were small and, despite some financial loss by a few farmers, the worst damage was to the industry's pride).

Ironically, Danie de Wet of De Wetshof had just won an award for his 1985 Chardonnay at the 1987 French wine-trade fair Vinexpo when the findings of the Commission (to which he had testified) were published. It must have been with no little amusement that he admitted that the '85, like its predecessors, contained a fair amount of Auxerrois.

Not that the Cape vintners and Vinexpo wine judges were alone in having the wool pulled over their eyes. For in regions of Alsace, from where

the variety hails, Chardonnay is sometimes called Auxerrois Blanc (Pinot Gris is also known as Auxerrois Gris). In fact, some Alsatians maintain that Auxerrois Blanc is related to Chardonnay. It is one of the most widely planted vines in Alsace, and does bear a resemblance to the noble white Burgundian grape.

It grows well, cropping generously, and the wine it makes has the same body and essential neutrality of an ordinary, unwooded Chardonnay.

Acid and alcohol are high, commending it to blenders. Which is exactly what Hartenberg did with its remaining few hectares of Auxerrois, using it in its fairly full-bodied, dry-white Chatillon and filling out its Bin 3 'house' wine, a dry, unwooded white. As a swansong, winemaker Carl Schultz bottled it as a varietal wine in 1997. Maverick winemaker André van Rensburg of Vergelegen did the same before leaving Stellenzicht in Stellenbosch. In both cases, the variety produced a dry wine of some weight, fairly juicy, with Muscat overtones not uncommon to specific Chardonnay clones and an attractive spiciness. The Stellenzicht also showed a Chardonnay-like propensity to bloom under the influence of wood.

It is a wine well worth vinifying for pleasurable and easy drinking, demonstrating a belief that farmers were maybe a little hasty in condemning the variety outright.

VERGELEGEN SPORTS AN OCHRE LIVERY RATHER THAN THE TRADITIONAL WHITE-WASH. THE COLOUR WAS ORIGINALLY INTENDED TO HIDE THE STAINS CAUSED BY RAIN-DRENCHED THATCH.

CHENEL

This is a Cape creation, the result of a crossing by viticulturist and researcher Prof Chris Orffer of classic Chenin Blanc with the Cognac variety Ugni Blanc. The name? The role of Stellenbosch winemaking education and research institution Elsenburg is acknowledged in the last syllable.

Conceived to cope with South Africa's warm, dry climate, it succeeded handsomely, being a vigorous grower, a big yielder and disease-resistant. What it lacks is character, however, to the extent that varietal wines are no longer bottled commercially.

First released in the 1970s after about 20 years of research, Chenel was expected to appeal to growers in areas where irrigation was required.

Too many other varieties, however, soon proved more rewarding to the winemaker as well as to the wine lover.

CLAIRETTE BLANCHE

This variety has proved most popular in the western Cape and in the southeast regions of France, but it served a very different purpose here than it did in Europe. It was once used for vermouth as well as for sparkling wine in France, while serving primarily as an ordinary table wine in the Cape (although this is now its new-found guise in its homeland, too, predominantly in Provence).

Of Mediterranean origin, it is a common-or-garden variety, attractive to growers because of its adaptability to poor soils, though it has done well locally in fertile ground. But it can be more trouble than it is worth in the cellar, as it oxidises at the drop of a hat. South Africa has solved the problem with its pioneering, in the 1950s, of the cold-fermentation technique and early use of stainless-steel tanks.

A degree of fame has been achieved by Clairette Blanc (as the variety is known in France) as an ingredient in a sparkling wine in the Rhône called Clairette de Die, but this has since faded with the realisation of the merits of so many other more worthy varieties, such as Chenin Blanc.

Few varietal examples in South Africa remain, although the simple, soft, flowery character of this grape, which is low in both alcohol and acid, will still be found at De Wet and Goudini co-operatives in Worcester, where the hot, dry conditions made Clairette a viable option in the early days. You may also discover it in uncomplicated white blends, such as the Swartland Premier Grand Cru and Simonsig's off-dry Mustique, which is an interesting mix of many other lesser-known varieties, including Muscat Ottonel and Schönburger.

EMERALD RIESLING

This variety is the result of a cross between the noble Weisser Riesling and the Bordelais Muscadelle (no relation to the Muscat family of grapes). Devised by Californian viticultural researcher Prof HP Olmo around 1950 as a white companion to his Ruby Cabernet, it produces wines that combine the grapey, Muscat aroma of one parent with the full-bodied character of the other. A firm acidity can result in a Riesling-like raciness in cool areas.

Experimental plantings in South Africa confirmed its potential as a characterful wine. Roodezandt Co-op in Robertson bore this out in the 1980s with a dry white, fruity and slightly savoury. But, with no distinctive features that are not met by our Muscat varieties or the noble whites to which Cape winemakers are committed, Emerald Riesling has attracted scant interest.

THE REALITY OF MODERN WINEMAKING: GLEAMING STEEL TANKS WITH COOLING JACKETS – SUCH AS THESE IN THE GRAHAM BECK CELLAR IN ROBERTSON – HAVE ENABLED THE PRODUCTION OF QUALITY WHITE WINE IN WARM CLIMATES.

A few other wines were bottled during the '80s, mostly by lesser-known co-operative wineries such as Lutzville in the Olifants River Valley, Vaalharts in the Orange River Valley and Porterville in the Swartland. They were simpler, lighter wines, with the Andalusia Emerald Riesling from Vaalharts picking up some of the spiciness or muskiness of its Weisser Riesling ancestry. Porterville persisted, though, and is now the only cellar where you will find a varietal Emerald Riesling: a novelty.

MALVASIA REI

Malvasia Rei is highly recommended in Portugal for white port, yet since its importation about 50 years ago it has not been much used for the little white port that is made in the Cape. Instead, it has joined fellow red grapes in the more multi-variety port blends such as Allesverloren (with six) and Overgaauw (with five, soon to be six). These are cellars that have always crushed and fermented their port varieties together, following the old Portuguese tradition.

As it turns out, the Cape may have adopted a variety under a misapprehension perpetuated by the Portuguese. Malvasia Rei is not related to the much more well-bred Malvasia of Italy and Spain. It is actually a Portuguese crossing called Seminario, created to produce high yields – which it does in South Africa.

Unfortunately, its big bunches of soft-skinned grapes also rot easily, which is one of the reasons why Overgaauw is finally giving up on it. Cellarmaster Braam van Velden suggests that growing it on poor soil may counteract its overbearing nature. The Malans of Allesverloren reckon it may make a reasonable Tawny port, which is often a blend of red and white ports; their Malvasia Rei has mysteriously refrained from rotting, no doubt due to the scarcity of summer rain in the Swartland.

With other non-port varieties being used for the handful of white ports in the Cape, Malvasia Rei may become an Allesverloren oddity.

MORIO MUSCAT

A modern German cross between Pinot Blanc and Sylvaner, Morio Muscat is another '70s child from the age of Germanicus at the Cape. The viticulturist to whom it owes its name as well as its identity did not intend to suggest a link with the Muscat family of grapes; rather, it is the variety's surprisingly strong aromatic character that prompted the suffix (the original spelling was Morio-Muskat).

Frans Malan, patriarch of Stellenbosch estate Simonsig, founding father of the Cape wine-route concept and inveterate experimenter, was one of the first to try out this forward young grape. The first varietal wine, in the early 1980s, was a flowery semi-sweet. As a natural sweet dessert wine in the hands of the German-owned Buitenverwachting towards the end of the decade, it came up with some complexity and a mélange of floral, citrus and pineapple flavours. Landskroon fortifies it Jerepigo-style. This is the only varietal example of Morio Muscat in the Cape; the rest have been relegated to slightly sweet blends such as Hartenberg's Bin 6 and Stellenzicht's Fragrance.

MUSCAT OTTONEL

Muscat Ottonel is a mid-1800s French cross between Chasselas and one of the Muscat family members. From the latter it inherited some Muscat aromatics, though not enough to usurp some of the other more established cousins such as D'Alexandrie and De Frontignan.

Typically, it is made as a dry white in Alsace, showing some likeness to Gewürztraminer. But in the Cape the few winemakers who planted it, such as those at Simonsig and Blaauwklippen, made simple semi-sweets. Grape aromas, with fairly strong Muscat and floral scents, were its greatest appeal.

Now only Blaauwklippen perseveres with a varietal wine, which is a fair mouthful with tropical-fruit flavours. Simonsig still uses its remnants in its off-dry Mustique.

SCHÖNBURGER

A German cross of doubtful merit, Schönburger (or Schoenberger, as the Cape vernacular spelling would have it) has shone at Simonsig. A starlet of the '70s, it cavorted about like a Gewürztraminer, all pink berry and spicy, rose-petal fragrance. This, despite its Pinot Noir paternal genes, but probably because of father's fling with the table grape Pirovano.

A little-known but apparently pleasing Special Late Harvest was made at Simonsig in the early 1980s, but the popularity – and shortage – of the farm's real Gewürztraminer persuaded the cellar to put its Schönburger to more practical use as a blending partner. It still co-stars, but now under its own name, in Simonsig's off-dry white Mustique, and until recently did a stint in Hartenberg's dry house blend, Bin 3.

WITH ITS ABUNDANCE OF JUICE, THERONA IS ESSENTIALLY A GRAPE FOR DISTILLING WINE, YET IT HAS FOUND FAVOUR AS A TABLE WINE AT WELTEVREDE IN THE BREEDE RIVER VALLEY.

THERONA

Pinotage protector Prof Chris Theron (head of viticultural and vinicultural studies at Stellenbosch University in the 1940s and '50s) took the liberty of lending his name to this curious cross of Chenin Blanc and Crouchen Blanc (Cape Riesling to the traditionalists). Therona Riesling was essentially an experiment: its large bunches of big sappy berries earmarked it as a mass producer of rebate wine, the base for brandy.

This is why it found its way to wine-growing regions with water on tap, such as the Breede River Valley with its irrigation canal, and how it came to catch the attention of Weltevrede's Lourens Jonker, who was looking for interesting wines with which to woo a new generation of wine lovers thirsty for as much as the burgeoning wine routes could offer in the '80s.

Needing to bolster the ranks of the sweeter wines in his range, Jonker turned some of his Therona into a Special Late Harvest in 1986.

The wine has endured, alternating between this and the slightly less-sweet Late Harvest style, and offering a lightness of touch and delicacy of flavour lacking in many of its ilk.

A characteristically nondescript wine with low acidity and therefore ideal for rebate, Therona clearly benefits from as long a hanging time as possible in order to develop sugars and some fruity flavours. A dash of acid out the bag, legal in the Cape, helps achieve the required balance, and a bit of bottle-age settles and enriches the wine. Its typical aromas and flavours include candyfloss, peach, spice, citrus and fudge.

RED VARIETIES

CARIGNAN

Although a Spanish variety (taking its original name from its hometown of Carinena in the northeast), the Gallic-sounding Carignan is an adoptive of France, at least as early as the 12th century.

It is California's third most widely planted red grape, and stands alongside Merlot as Chile's most popular red wine.

Carignan gets first prize for productivity: only Italy's Trebbiano is naturally more prolific. But it requires attention from the vintner in the vineyard to protect it from rot as well as downy and powdery mildew. A rich red colour and firm tannins make up for this susceptibility, which is probably why it remains the grape of choice for Languedoc-Roussillon winemakers wishing to blend it with the fruitier Cinsaut and more gracious Grenache.

The isolated plantings of Carignan in the Cape are found in the Wellington Valley, where the excessive summer heat probably helps in the battle against bugs. It is here that the only local varietal wine is bottled. Introduced in South Africa in the mid-1970s to add colour to red blends, it was generally planted in areas where the soil and rainfall were good. But some winemakers believe that the variety is better

suited to more arid sites – which is the profile of the two hectares of 20-year-old vines on Welgegund farm in Wellington.

Just two vintages have been bottled here, with the second, in 1998, showing much more body and character than its predecessor, a flavourful, easy-drinking red reminiscent of Beaujolais. Only some 500 cases are made.

CORNIFESTO

Regarded as one of the better red grapes for port in Portugal, Cornifesto is a rarity in the Cape, confined mainly to Overgaauw in Stellenbosch. It makes up Overgaauw's Cape Vintage blend with other choice port varieties Tinta Barocca, Tinta Francisca, Souzão and Touriga Nacional, plus some Malvasia Rei. Glen Carlou also selected Cornifesto as an ingredient in its first few blends of a Cape Vintage style from 1993.

Cornifesto's small black berries produce a wine of concentrated colour, which is the main incentive for its release to Cape port-wine makers post World War II (after extensive experimental plantings of several 'new' port varieties by viticulturists Perold and Theron).

GRENACHE

A small vineyard high up in the Devon Valley hills in Stellenbosch is the cause of some serious manoeuvring by Cape winemakers eager to lay their hands on what is a rarity in the Cape: Grenache good enough to add to a quality red blend. Grenache was one of the varieties that found its way to the Cape Colony, apparently for port making, in the 19th century, but it was only in the early 1900s that the estimable Abraham Perold, professor of viticulture at Stellenbosch, confirmed that it was the same as one of the major red varieties in southern France and Spain.

CANALS FROM THE BREEDE RIVER HAVE ALLOWED FARMS SUCH AS VAN LOVEREN TO HAVE WATER ON TAP, TO FRESHEN UP THEIR VINES DURING DRY SUMMERS.

Grenache took hold in other New World wine regions, such as Australia and California, but it has all but disappeared in the Cape. The characteristics that came through for it elsewhere did not endear it to local winemakers.

Grenache is a hard-working grape, coping well with hot, dry conditions, growing vigorously and cropping generously. As such, it has proved ideal for stretching volumes of everyday drinking wine. But Cape winemakers were not impressed with its general lack of colour and tannin (plus a susceptibility to mealy bug and downy mildew). It is a thin-skinned grape, often more pink than red in colour, although as a bush vine in harsh, windy, arid conditions small yields allow it to ripen into a deep red, more concentrated fruit. In Spain, where it is tailor-made to thrive in this country's rugged landscape and is the most widely planted red grape, it can turn up as a seriously high-alcohol wine.

But it is that soft fruitiness and light colour that has served Grenache so well as a blending ingredient in Europe. It is also why it makes a very respectable Rosé, its most common form as a varietal wine – which is indeed what most of the Grenache in the Cape is used for.

THE HOT VALLEY FLOOR OF THE OLIFANTS RIVER REGION NEAR KLAWER, WHERE SITES WITH LIME-RICH SOIL ARE PRODUCING GOOD FRUIT.

With most of the meagre plantings of Grenache concentrated in the suitably hot, dry, sometimes-irrigated region of the Olifants River Valley, several co-operative wineries rely on it to make some fairly respectable Rosé and Blanc de Noir wines. Goue Vallei in Citrusdal has both, while Klawer Co-operative Winery makes an easy-drinking, fragrant Grenache Blanc de Noir that can lay claim to the only Veritas gold medal awarded to this style of wine in more than five years. Lutzville bottles a pale-crimson, semi-sweet Grenache Blanc de Noir under its Fleermuisklip label.

There is renewed interest in this grape among Cape wine growers as a varietal wine (Ken Forrester's debut) or as a potential asset to a red blend, be it a fruity easy drinker or a more serious Rhône look-alike, like that of Welgemeend's Amadé. With local winemakers still struggling to achieve the soft, ready fruit that seems to come so easy elsewhere in the New World, Grenache could be just what they are looking for.

MOUVÈDRE

Now accepted as a southern Rhône variety, it has been thoroughly at home there for at least four centuries (Mouvèdre was once thought to hail from Spain). It is also known as Mataro, the chosen nomenclature in Australia (where it is quite widely planted), hence the theory that it must have originated in either Murviedro near Valencia or Mataro in Catalonia.

Mouvèdre is a new arrival in South Africa, brought in at the beginning of the '90s on order by a few energetic experimentalists eager to prove its suitability to the Cape's naturally warm climate; they were also after its potential contribution to serious, Rhône-like reds. It enjoys a warm climate, is fairly hardy – thick skin makes it impervious to most bugs and pests – and grows 'like a bat out of hell', as one winemaker puts it.

Not unexpectedly, Fairview's dynamic Charles Back has just produced his first tiny crop with the help of assistant winemaker Anthony de Jager, who has working experience in the Rhône. Beamont winemaker Niels Verburg has also planted a smidgen of Mouvèdre, with plans to incorporate it into a Rhône-style blend. The variety is also in the job jar of the Spice Route Company, a part-time partnership – the busy Back and wily Gyles Webb of Thelema are involved – geared towards putting Malmesbury on the map as a fountain of fine, fruity red wine.

CARIGNAN VINES ON WELGEGUND FARM IN THE WARM WELLINGTON VALLEY; THEY ARE THOUGHT TO PRODUCE BETTER WINE WHEN GROWN IN DRIER, MORE ARID CONDITIONS.

The first experimental wine at Fairview, made from a standard French clone cleaned up for virus-infection by the KWV, surprised with its unexpectedly soft, smooth tannins – but the typical spicy Shiraz-like aromatics and rich, blackberry fruit were there.

It is early days yet, but the first dispatches have been encouraging. With the Cape's capability of making fine Shiraz and the availability of Cinsaut, the addition of Mouvèdre to the mix should see some stunning new Shirazes, a few really good Rhône reds and maybe even a varietal Mouvèdre or two in the future.

MUSCAT DE HAMBOURG

What is ampelographically identified as Muscat Hamburg is most common as a table grape, so dark it is almost black. In South Africa a lone cellar in Robertson works a bit of magic and turns it into a well-rated fortified dessert wine.

Weltevrede's Lourens Jonker adopted this lesser Muscat grape (known locally as Muscat de Hambourg) and has managed to make from it a dead ringer for a Red Muscadel for the past couple of decades. Left on the vine to ripen fully, the large bunches of big black berries respond with high sugars and good fruit. After all, Jonker is no slouch at vinifying Muscat grapes; in 1976 he produced the country's first fortified Red Muscadel sweet wine. No wonder the humble De Hambourg rose to the occasion.

For there is some substance to this novelty. Besides being the first – and only – wine made here from this variety, it was also the first fortified wine to be selected for sale at the exclusive annual Nederburg Auction: the maiden 1977 appeared in the 1981 catalogue. Early vintages were heavyweights; full-bodied, rich and raisiny, but the latest bottlings are lighter, slightly spicy and still not excessively sweet. It is invariably a more delicate alternative to many Muscat de Frontignan Muscadels.

An old slave bell from early winemaking days at Altydgedacht in Durbanville; here wine-making dates back to the early 18th century.

NEBBIOLO

One of the Italian greats, Nebbiolo is currently being vinified on an experimental basis in the Cape, but it is already bringing a gleam to the eye. Nebbiolo is the grape that makes the robust Barolo and more delicate Barberesco wines of Piedmont, and has been at home there since at least the early 1500s. Its growing conditions are curious, high up on Alpine slopes along tall trellises, hence the allusion to mist or 'nebbia'.

While Italy's most-planted red grape, Barbera, has been vinified by the Parkers of Altydgedacht estate for years, Nebbiolo and Sangiovese represent a fresh interest in Italian varieties. Bouchard Finlayson's Burgundian fanatic Peter Finlayson is looking to Nebbiolo and Sangiovese for inspiration in his Walker Bay vineyards.

And it is Nebbiolo that seems set to engage him most seriously, having impressed with its deeply coloured wine from big, scarlet-red berries, a strongly perfumed nose, strawberry fruit flavours, high acids and 'marvellous' tannins, firm but ripe, promising longevity.

Problems with sunburn have underlined this grape's preference for chilly conditions, which is why the new Steenberg vineyards in cool Constantia also boast some Nebbiolo plantings. A long, slow ripening process is a particular requirement for this variety, as it needs full-ripeness to counteract its natural high acidity.

While the Italians opt for big vats to wood-mature a wine already bolstered by firm tannins, Finlayson tried his Nebbiolo in small barriques and was happy with the result. In the search, as he puts it, for wines without hard tannins and with structure instead of weight, Nebbiolo may very well fit the bill, as a varietal wine and as a blending component.

ROOBERNET

This is another Cape creation, although brand new and nowhere near achieving the panache of Pinotage. Perold's successor as the Cape's viticultural guru is the recently retired Prof Chris

Orffer, and it is he who crossed two Cape classics – Cabernet Sauvignon and the historic Pontac – to come up with Roobernet.

It has been available to wine growers only since the early 1990s and no wine – varietal or blend – has yet been bottled. But it has caused some excitement among those who have planted it, including two highly rated red-wine cellars in Stellenbosch, Uiterwyk and De Trafford, as well as Laborie in Paarl, KWV's former experimental farm now emerging as a fine-wine producer.

Roobernet has proved to be a better bearer than both its parents, happy in warm and cool areas alike and pleasingly resistant to common diseases such as rot and powdery and downy mildew. The juice of the grape is a deep, rich red – no doubt inherited from Pontac, which is one of only two varieties to have red flesh – and it does not need lengthy skin contact. The first experimental wines have been surprisingly soft, though with typical Cabernet characteristics: good structure and flavour, complexity, natural fruit density and acid.

While the colour alone promises a great future as a blending component, its prominent Cabernet Sauvignon aromas and flavours could soon be confusing wine lovers in a top-quality varietal red.

THE PARKER FAMILY HAS FARMED ALTYDGEDACHT FOR FIVE GENERATIONS AND IS INTENT ON PRESERVING BOTH TECHNIQUES AND EQUIPMENT, WHILE STILL PRODUCING WINE FOR MODERN TASTES.

SANGIOVESE

This Italian red variety has been on order since the late 1980s, and finally arrived as the millennium approached. Sangiovese is the grape of Chianti, with origins in Tuscany, and, together with Barbera, is Italy's most widely planted red.

Grosso is one of two variations of Sangiovese, named for its larger yields of lesser quality than the fruit of the shyer Piccolo. Of course, there are exceptions, but the first experimental wines in the Cape seem to indicate that the long-suffering winemakers have been saddled with the Grosso. The KWV's mother block on Vergelegen is on good, clay-rich but well-drained, gravelly soil.

It rewarded with prolific yields of compact bunches with fat, thin-skinned berries, and made a rather thin wine with the pale garnet hue more common to Pinot Noir, and not at all uncommon in the ordinary Sangiovese wines of Italy.

Similar results have been obtained at the new Rupert and De Rothschild cellar at Fredericksburg in Paarl. Here winemaker Schalk Joubert found the wine to be fuller and surprisingly soft and velvety for a variety noted for its high acidity and fairly harsh tannin. This may have been the good influence of the small amount of another experimental Italian grape, Nebbiolo. He also blended in some Merlot.

THE VIEW THAT GREETS VISITORS AS THEY DRIVE UP TO UITERWYK IN STELLENBOSCH, HOME OF THE DE WAAL FAMILY FOR THE PAST 130 YEARS.

Peter Finlayson of Bouchard Finlayson planted his Sangiovese on Malmesbury shale, put it in new wood and also touched it up with a bit of Nebbiolo for an experimental 1997 vintage. A warmer '98 summer in his cool-climate Hemel-en-Aarde Valley vineyards may give more concentration to the wine, which shows quite coarse tannins. This, and its acidity, makes it the perfect companion for traditional Italian fare. But it is still very much in the trial phase.

The Italians have proved that the grape is capable of breathtaking blends with Cabernet Sauvignon. With the right clone, South African Sangiovese could yet go places.

TOURIGA FRANCESA

Like its relative, Touriga Nacional, Touriga Francesa is also a proud member of the selected six varieties most highly esteemed by the quintas (estates) in the Douro Valley; it is more productive than its big brother but is lighter in colour and not as concentrated. Its charms are more feminine, starting with the pungency of its perfume. It adds vitality to a port, but has hidden depths that emerge only under loving care. Firm acidity and intense fruit flavours are two of the variety's most valuable assets – of inestimable value to the blender.

Its support role is considered invaluable by seasoned growers in Portugal, who play it at number two to Touriga Nacional's number one in their blends.

Cape winemakers have been slow to woo this one. Perhaps the ease with which it is confused with Tinta Francisca (which arrived in South Africa about 50 years ago), together with a whole host of reputable port varieties (including the well-established Tinta Barocca), is to blame. Whatever the case, our port makers are on the warpath to show their Portuguese brethren that whatever they can do, we can do just as well – and they looked to the king of Calitzdorp for leadership. Carel Nel, typically quick on the uptake when it comes to trying new wine ventures, promptly planted a patch of Touriga Francesa. Anton Bredell in Stellenbosch soon followed. The material was obtained through their recent close contact with the Symingtons, the venerable English family that put the ports of Warre's, Dow's, Graham's and others on the top of the heap.

Like all the port varieties, at Boplaas Touriga Francesa has been allocated the Karoo soils, the gravelly shale with its clay sub-structure found on the outer edges of the valley in which Calitzdorp is situated. No wine has yet been made from it, but there have been concerns about its seeming susceptibility to diseases. But, given the success of its fellow port players in this part of the world, it should do as well here as it has under the similar conditions of the Douro.

TOURIGA FRANCESA PRODUCES A LIGHTER-COLOURED, MORE FEMININE WINE THAN ITS BIG BROTHER, TOURIGA NACIONAL.

WINE STYLES

SINGLE VARIETAL WINES ARE WHAT THE world seems to want right now. It is a fashion born of the New World, where marketing is the name of the game and image is everything. The wine you drink, like the car you drive, the clothes you wear and the suburb in which you live, has been invested with the power to impress. Yet many forget that wine is the drink of the peasant: home-grown as an integral part of daily sustenance, a panacea and a pleasure, a slaker of thirst and a means of celebration. The still-great wines of the world, led by the Chateaux of France, have been bent but not beaten into divulging

the type of grape from which their wines are made. Château Margaux is simply what it is: one of the most wonderful red wines in the world. Who cares whether it is made from noble Cabernet Sauvignon, or whether the winemaker added 20 per cent Merlot this year, or whether the *encépagement* (recipe) is the same each vintage.

A recent scene in an otherwise pleasing movie (which will remain unnamed) fell into the trap of pretension when a character, after carefully perusing a proffered winelist, airily requested 'a Chardonnay, please'. It must have been a novel winelist. Or maybe our hero was a beer drinker, used to ordering by 'brand'.

There are wines that are defined by style rather than grape variety (and Chardonnay is not one of them!). Ironically, this is the area in which South African wines, though striving to equal the world's best in the singles stakes, perform particularly well. The Cape's Cap Classiques, ports, Noble Late Harvests and Muscadels are specialist wines that deserve a regular place at the table.

IN SEARCH OF THE PERFECT BUBBLE

It was apparently first found by the Benedictine monk Dom Pérignon, an amateur viticulturist (according to records of activities at the Abbey of Hautvillers in Champagne around the mid-17th century). A particularly cold winter had arrested fermentation of the Abbey's stock of wine – in those days wine was fermented in the bottle – and, with the onset of spring, a second fermentation started up again. Unable to withstand the building pressure of the carbon-dioxide, the bottles started exploding and drew the attention of our hero. The rest, as they say, is history.

The Champagne industry really got going only early in the 19th century when German merchants such as Bollinger and Krug joined the Widow Clicquot in developing a market for their special wine.

'Bubbles' is how Cape wine-industry doyen Dave Hughes happily refers to any still white wine that has been unduly influenced by carbon-dioxide, whether a lowly carbonated bubbly or a fine, bottle-fermented Champagne. But he will be the first to single out the nuances of quality and style effected in this most delicate of wines by the different production methods.

CAP CLASSIQUE

The term 'sparkling wine' has been adopted here, and elsewhere, as an alternative name for Champagne, a term permissible only in reference to the 'real thing' – which is sparkling wine made in Champagne, France, according to strict requirements by the Champagne producers themselves. The Champenoise, however, regard their Champagne as a specific wine rather than a style, and therefore expressive of certain varieties grown in a particular terroir. Hence their continuing and largely successful attempts to reserve that term solely for their produce. Other countries, including South Africa, were left to label the fruits to their labour as Méthode Traditionelle or Classique; even Méthode Champenoise was banned for all wines produced or sold in the European Union. Cape winemakers, well on their way to producing sparkling wines not far off the classic Marques of Champagne, coined the term Cap Classique.

About 20 Cape winemakers subscribe to the tenets of the Cap Classique Producers' Association, which encourages the application of true Champagne winemaking methods. The varieties recommended are Chardonnay, Pinot Noir and Pinot Meunier. Often, only free-run or lightly pressed juice is used to capture the purest essence of the grape. Each variety is fermented separately, usually in stainless-steel tanks, resulting in a bone-dry wine with a high acid and very little flavour.

Then comes the blending: Chardonnay for its steely strength, finesse and longevity; Pinot Noir for its body, depth and rich fruit; Pinot Meunier for its softness, fruit and touch of spice. Sometimes reserve wines, either tank- or barrel-fermented in previous vintages, are added for greater richness, complexity and maturity. Finally, the *liqueur de tirage* (a measureful of specially selected yeasts, still base wine and cane syrup) is added and the wine is bottled and sealed with a metal crown-cap (like a beer bottle top).

In the bottle, the wine then undergoes a second fermentation. Precipitating dead yeast cells are guided down to the neck of the bottle as it is slowly canted over onto its head in a process called riddling or *remuage*. Once this process is complete – the time on the lees, be it months or years, determines the quality of the final product – the neck of the bottle is frozen and the crown-cap removed. The pressure build-up of the carbon-dioxide released in the sealed bottle during fermentation expels the plug of frozen sediment and the bottle is quickly corked. The bit of wine lost during *dégorgement* is replaced by the *dosage*, a mixture of base wine and cane syrup that also brings the bone-dry wine to a generally acceptable sweetness level. A bone-dry bubbly has less than 4g/l residual sugar, an extra-dry 15g/l or less, a dry 15 to 35g/l and a semi-sweet 35 to 50g/l.

It is during this second fermentation that the 'perfect bubble' that marks a fine, bottle-fermented sparkling wine is achieved: that fine stream of tiny bubbles, like a string of pearls or the dewdrops on a spiderweb. You are bound to find it in Cap Classiques such as Graham Beck, Pongrácz, Simonsig Kaapse Vonkel, Twee Jonge Gezellen Krone Borealis, Cabrière's Pierre Jourdan and the Villiera Tradition range. And, like the Champagne houses, a few of the estates are also exploring the single-varietal option, such as the pure Chardonnay Blanc de Blancs

from Cabrière and Graham Beck and the vintage Chardonnay and Pinot Noir from South Africa's first Cap Classique 'House' of JC Le Roux.

More than the bubbles, it is the aroma and flavour that sets a Cap Classique apart from all other bubblies: the fresh scent of green apples and the toasty, biscuity, yeasty aromas of freshly baked bread; the seamless blend of freshness and creaminess, elegance and richness and delicate fruit, all of which lingers on and on.

Unorthodox varieties do also appear in some rather fine Cap Classiques. Villiera's consistently

BOTTLES OF BUBBLY UNDERGO THEIR SECOND FERMENTATION IN PUPITRES AT TWEE JONGE GEZELLEN, WHERE RIDDLING IS STILL DONE BY DEXTEROUS HANDS.

good-quality Tradition Carte Rouge shows what can be done with a dash of Pinotage and a shot of Chenin Blanc. The Cape's first foray into sparkling wine started with stalwarts such as Chenin Blanc, particularly when the advent of stainless-steel tank fermentation in the 1930s allowed for mass production of carbonated sparkling wine. Chenin is still the base for many carbonated bubblies, including best-seller Grand Mousseux. Before that, what little sparkling wine was made here actually went through the second fermentation in the bottle.

Simonsig brought the variety and method back together in 1971 with the first 'official' Méthode

Champenoise wine, which it called Kaapse Vonkel. And it is Simonsig that is close to including the Cape's first Pinot Meunier in a Cap Classique.

The French have kept the strongly supportive role of this specialist variety in their early-maturing non-vintage Champagnes very quiet. But, with the first experimental wine made from the Cape's only commercial planting to date showing promising results, Simonsig's success may persuade other Cap Classique proponents to invest in PInot Meunier, despite its lack of versatility as a still wine compared with colleagues Chardonnay and Pinot Noir.

THE CHARMAT (TANK) METHOD

Bellingham and Nederburg Kap Sekt have proved their success with the Charmat (or tank) method in combining quality with quantity; both are greatly underrated alternatives to the mostly more-expensive classics.

Here the second fermentation takes place in a pressure tank rather than in each individual bottle, and instead of the ritual of riddling, the Charmat practitioners transfer the wine into a holding tank. The sweetening *dosage* is added, and the finished wine is decanted into glass. It involves a complicated set of pressure systems to maintain the carbon-dioxide in the wine.

CARBONATED SPARKLING WINE

This simply involves the injection of carbon-dioxide into a tankful of wine, in the same way that fizzy cooldrinks are made. It is one of the easiest and cheapest methods and is in common use in the Cape for many of the uncomplicated, mostly semi-sweet or sweet bubblies.

These sparkling wines are marked by large, languorous bubbles that either collapse or turn into a frothy mass in the mouth. The nose and palate are often neutral, although sometimes they have not unattractive herbaceous or tropical fruit aromas and flavours depending on whatever non-Champagne grape was used. JC Le Roux uses Sauvignon Blanc and Pinotage and Van Loveren's Papillon Brut includes Colombard. Grand Mousseux relies on Chenin Blanc, while Muscat de Frontignan crops up all over the place.

WINEMAKER'S COMMENT

Pieter Ferreira, Graham Beck: 'When I think of Champagne, I think of those magical bubbles so unique to the wine. I am constantly in search of that perfect bubble. I work inside the bubble when I am structuring the wine and then I leave it for a while, walk away from it and inspect it objectively from the outside to assess whether I have achieved that synergy and complexity.'

WINE WRITER'S COMMENT

Dave Hughes, SA writer: 'It gives lift and life.'

AT THE GRAHAM BECK WINERY, THE GREENS, OCHRES AND PLUMS PICK OUT THE COLOURS OF THE SURROUNDING FYNBOS, ALOES, VINES, BOUGAINVILLEA AND FRESHLY FERMENTED RED WINE.

THE TRANSFER METHOD

Used until recently by a few Cape cellars but common in the USA, this technique also allows for a second fermentation in bottle. Instead of riddling each bottle to dispatch the sediment, however, the wine is transferred into a tank designed to cope with the increased pressure caused by the now naturally carbonated wine being injected into it. The sediment subsides and is filtered out. The *dosage* is added and the wine is again bottled, using a counter-pressure filter that regulates the pressure level, bringing it down to a level that can be handled by a bottle sealed with its special wired cork.

OPENING THE PORTALS TO PORT

As with Champagne, it was a member of the clergy who gave us port. The Abbot of Lamego, holed up in the arid Douro Valley in Portugal in the last half of the 17th century, was found by two English wine traders to be doctoring his wine with brandy. What was, in fact, a local Portuguese practice was turned into a thriving industry by the English by the early 1700s. And, as with Cap Classique, the Cape is being bullied.

This time it is Portugal that is flexing its muscles, though in an awfully proper way, given the long domination of the port industry by good English families who made Cockburn's, Graham's, Dow's and Taylor's so famous. Plans have been mooted to have the generic term 'port' reserved purely for the product from Portugal. This is probably in no small degree due to the fact that South Africa not only has the right terroir and grape varieties but also the ability and a strong desire to match the quality of its northern-hemisphere competitor on world markets.

The heart of Cape port production lies in the Klein Karoo, around the little gem of a town called Calitzdorp. The heat, the scrub, the schist-like shale soils, all are pure Douro. Visiting Portuguese port producers have found, to their undisguised amazement, that Tinta Barocca and Touriga Nacional grown in the Cape produces wine easily mistaken for Portuguese port. Indeed, local winemakers are particularly adept in their methods, and are intent on establishing authentic port styles. Encouraged by their own SA Port Producers' Association (SAPPA), over 30 wineries are turning out traditional Ruby, Tawny, Late Bottled Vintage, Vintage and Vintage Reserve ports. And more and more labels are carrying the prefix 'Cape' to pre-empt any future legislation forcing the local industry to drop the word 'port' from their nomenclature.

Port wine makers start the production process with full-ripe grapes, preferably the authentic port varieties with exotic names such as Touriga Nacional, Touriga Francesa, Tinta Barocca, Tinta Roriz, Tinta Francisca, Souzão, Cornifesto, and Malvasia Rei. Stand-ins such as Shiraz, Pinotage, Cabernet Sauvignon and Ruby Cabernet are still used by Cape winemakers, though this will now cause raised eyebrows among their colleagues newly committed to using only traditional port varieties. Port lovers will still find pleasure in these more unorthodox wines, though, from Boland's Ruby Cabernet and Bloemendal's Shiraz to La Cotte's Pinotage; or the mixtures from Villiera (Shiraz, Gamay and Pinotage), Simonsvlei (Pinotage, Shiraz and Tinta Barocca) and Blaauwklippen (Pontac and Zinfandel).

Crushed and fermented until the desired sugar level – around 100g/l – is reached, the wine is then fortified with fine grape (brandy) spirit and matured in wooden barrels. The purists, including a growing number of Cape specialists, swear by the gentle approach: footstomping and cap punching. Translated into English, this means crushing the grapes by foot instead of in a mechanical crusher and using a long wooden staff to continuously push the layer of skins on top of the fermenting juice back down into the purple morass, rather than pumping the juice back over the skins. In both cases, the aim is the same: to extract that rich, opaque, full-red colour and deep, fruity flavour that is the beginning of a fine port. After all this, it boils down to wood maturation, which separates the Vintage men from the Ruby boys.

CAPE RUBY

This is a blend of young, full-bodied, round and fruity port with components aged in wood for between six months and three years, averaging not less than a year. The vintage is irrelevant, as the wine can be blended from several crops. It is made to be drunk in the flush of youth, and something fruity, peppery, spicy and warm is what you should expect. Try the De Wet Ruby, voted top-of-the-class in a Ruby category tasting by an SA Port Producers' Association panel at the annual SAPPA symposium in 1998, despite being 100 per cent Shiraz. Or try Die Krans Cape Ruby, which is pure, classic Tinta Barocca.

CAPE VINTAGE

This is a wine from a single harvest which shows outstanding character and concentration. The wine is aged in small barrels or large vats and is usually bottled within two years of the vintage date on the label. It is altogether richer than a Ruby, retaining its largesse for many years in the bottle. Landskroon, Vergenoegd, Die Krans, Villiera, Overgaauw, Glen Carlou and KWV are good exponents of this style.

CAPE VINTAGE RESERVE

One step up from the Cape Vintage, this port-style demands a minimum of a year in oak and is usually released only after several more years of ageing. This comes closest to the pure Portuguese Vintage, the ultimate in ports, which is designated as the product of a particularly outstanding vintage officially so 'declared' by all the major port houses. Leaders in their field are the port wines from Die Krans, JP Bredell and Boplaas. The single-varietal Touriga Nacionals from both Boplaas and Overgaauw are made in the Cape Vintage Reserve style.

COMPARE THE DIFFERENT HUES OF AN UNCOMMON CAPE WHITE PORT, A CAPE VINTAGE AND A CAPE RUBY.

CAPE LATE BOTTLED VINTAGE

A Late Bottled Vintage (LBV) has just missed the boat in becoming a true Vintage, so was subsequently left in oak for at least a second year, and may have been aged for up to six years before bottling. Good, but not great, it has much of the Vintage character, if a little less of its staying power. Allesverloren port is traditionally a Cape LBV, while Rooiberg's Rubies sometimes adopt LBV characteristics with age. Morgenhof recently introduced an LBV, as did port 'négociant' Theo Rudman under his Rudman's label.

CAPE TAWNY

A blend of wine from various vintages, it must be matured in wood. You will know a Tawny by its translucent amber colour, its relatively light, ultra-smooth texture and its delicately nutty flavour. A Cape Dated Tawny is from a specific year. Portuguese Tawnies make some of the best drinking ports around. True Tawnies are not common in the Cape. Boplaas makes one, but if you can get your hands on some of the old Monis vintages, such as the 1983 Reserve (made from old Cape stalwarts Cinsaut and Pinotage), you'll taste something akin to a Tawny.

CAPE WHITE

Cape White port is a rarity, and not that good – yet. It is made from any non-Muscat grape variety that has received the nod from the Port Producers' Association, with a required minimum of six months' wood maturation. Malvasia Rei is okay, say the Portuguese, and it lurks in local vineyards. The South Africans still rely on old stalwart Chenin Blanc. Some winemakers have been known to sneak some white port into their red port to make an amber 'Tawny' – this is definitely now regarded as a no-no. Boplaas is one of the few cellars that offers a white port; try it chilled, as an apèritif in the Portuguese style.

Cape port-wine makers have taken to heart the reminder that a fine port is not sweet; it is rich. Many new-wave Cape ports have brought their sugars down to the desired 90g or even less per litre, delicately balancing it with a slightly higher minimum alcohol of 19 per cent, which provides greater firmness of structure and extra grip.

WINEMAKER'S COMMENT

Anton Bredell, JP Bredell Wines, on Vintage character: 'You just know. It's an intensity of colour and complexity on the nose and on the palate. It just seems to have everything: fruit, spirit, wood; but all in balance.'

WINE WRITER'S COMMENT

Roger Voss, UK author: 'Probably no other wine apart from Champagne has so imbued a way of life.'

MAKING MAGIC WITH MUSCADEL

The Cape has made Muscadel its own. It is a style of wine so entrenched in local wine-making culture that it has become the common name for the specific grape variety used: Muscat de Frontignan.

It was one of the first vines to arrive in the Cape when founding father Jan van Riebeeck requested vine cuttings back in the mid-17th century. For the farmers who pushed back the boundaries of the Cape colony, the heat of the Cape hinterland must have encouraged the technique of fortifying wine. Whether to balance the rich sweetness of the sun-ripened grapes, preserve the wine or simply give their daily tipple a bit of a kick, winemakers adopted it on a broad scale. Hence the home of Cape Muscadel was firmly founded around Worcester and Robertson and in the arid Klein Karoo. With co-operative cellars being the most common wine-production system in these areas, Muscadel

PORT SHOULD BE POURED TO FILL TWO-THIRDS OF A MEDIUM-SIZED GLASS WITH A SLIGHTLY CONCAVE LIP; THIS LEAVES ROOM FOR A BIT OF A SWIRL AND A SNIFF.

has almost become a co-op speciality. This is probably partly the reason for its undeserved lack of cachet. It is also rather more alcoholic than natural wine, with an average of 18 per cent versus 13 per cent per volume. Nevertheless, it has its place in your cellar or drinks cabinet or even – to be on-hand for a spontaneous tipple – in your fridge.

Co-ops and cachet aside, Muscadel has made it into the top-quality bracket. Critics across the board have given it their highest rating, from the pick of the bunch in the *John Platter SA Wines* guide to a rare five-star rating in *Wine* magazine and Veritas double gold medals.

Of all the many talented makers of Muscadel, Wilhelm Linde of Nuy in Worcester is the one to have turned it into an art form. Recognition

finally came the way of both Linde and this style of wine in 1988 when Diners Club selected Muscadel as the category for judging and Linde as its Winemaker of the Year. And it was the Nuy 1996 White Muscadel that recently earned *Wine* magazine's five-star rating.

The preference for red or white Muscadel is purely personal. In general, though, red Muscadels can be fuller, richer and more raisiny, while the whites are lighter, fresher, more elegant and, sometimes, spicy.

The two Nuy Muscadels prove the point perfectly. Nuy is just one of a band of merry Muscadel makers in the Breede River Valley, which includes Rooiberg, Robertson, Du Toitskloof, Bon Courage and Weltevrede. In fact, the latter was the first to sell a certified

THE VINEYARDS OF NUY, HOME OF CHAMPION MUSCADELS, MARCH ACROSS THE BREEDE RIVER VALLEY TOWARDS THE KEEROM MOUNTAINS.

for a 375ml bottle! Never mind Graham Beck's Rhona White Muscadel: R30 a bottle! Granted, it is 500ml and the long-necked, clear glass bottle is imported from Italy... What these producers are doing is putting Muscadel in its rightful place as a rather special after-dinner drink, a dessert wine of the highest social standing.

What of Jerepigo? Invariably spoken of in the same breath as Muscadel, and often quaffed as a replacement but sometimes disputed as being anything like Muscadel, Jerepigo sometimes appears labelled as Muscadel Jerepigo (just to further confuse the already confused).

They are technically not the same animal; some would go further and say Jerepigo is technically not even a wine but a preserved grape juice! Well!

What is labelled Muscadel is usually made from the Muscat de Frontignan grape, fermented to the desired sugar level and then fortified with a natural grape spirit. Jerepigo is fortified before fermentation actually starts (hence the rather derogatory reference to 'preserved grape juice'). And the grape of choice is invariably the lesser Muscat variety Muscat d'Alexandrie, known as Hanepoot in South Africa. Thus a Soet (sweet) Hanepoot is the same as a Jerepigo (or Jerepiko). A Muscadel Jerepigo, on the other hand, is a Jerepigo made from Muscat de Frontignan (or Muscadel). In the end, Jerepigo makes for a delicious sweet dessert drink, but Muscadel has an elegance, balance and complexity that makes it more than just sweet, and so much more of a wine.

WINEMAKER'S COMMENT
Wilhelm Linde, Nuy: 'Our Muscadels will age for up to 12 years, but they lose their fresh Muscat flavour, becoming deep and rich. The younger Muscadels will appeal to popular taste, while older bottles should be kept for special occasions.'

WINE WRITER'S COMMENT
David Biggs, SA columnist: 'Bottles of sunshine that bring warmth to our winter days.'

Red Muscadel under the Wine of Origin certification system introduced in the 1970s, and it carried the sought-after gold Superior sticker under the old quality-rating system. The cellar's White Muscadel matches it in quality – the 1997 is a Veritas double gold medallist.

Another aspect of Muscadel that has done nothing to up its image as a classy drink is the little matter of money. Muscadels are ludicrously cheap; there are few going for more than R15 a bottle from the cellar door and some barely scraping R10. And this for a 750ml bottle. One or two cellars are shaking things up, though. Eyebrows have been raised at Simonsvlei selling its Premier White Muscadel for R30-plus. They have hit the roof with the new releases from De Wetshof and Graham Beck in Robertson. The Muscat de Frontignan Blanc is over R20, and that

THE NECTAR OF THE GODS: NOBLE LATE HARVESTS AND NATURAL SWEETS

If, as Louis Pasteur remarked, a meal without wine is like a day without sunshine, then a Noble Late Harvest or Natural Sweet wine for dessert is like tasting the sun itself. Only chilled. These must have been the wines described by legend as ambrosia: the nectar of the gods.

The colour is burnished gold, with hints of lime green. The aroma combines wafts from a honey pot and jars of marmalade and peach and apricot preserves. The flavour is pure honey and tart fruit, rich and fresh, sweet and sour. It is all the result of a fungus the scientist calls *Botrytis cinerea* and the vintner knows as noble rot.

Noble Late Harvest is the South African nomenclature for what the French call *Pourriture Noble* and the Germans *Trockenbeerenauslese* (short for 'selected dried or raisined berries'). These are the wines made from grapes left on the vine until full-ripe when, in humid conditions, the rot takes hold. It is horrible to look at, a brownish-grey, cobwebbed mass that, unless given a dry spell to develop properly, quickly turns into a grey or sour rot that ruins the crop. The concentrating effect of the fungus that digests the skin, dehydrating and shrivelling the berry, results in large numbers of grapes yielding a small quantity of juice. Sometimes only part of the bunch is affected, necessitating hand-sorting of the berries.

White grape varieties with thin skins that are easily split or achieve high sugars are most readily affected by *Botrytis cinerea*. It has been Germany's Riesling and Sauternes Sauvignon Blanc and Sémillon that has influenced the Cape's finest Noble Late Harvests, led by Neethlingshof and Stellenzicht. It was a German, Günter Brözel, who pioneered what was a new wine style in the Cape in 1969 with his Nederburg Edelkeur, forcing the rewriting of wine and spirits laws to accommodate a natural, unfortified wine with a residual sugar exceeding 20g/l. Yet, ironically, he used not Riesling but Chenin Blanc.

Ultimately it is nature that dictates which grapes are to be blessed by a fungal attack, making each bottle of Noble Late Harvest a little treasure. L'Avenir's Vin de Meurveur is Colombard, Simonsig uses Bukettraube, Lievland has used Riesling, but found Chenin Blanc and Bukettraube most suitable. The consistently fine Fleur du Cap relies on Chenin Blanc, and so does Nederburg Edelkeur, sometimes containing a dash of Muscat de Frontignan. Buitenverwachting in cool Constantia is rarely attacked by botrytis, which, when its strikes, has Weisser Riesling in its sights and results in the very elegant Noblesse in its antique green bottle with gold filigree.

Noble Late Harvests can sometimes push the sugar limit to 200g/l, though the trend is to find a level between 80–120g. This, plus the distinctive character imparted by botrytis, sets these wines apart from the semi-sweet Special Late Harvest and Late Harvest wines. But it is the art of balancing that rich sweetness with a bracing acidity that occupies the winemaker. And now wood has come into the equation, effecting an often more elegant, drier style of Noble Late Harvest in the vein of Sauternes, as achieved most notably by Lievland.

For those times when the fungus chooses to hibernate, there is a new style of natural sweet dessert wine to fall back on. Not unexpectedly, it is called Natural Sweet (sometimes Sweet Natural). This category was created in the Cape in 1990, especially to accommodate wines that had all the attributes of a Noble Late Harvest (barring that particularly luscious complexity imparted by botrytis) but with a higher sugar than the maximum of 50g/l set down for a Special Late Harvest (like the Vlottenburg, for example). Never think that the Natural Sweets are inferior to the Noble Lates, as there are some gems out there. Klein Constantia's Vin de Constance, as far as possible a recreation of the original 18th-century sweet wines, has reclaimed the world attention afforded its ancestors.

ABOVE: A NOBLE LATE HARVEST GLOWS IN AN ELEGANT, UNEMBELLISHED DESSERT-WINE GLASS.

OPPOSITE, TOP AND BELOW: THE MODERN GRAHAM BECK WINERY IS A CELEBRATION OF LIQUID LIGHT AND COLOUR, WITH STYLISH SOPHISTICATION REFLECTED IN 'THE AFRICAN MASK', A STEEL SCULPTURE BY EDUARDO VILLA AT THE TASTING ROOM ENTRANCE.

It is not the only one to do so. Cellars are now no longer constrained by the rare combination of warmth and rain that causes the humidity in which botrytis thrives, so are able to come up with a Natural Sweet most vintages.

Nederburg took the gap by producing its Eminence, now almost as sought-after on the Nederburg Auction as the Edelkeur. You may sometimes pick up a hint of botrytis in some of these wines, such as the Beaumont Goutte

BELOW: DEHYDRATED AND SUN-DRIED GRAPES PROVIDE THE ESSENTIAL FLAVOUR FOR A NEW CAPE RARITY IN THE STYLE OF THE FRENCH 'VIN DE PAILLE'.

OPPOSITE: 'ALL ROADS LEAD TO NEDERBURG,' AS THE ADVERTISEMENT WOULD HAVE IT. THE BEAUTY OF THIS PAARL FARM'S CAPE DUTCH MANOR HOUSE, HOME OF THE NOBLE EDELKEUR, IS BREATHTAKING.

d'Or (drop of gold) and the Saxenburg La Reve, which just adds to their charm. Several, including Vin de Constance, Goutte d'Or and a delightfully luscious wine from new Stellenbosch cellar Laibach, have treated their Natural Sweets to some time in the barrel.

One intrepid young Stellenbosch winemaker, David Trafford, has instigated the creation of a new category of naturally sweet wine, somewhat laboriously listed as 'Wine from Naturally Dried Grapes'. The French, more romantically, call it *Vin de Paille* (straw wine), while the German term is *Strohwein*. The name indicates the ancient method of sun-drying full-ripe grapes on straw

mats or racks (or strung up on rafters in a loft). As the grapes shrivel and dry, the sugar, acid and fruit flavours become highly concentrated, resulting in wines of similar alcohols and sugars as the Noble Lates, averaging 13 per cent and 100 g/l respectively. After about three weeks, the grapes are crushed, pressed and transferred into small oak barrels where fermentation takes place. The wine is then left to mature for a year. Trafford's wine, made from Chenin Blanc, is currently the only 'straw wine' made in South Africa.

WINEMAKER'S COMMENT
Schalk van der Westhuizen, Neethlingshof: 'Botrytis is a difficult one: every year is different and a lot has to do with the weather. There are times when the sugars are high and I can't get the fermentation going; other times I have to warm the tanks. But our one Weisser vineyard against a southerly slope gets noble rot every single year, like clockwork. It's amazing.'

WINE WRITER'S COMMENT
Huon Hooke, New Zealand writer: '[Cape Noble Late Harvests provide] a feast of gorgeous, luscious, complex and drinkable wines.'

FINDING THE EYE OF THE PARTRIDGE IN BLANC DE NOIR AND ROSÉ
Colour is at the core of the attraction of Blanc de Noir and Rosé wines. The different shades of translucent salmon pinks and rosy reds reflect perfectly the lightly fruity, delicately fragrant and essentially feminine delights of a style of wine that is tailor-made for salad days and summer lunches. There is, however, a slight difference between the two.

Both are styles of the modern era, in answer to consumer demand for fashionable, quaffable summer wines. Rosé can be made by blending white and red wine, as is still the case in Champagne. This technique is rarely used in the Cape, as there are three other methods that make fresher, fruitier wines.

RIGHT: LANZERAC IN
STELLENBOSCH IS AS POPULAR
AS ITS TEAR-DROP ROSÉ
BOTTLE; IT IS A GOOD
EXAMPLE OF A NEO-
CLASSICAL CAPE DUTCH
GABLED FARMSTEAD DESIGN.

THE APTLY NAMED ROSÉ WINE:
THE WHITE JUICE IS DELICATELY
COLOURED BY A SHORT
SOAKING ON THE SKINS OF
THE RED GRAPE.

Bleeding is the recovery of juice from red grapes that are crushed by their own weight, resulting in the most delicate of pinks. Limited pressing allows the winemaker to extract colour as required. Maceration entails initial fermentation on the skins until the right colour is achieved – not more than 24 hours – after which the fermentation is continued off the skins.

The latter is the most common and preferred practice and results in a far more authentic flavour, true to the varieties from which the Rosé is made.

Blanc de Noir was made famous as a still wine by the Californians, although it has its roots in classical winemaking. Blanc de Noir is a Champagne term: the white wine made from red (or black) grapes, usually Pinot Noir and Pinot Meunier. In the Cape, Blanc de Noirs and most Rosés are now made from red grapes left on the skins for just enough time – hours or even minutes – to extract some colour. This explains its characteristic hue: not the rosy pink of the Rosé but that elusive salmon pink or onionskin shade most evocatively described by the French as the *Oeil de Perdrix* (the eye of the partridge).

Some of the most famous labels in Cape wine, such as Nederburg, Lanzerac and Bellingham, have included a Rosé in their ranges from as far back as the '50s. Blanc de Noir is more recent, introduced by Boschendal in 1981, when sparkling wine specialist Achim von Arnim of Cabrière was the winemaker there.

While Rosé wines come in varying degrees of sweetness, Blanc de Noirs are invariably dry or off-dry. The fact that numbers have increased is one more illustration of the change in tastes from sweet to dry. Boschendal, Neethlingshof and Van Loveren remain the best bets.

This is not to say that a Blanc de Noir is necessarily of better quality than a Rosé, for many cellars commandeer some fine red grapes for their Rosés, from Cabernet Sauvignon at

Warwick to Cinsaut and Gamay at Nederburg and Fairview. The popular semi-sweet Rosé from Delheim is pure Pinotage. And if you cannot find a pink to please, there is invariably one on the shelves of Woolworths.

WINEMAKER'S COMMENT
Bussell Retief, Van Loveren: 'Our slightly sweeter Muscat Blanc de Noir is more appealing than the dry one we make from Shiraz. The alcohol is around 11%, so it's a good lunchtime wine.'

WINE WRITER'S COMMENT
David Biggs, SA columnist: 'Those "pinks" with some sweetness are preferable, offering a longer aftertaste, more complexity and hinting at a fruit-salad character.'

WINE TASTING

THE MIRACLE OF WINE IS THAT IT OFFERS the diversity and complexity that bears such close scrutiny: it is where art and science overlap. The variables that come into play start with the natural elements of soil, climate and fruit. Then comes the craft: vine management, cellar techniques, vintner's skill and choice. Once in the bottle, it remains a live product, changing, developing and regressing. At the time you sip it, it is not the same as it was – nor the same as it will be. This is the stuff of serious discourse.

PREVIOUS PAGES: THE VAULTED
UNDERGROUND SPARKLING-
WINE CELLAR AT TWEE
JONGE GEZELLEN IN
TULBAGH — INSPIRATION TO
ALL WINE LOVERS WISHING
TO TRANSFORM THEIR OWN
HUMBLE HOME CELLARS.

BELOW: GRADATIONS OF
YELLOWS AND REDS GUIDE
YOU TOWARDS IDENTIFYING
THE STYLE OF WINE IN
YOUR GLASS.

But no matter how academic, pinning down this mercurial liquid is always fun. Whatever tack you take, tasting wine is simply not something you do on your own. Wine is a matter of opinion – and opinions have to be shared to be worth having. Some knowledge about basic procedures, terms and techniques, however, will help you make sense of all the sniffing and spitting that may be going on around you. It is also guaranteed to make you enjoy your glass of wine that much more.

METHOD

To non-winos there is madness in the method of wine tasting. The sight of sniffing, swirling, spitting and scribbling figures hunched over a dining-room table is enough to send a spouse or housemate in search of a psychologist. Should they stick around, however, they are sure to find out why there's all this seriousness and concentration. Because there *is* method in the madness. If you do not spit and scribble, you will barely be able to recall the fundamental flavour

of the first wine in the line-up, let alone the finer nuances of character that will allow you to proffer a varietal or vintage identification with at least some degree of confidence during 'discussion time'. Because if you like wine, you see, you cannot help but drink it, and no matter how formal the proceedings or how expert the tasters, no tasting ends quite as it began.

Tasting is fun, but its primary purpose is to learn something more about what you are putting in your mouth. If anything, a tasting is a practical opportunity to find out what you like and what you do not. The tilting of the glass, the nosing through one nostril and the sucking in of air through pursed lips may seem either pretentious or simply a bit of a scream. But there are good reasons for it.

THE SENSES

Sight is the sense that comes into play first. The broad categorisation of wine into white and red belies the variety of hues and shades that appear when you really begin to study the colours of wine. Colour is the first 'give-away' if you are playing the guessing game of vintage and variety: a pale straw-yellow wine suggests a white wine that is young, for example, and you can smell the difference between a Chenin Blanc and a Chardonnay. A Pinotage is like a gemstone, taking you through gradations of red, starting with the vibrant young purple of amethyst, through ruby and garnet on to aged amber.

Light is integral to colour perception. Holding a glass of wine against a bright light or a clean sheet of white paper gives you a true reflection (wine in the glass picks up colour from clothing and walls). Tilting the glass allows the eye to travel from the deeply coloured core of the liquid to the edge (the changing shade and intensity gives a clue to age and quality: a watery rim does not auger well, while an opaque centre or rich colour throughout promises quite a mouthful).

Brilliance of colour is also important. A dull appearance may mean that the wine is equally boring. A murky, milky look usually means that the wine is off. Prepare to spit.

Aroma either confirms or confuses your initial guess: this is the 'nose' that tasters are always on about. Do not confuse aroma and bouquet: aroma refers to the more primary, basic, vinous grape smell of a young wine; the bouquet encompasses a variety of smells given off by a complex, mature wine. And that is why everyone just talks about 'the nose'; it is much easier.

To get a good ingestion of 'nose', swirl the wine in the glass, which allows air to circulate through the liquid, releasing more of its bouquet. This is where the single-nostril action comes into play. It looks funny, I know, but it works, seeming to concentrate and separate the array of smells that can assail the olfactory senses when 'nosing' the wine to try and identify the variety of whiffs. (That is the correct verb to use, by the way: 'smelling' is gauche).

Speaking of noses, this is also the time when the super-serious look out for legs. No one is quite sure what causes these tear-shaped globules that sometimes form on the side of the glass after swirling the wine; some say it is a sign of high alcohol, others that it promises a wine of richness and extract. It can simply indicate that the glass may be a bit grubby or soapy. Best to just ignore.

The actual sniffing: just do it any old way that comes naturally and provides enough information to pick out and describe whatever it is that you find.

The taste is what you have been waiting for; it is what really counts. The right word to use here is 'palate'. Take a reasonable mouthful and swirl it in your mouth (with a few intakes of air to go with it); this allows the release of all the wine's flavour components. It also covers all the taste-buds, which is important as the tongue has very specific areas to pick up the basic elements of taste that apply to wine: sweetness on the tip; sourness (acidity) on the sides; and bitterness at the back. The palate is the arbiter of the body, weight and texture of a wine. Is it light, fresh, chewy, full, round, weighty or what? As for quality, it is surprising how many will settle for a fine nose (Cleopatra had more in common with wine than she knew), while there are those who look for a long finish, the lingering of the wine's essential flavours long after it has been expelled or swallowed. Try going back to your by-now advisedly empty glass for another whiff; it is edifying how a simple wine leaves little trace while a noble cru can immediately be identified and savoured anew, even in its absence.

ABOVE LEFT: A GOOD-QUALITY RED WILL REFLECT A DENSITY OF COLOUR RIGHT TO THE RIM.

ABOVE CENTRE: TILT YOUR GLASS AGAINST A WHITE BACKGROUND TO SHOW UP THE TRUE COLOUR.

ABOVE RIGHT: BRIGHTNESS OR BRILLIANCE OF COLOUR SUGGESTS A WELL-MADE WINE.

ABOVE LEFT AND CENTRE:
A GOOD SWIRL HELPS TO
AERATE THE WINE, WHICH
RELEASES ITS BOUQUET. DO
NOT BE SHY TO DIP YOUR
NOSE RIGHT INTO THE GLASS
TO GET A GOOD WHIFF.

ABOVE RIGHT: A HIGHLY
EXTRACTED, DENSE RED WINE
AND A SWEET, UNCTUOUS
WHITE TEND TO FORM RIVULETS
DOWN THE SIDE OF THE GLASS:
THE LEGS.

SCRIBBLES AND SCORES

Memory is everything in tasting wine, be it
the association of a scent or a flavour once
experienced and now rediscovered, or the
recognition of a distinctive characteristic in a
specific wine picked up again many tastings
hence. Even the best memory needs practice,
which is a good excuse to have many, many
wine tastings. But any memory needs a back-up,
especially when its owner imbibes. And even if
you refrain from swallowing, a minuscule amount
of alcohol does find its way into the bloodstream
through the interior surfaces of the mouth, while
the fumes in a closed room during a tasting are
sufficient to make you feel a little light-headed.
This is the motivation for the awfully formal
scoresheet and manic scribbling at any self-
respecting wine tasting. It helps you remember
and provides a record of what you have tasted.

South Africa uses the 20-point scoring system
rather than the 100-pointer favoured in the UK
and US. Users of the 20-point system usually
confine themselves to the upper end of the scale;
anything rating less than 13 is regarded as not
worth drinking. A full-house is as rare as hen's
teeth, no matter what the point allocation.

Like so many aspects of wine, scoring is a
subject of heated debate. At competitions,
opinions fly about what constitutes a five-star,
double gold, world-class wine, and whether this
is arrived at by majority vote, median score,
straight averaging or consensus. Luckily, you
can leave these earth-shattering decisions to the
professionals. The rest of us have quite happily
agreed to give a truly wonderful wine 18 or
higher, a really fine wine 16 or 17, a very nice
wine 15, an average, acceptable wine 14, an
arbitrary wine 13 and an undrinkable wine 12.
Of course, being wine and each person being
in possession of a collection of tastebuds as
individual as a set of fingerprints, there are
degrees even of undrinkability, depending
on the imbiber.

The division of points falls into three groups,
addressing the three major quality components
of a wine: colour is scored out of three, the nose
out of seven and the palate out of 10.

Some professional scoresheets have an
extra column down the right of the page, which
professional tasters have to be reminded –
often begged – to fill in: what is required is a
recommendation as to when to drink the wine

being evaluated, or how long to lay it down. Now this is no easy task, no matter how experienced or knowledgeable you are. The truth is that no one really knows! Anyone who buys good wine cannot be blamed for wanting to know how long they can stretch the pleasure of opening the next bottle. There is only one thing more disappointing in a wine lover's life than opening a treasured red to find it still a bit rough around the edges – and that is the long-delayed opening of a last precious bottle and finding the wine all dried out.

Suffice it to say that it is best to underestimate rather than overestimate, especially these days when wines are being made to drink younger than they once were. As for those scoresheets: when in doubt, leave out; any suggestions or ideas on the wine's development potential can be incorporated in your description.

ETIQUETTE

Wine tasters do some pretty disgusting things that may shock the novice.

It is the one time when sniffing loudly in public is allowed. Assailed with so many aromas that need identification, the nasal passages need all the help they can get. But keep it delicate. Vigorous sniffing will not help, but clearing the nose, with little light exhalations, does help to open the passages which can become congested, especially when tasting a fair number of wines and particularly intense, robust reds.

Gurgling is the quite acceptable result of sucking in air with a mouth full of wine. It aerates the wine, releasing and enhancing its flavour components for more ready identification. But beware: inhale too vigorously and you will choke; breathe in too gently and you will dribble wine out of the corners of your mouth, especially if you have taken too big a slug from your glass.

Gargling is out. So is rinsing; foaminess does nothing to enhance the feel or flavour of a wine. Better to gently swirl the wine around the mouth with your tongue and let it quietly lie there while you note the various characteristics as they impinge themselves on your tastebuds.

Spitting requires practice – it is not something that is easily relearned so many years after playground competitions. Accepting that it is part and parcel of a professional taster's repertoire will go a long way towards making you spit with confidence. Because that is what it takes to be a successful spitter. Spitting surreptitiously will bring on another bout of dribbling or leave you with one of those long, dangling threads of saliva you thought you only had to cope with in the partial privacy of the dentist's rooms!

Wine tasters also have some rather pretentious mannerisms that, in fact, owe more to practicality than to image.

Holding the glass by the stem rather than around the bowl has several purposes. It allows for unhindered scrutiny of the wine's colour when tilting the glass, and it is also easier to rotate a glass by its stem when swirling the wine before nosing. Cupping it in the hand warms the contents, something to bear in mind when you *do* want to put the heat on a wine that is too cold to show off its aromas and flavours to best advantage. Some professionals even avoid the stem, preferring to grip the glass at the base between thumb and forefinger. This calls for dexterity and digital strength somewhat beyond the bounds of practicality and comfort.

Some tasters like to lean out from their chair and away from a line-up of ready-poured wines in front of them before applying nose to glass. This acutely angled, dramatic pose does have the advantage of removing the nose from close proximity to conflicting aromas.

TASTING TERMS

There is no right or wrong way to describe wine; the best wine tastings are rife with original, outrageous descriptions. A personal favourite emerged at a tasting by committed but no less irreverent wine lovers. A delicious Cape Noble

CLUTCHING THE GLASS AROUND THE BOWL LEAVES YOU WITH A LUKEWARM WINE – AND A RATHER GRUBBY GLASS.

HOLDING YOUR GLASS BY THE STEM ALLOWS YOU TO MANIPULATE THE LIQUID TO PLEASE ALL YOUR SENSES.

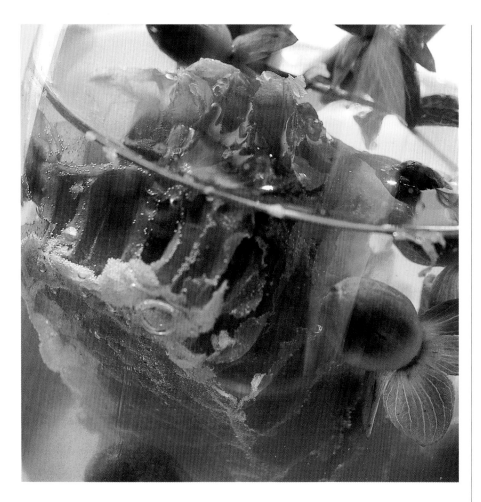

you like or dislike about what is in your glass. Many of those colour, aroma and flavour characteristics are directly linked to the physical or chemical make-up of the wine: clone, acid, wood, tannin, yeasts, youth and maturity... The same grape reacts in different ways to the soil and climate in which it is grown as well as the various winemaking techniques.

What follows is a list of terms most commonly used and generally regarded as standard to describe the colour, nose and palate of a wine. First up are the typical aromas and flavours peculiar to the specific varieties bottled as varietal wines in the Cape, or those that add a distinctiveness to a blend. These characteristics are the thumbprint of the grape, but also reflect the way it is generally grown, and are based on the actual physical and chemical make-up of the wine that is usually made from them. They include style pointers, such as the honeyed aroma and flavour of a sweeter or bottle-aged version of the wine, or the vanilla of a wooded wine. These varietal characteristics are followed by a list of general terms, which say a lot about the quality of the wine, the way it was made and whether you like it or not.

Late Harvest was described as reminiscent of 'sticky mango fingers': these three words evoked not just the aromas, flavours and textures of the wine in the glass but all the attendant sensual delights of drinking that wine.

Perception of colour, smell and taste is as subjective in wine evaluation as in anything else. And what is extraordinary about wine, as opposed to beer or tomato juice, is that one product, made from a single fruit type, can yield such a vast array of sensory information. Equally amazing is that, subjective as sensory analysis can be, it finds resonance among so many noses and palates the world over. This is how, over time, more and more terms to describe wine come into popular use.

Identifying these specifics is not integral to the enjoyment of wine, but recognising them is important when it comes to describing what it is

TYPICAL VARIETAL AROMAS AND FLAVOURS

BARBERA
Ripe cherry, blackberry, sweet vanilla, herbs, brambly, savoury, organic, earthy

BUKETTRAUBE
Muscat, grape, peach, pear

CABERNET FRANC
Raspberry, violets, pencil lead shavings, herbaceous, weedy (positive), spice (cinnamon), cedarwood, cassis, tobacco, chocolate

CABERNET SAUVIGNON
Blackberry, cassis, ripe plums, green pepper, grassiness, herbaceous, mint, eucalypt, menthol,

liquorice, cedarwood, cigarbox, tobacco, pencil lead, tea leaves, sweet wood vanillins, oak spice

CHARDONNAY
Citrus (lemon, lime), marmalade, tropical fruit (melon, pineapple), butter, butterscotch, toffee, caramel, honey, spice (cloves, cinnamon), toast, nuts (almonds)

CHENIN BLANC
Guava, melon, tropical fruit, fruit salad, candyfloss, floral, peach, apricot, honey, almond

CINSAUT
Raspberry, jellybabies, sugarwater, candyfloss, spice (cinnamon), nuts

COLOMBARD
Guava, tropical fruit (melon, litchi and granadilla), floral (rose)

CROUCHEN BLANC (CAPE RIESLING)
Fruit cordial, hay, thatch, grass, herbs (thyme), geranium, honey

FERNÃO PIRES
Pepper, spice, Muscat, citronella, lemon

GAMAY
Fresh cherry fruit, raspberry, boiled sweets, savoury, spice, herbs, herbaceous, bacon, gamey

GEWÜRZTRAMINER
Rose petal, honeysuckle, spice (musk), Muscat, apricot, litchi, grape, honey, slightly bitter pith of a citrus fruit

HÁRSLEVELÜ
Herbs, fynbos, grapefruit, lime, pineapple, peach, honey

MALBEC
Blackberry, spice, savoury, grass, mint

MERLOT
Mint, eucalypt, chocolate, coffee, violets, mineral,

spice (cinnamon), fruit cake, plummy fruit, blackberry, cassis, smoked meat

MUSCAT D'ALEXANDRIE (HANEPOOT)
Muscat, sun-ripe grapes, tropical fruit (litchi, pineapple, melon), honey, raisins

MUSCAT DE FRONTIGNAN (MUSCADEL)
Muscat, floral, spice (musk), dried apricot and peach, grape, honey, raisins, nuts

PETIT VERDOT
Spice, pepper, blackberry

PINOT BLANC
Spice (musk), Muscat, honey, butter, toast, dried nuts

PINOT GRIS
Faint citrus fruit, peach, spice, earthiness, thatch, fynbos

PINOT NOIR
Cherry, cranberry sauce, strawberry, boiled sweets, violets, organic aromas (mushrooms, truffles, forest floor, compost, damp leaves), liquorice, spice

PINOTAGE
Strawberry, raspberry, boiled sweets, banana, paw-paw, spice, acetone (nail varnish, paint), jam, vanilla

PONTAC
Perfumed, spicy, herbaceous, organic, wild redberry fruit, smoky, liquorice,

SAUVIGNON BLANC
Gooseberry, cat's pee, tropical fruit (capsicum, melon), herbaceous, grass, nettle, green pepper, tinned peas, asparagus, figs, flint

SÉMILLON
Lemon, honey, spice, lanolin, beeswax, butter, butterscotch, vanilla, citrus, peach, melon, dried grass, hay, thatch, almonds

SHIRAZ
Spice (cinnamon, oak), black peppercorns, sweet pimento, violets, caramel, fudge, blackberry, smoke, gamey meat, tar, leather, sweet vanilla

SYLVANER
Muscat, tropical fruit (melon, pineapple), apricot, spice, honey

TINTA BAROCCA
Red-berry fruit, prune, vanilla, spice, pepper

VIOGNIER
Apricot, dried peach, honeysuckle, may blossom, violets, rose, fresh honey

WEISSER (RHINE) RIESLING
Floral, fragrant, sweet honeysuckle, limes, apples, spice, herbs, honey, terpene or kerosene, peach and apricot (botrytis)

ZINFANDEL
Raspberry, plum, bramble berry, spice, pepper, savoury

GENERAL TASTING TERMS

Accessible: soft tannins and acids, no harsh flavours, easy-drinking
Acetic/acidic: sharp, acidic, tart, vinegary
Acetone: the nail varnish smell of an ester, ethyl acetate or amyl acetate
Aftertaste: the flavours that linger after the wine has been spat out or swallowed
Aggressive: pungent, tart or tannic
Alcoholic: detected by the heavy weight of the wine in the mouth and a burning sensation on the tip of the tongue; not favourable
Aromatic: delicate, fragrant, sometimes spicy
Astringent: the mouth-puckering effect of high acid or the dryness of high tannin
Attack: the first aromatic sensations
Attenuated: a drying out or thinning of flavour; a lack of flesh and weight
Austere: lacking complexity, hard, ungiving

Backbone: the strength to last in the bottle, usually the tannin/acid combination
Baked: a 'hot', earthy, burnt smell of excessively alcoholic wines, usually from hot areas where the grapes ripened too quickly to develop balance
Balance: the harmonious relationship between the wine's major elements of fruit, sugar, acid, tannin and alcohol
Beefy: heavy, full-bodied wine with high extract of fruit and tannin
Big: full-bodied wine, with lots of everything: fruit, acid, tannin, alcohol
Bite: high acid or tannin, good in a lively wine, bad if excessive
Bitter: unpleasant taste from harsh pressing of grapes (pips and skin tannins), which can soften with maturation, or from dirty barrels
Blowsy: a very fruity, over-the-top wine, lacking in acid and tannin to balance
Body: the feel or weight of the wine in the mouth due to high extract and alcohol
Bottle-age: the mellowing effect on the wine of time spent in the bottle, picked up in the golden colour and slightly musty aroma of a white and the browning colour and dusty aroma of a red
Bottle shock: the temporary loss of aroma and flavour in a wine during the first few days or weeks after bottling due to excessive contact with the air
Botrytised: the honeyed aroma and flavour of a wine made from grapes advantageously affected by the *Botrytis cinerea* fungus
Brick red: the colour of a red wine; a dark red with a coppery, amber, orange tinge, browner than garnet; denotes age
Brilliant: shininess, brightness of colour, indicating a clean, well-made wine
Browning: a red wine with a slightly amber, brownish tinge or rim. Indicates advancing age or oxidisation, which can be a fault in a young wine
Burnished: the lustre of a white wine with a gold colour, indicating quality or bottle-age
Buttery: the rich, fat smell and taste developed by some white wines that have undergone malolactic fermentation or been barrel-fermented or -matured

Classic: any wine that is authentic in variety and style, of high quality and great finesse

Character: a good-quality wine that has the distinctive characteristics of its provenance

Cheesy: a positive aroma in mature Champagne, indicating time spent on the lees; can be picked up on whites left on their lees, especially if they were unracked or unfiltered

Chewy: heavy with so much extract and body you feel like chewing it

Clean: a wine with no off-odours, odd flavours or faults, showing technically skilled winemaking

Cloying: the mouth-coating effect of an overly sweet wine lacking acid to balance it

Cloudy: wine with suspended particles, denoting poor quality or faulty winemaking

Coarse: a rough wine, lacking harmony between its elements, showing careless winemaking

Commercial: simple, uncomplicated, with no distinctive character to make it stand out in the crowd

Complex: a wine that offers a range of aromas and flavours

Cooked: the unnaturally sweet smell of a wine that has been fermented at high temperature

Corky: the distinctively dusty smell of cork on a wine, only apparent if the cork is infected or of poor quality; if it has allowed air to seep into the bottle, the wine will be oxidised or 'corked', with a musty smell

Concentrated: an intensity of aroma and flavour in a fine wine

Creamy: the soft, smooth mouthfeel of a wine with soft fruit acids or that has undergone malolactic fermentation

Crisp: a wine with good acidity

Crimson/cerise: the pinky red colour of a youthful red wine, usually used to describe the colour of the rim of the wine; may indicate a Beaujolais style or a Pinotage

Developed: a wine that shows maturity; aromas and flavours at their height of intensity

Delicate: a good-quality wine with understated aromas and flavours

Dry: a wine with technically under 4g/l of residual sugar; if full-fermented with close to 0g, such as some sparkling wines, it is described as bone-dry

Dumb: usually a young wine with the weight and balance that promises quality, but no definitive aromas and flavours showing through yet

Dusty: can be tannin in a red, a lack of definitive varietal characteristics in a white, or a dirty glass

Dense: a concentration of colour, aroma or flavour in a fine young wine

Dried out: usually an older vintage in which the fruit has disappeared, leaving only tannin and acid

Dull: the colour of a wine, white or red, that may be faulty or of inferior quality

Earthy: a drying effect in the mouth, or an actual character derived from certain soils

Elegant: a wine of balance and finesse, with nothing overdone

Extract: all soluble solids, from proteins to tannins, extracted from the grape must, skin and wood that give body to a wine

Estery: a sweetness derived from compounds formed during fermentation

Farmyardy: a not unpleasant ripe, manure, vegetal, smelly smell, given off by an acid; typical of Pinot Noir and not uncommon in mature, developed wines

Fat: full-bodied, highly extracted wine

Finesse: an elegance of character marking top quality

Fresh: usually a wine with good acidity

Firm: a wine that has good acid and tannin to support the fruit

Flabby: a lifeless wine without acidity to give it freshness and lift; probably past its best

Finish: the aftertaste

Forward: a wine with aromas that seem to almost jump out of the glass and flavours that are readily apparent

Flat: lacking in acidity

Floral: flowery aromas, fresh and sweet

Fragrant: delicately scented

Flinty: reminiscent of gunflint, hinting at stony, shale soils, particularly in whites

Full-bodied: a wine that fills the mouth
Feminine: a delicate wine, with nothing in excess and out of balance
Fleshy: made from full-ripe fruit, high in extract, mouthfilling, textured, but smooth
Fruity: the essence of a good wine, the result of vinifying grapes at optimum ripeness to expose the full range of different types of fruit flavours, rarely that of grapes

Gamey: a sign of overripe fruit, over-development or a very mature red
Garnet: the colour of a red wine; like the gemstone, a combination of deep ruby and brownish red; usually a well-developed wine of some age
Gold: colour of a full-bodied, quality white wine, usually a Chardonnay; can indicate sweetness, as in Late Harvest or Noble Late Harvest, or bottle-age in any white wine.
Green: a desirable tinge in the colour of white wines showing youth or promising liveliness despite bottle age; also used to describe a wine with unripe fruit or tannins.
Grip: the combination of good alcohol and firm tannins, backed by full-ripe fruit, giving the wine a presence in the mouth and the promise of longevity
Grapey: ironically, uncommon in most wines, but it is typical of the Muscat varieties and their offspring

Hard: the feel of a wine with excessive tannin or that has had extensive contact with pips and skins during fermentation
Harsh: due to excessive tannin, or acid
Heavy: the feel of a wine with a lot of body and extract; can be positive or negative, depending on the requirements of the imbiber
Herbaceous: a freshness of character, combining grass and flowers
Hollow: a wine with appeal on the nose and initial flavour as well as some aftertaste, but lacking in flavour and character
Honeyed: the pleasing rich sweetness of an aged white wine of quality (not necessarily technically sweet) and a characteristic of fine sweet wines, such as Noble Late Harvests
Hot: see baked

Inky: the colour and density of a highly extracted quality red wine, opaque and almost black
Intense: a concentration of aroma or flavour

Lively: a wine with well-balanced acidity that makes for a freshness of flavour
Leathery: the toughness of a red with a high tannin content
Length: the period of time the flavour remains in the mouth; a lingering aftertaste is one of the surest signs of quality
Light: low in alcohol; or lightness of body
Luscious: the particular combination of rich fruitiness and fatness that makes a wine a delicious, succulent mouthful
Lean: a wine somewhat short of fruit, with the tannin or acid, or both, dominating
Leesy: a rich, yeasty character imparted to a white wine that has spent extra time on the lees (the sediment, including dead yeast cells, that forms during fermentation)

Meaty: a rich, dense red wine with a chewy, almost thick feel in the mouth
Musty: either a barrel or cork fault, or bottle-age, which may fade a bit if the wine if the bottle is left open a while before pouring
Maderised: a dullness of aroma and flatness of flavour, similar to oxidisation; usually the result of the bottle's exposure to heat
Masculine: a big, powerful wine with strong flavours and fruit, acid, tannin and alcohol in abundance
Mature: a wine in which, after time in the bottle, all the components have integrated, resulting in a mellow character
Mellow: a wine that is soft and rounded
Mercaptan: a compound in a wine formed by chemical reaction and resulting in an off-odour, likened to cabbage, garlic or burnt rubber
Metallic: a tinny flavour, usually due to some cellar contamination

Mouldy: an unpleasant flavour, usually the result of dirty barrels or rotten grapes

Mouthfilling: a richness of flavour and weight of body that spreads across the mouth

Mouthfeel: relates to the texture of the wine, whether smooth, supple, harsh or rough

Murky: the look of a wine caused by suspended particles, denoting either poor quality or faulty winemaking.

Nervy: usually a dry-white wine, invariably with high acid, that has yet to settle down into a finely tuned harmonious whole

Neutral: no distinctive aroma or flavour

Noble: a wine of excellent quality, usually from one or a combination of varieties proven to produce fine wine

New World: very subjective, and subject to developments in style, but is most often used to indicate a modern style of wine made for instant gratification, usually in which overt fruitiness and soft tannins and acids are paramount

Open: a wine with instantly apparent aromas and flavours, usually suggesting something of mediocre quality, no great complexity or one that has reached its optimum level of development

Oaky: showing distinct or excessive influence of barrel maturation, with the result that the oak flavours overpower the fruit

Off: bad odours or flavours due to faulty winemaking, contamination or unhygienic cellar practices

Oily: the smooth texture of a fat, viscous wine

Oxidative: the beneficial effect of exposure to air, one of the effects of barrel maturation, which softens and matures a wine

Oxidised: a wine that has gone flat and lost its flavour due to excessive or prolonged contact with air

Old-style: in South African terms, this can refer to a jammy, tarry, stewed-fruit style of red wine, or a wine that shows the effects of maturation in old vats

Opaque: a red wine of such a dense colour that nothing can be seen through it

Peaking: a wine that has reached optimum maturity; is at the height of its development

Penetrating: a strong aroma, often the result of high alcohol and volatile acidity

Perfumed: a delicately fragrant aroma, typical of varieties such as Gewürztraminer and the Muscats

Persistent: an aroma and flavour that lingers

Petillant: a wine with a slight sparkle, usually the result of carbonic gas, given off during fermentation or artificially added

Powerful: a strongly flavoured wine, usually supported by high alcohol and firm tannins

Pungent: an aroma or flavour that is piercing and strong

Porty: a red wine that has lost its fruit and is dominated by an alcoholic, spirits character, or is overripe and raisiny

Purple: the colour of a very young red wine; could indicate a tank sample

Racy: a lively, zesty wine, usually with good acidity

Reductive: white wines, usually unwooded dry wine like Sauvignon Blanc, that have had minimum exposure to air during vinification and are therefore particularly defined, fresh and lean

Rich: a fully flavoured wine, with high extract; not necessarily sweet

Ripe: can refer to fruit, tannin or acid (if it is natural fruit acid, rather than added, as is still the case in many Cape wines)

Robust: a full-bodied wine, but powerful, tough

Rounded: a full wine in which the acids and tannins are ripe and well-integrated

Ruby: the colour of a red wine; a rich red, reminiscent of the gemstone, denoting youth or good quality

Sweet: refers to the residual sugar content in the wine, or the perception thereof

Sour: a wine affected by acetic acid that has gone vinegary; can also refer to tart acidity, an advantage in the sought-after sweet/sour balance of Noble Late Harvests

Subtle: delicate, not overt aromas and flavours, the opposite of forward

Sappy: juicy, usually a white wine, but more in reference to the grape itself

Savoury: a rich wine that is spicy; tartly flavoured

Scented: a delicately perfumed aroma

Sharp: high acidity

Short: a wine with no aftertaste

Silky: a delicately smooth texture on the palate

Simple: a wine with not much complexity or few distinctive characteristics; can also refer to a one-dimensional wine

Smoky: usually an effect of wood on a wine, but can be a varietal character, of Shiraz, for example

Smooth: the texture of a rounded, integrated wine on the palate

Soft: a wine that has either few, or well-integrated acids and tannins

Solid: a wine with all its elements in generous quantities; just short of powerful

Sound: technically well-made; sometimes a polite term for a wine that has little else

Spicy: a varietal character of Gewürztraminer and Shiraz; or the result of maturation in new oak barrels

Stalky/stemmy: detected in a young wine that has had contact with the grape stalks during vinification; an also indicate a coarseness; can be slightly bitter

Steely: a sign of firm acidity, particularly in a lean white wine

Stewed: an overripe, mushy, stewed-fruit character in a red

Straw: a pale, almost colourless still or sparkling white wine. Denotes youth, varietal type such as Colombard or Chenin Blanc, or may indicate lack of depth and complexity in classics such as Sauvignon Blanc and Chardonnay

Strong: denotes high alcohol

Sulphury: rotten-eggs smell, indicating excessive use of sulphur to preserve the wine

Supple: refers mostly to the ripeness of tannins, usually balanced by juicy fruit and soft acids

Syrupy: a rich, sweet wine, perhaps just a little low in alcohol and lacking in acid

Structured: indicates firm tannins, alcohol and acid underpinning the fruit, designed to make a wine last

Tangy: a lively, zesty bouquet, often in a white wine with slightly volatile acidity

Tannic: the hard, mouth-drying effect of excessive tannins in a wine, gained from the grapeskin or the barrel

Tarry: the texture of a highly extracted, thick red wine, heavy in the mouth

Toasty: positive effect of barrel fermentation and maturation on the aroma and flavour of a wine

Tart: a wine with high acidity, not necessarily excessive, which can soften

Taut: often a young wine with firm acid and tannin, but with fruit that is either green or temporarily dominated by the other elements

Thin: a wine that lacks fruit and structure

Tough: a powerful wine with high alcohol and hard tannins that often needs time to soften and develop

Textured: a wine with body and a discernible mouthfeel

Varietal: a wine that exhibits the authentic aroma and flavour characteristics of the grape from which it is made

Vegetal: an earthy herbaceousness, more fecund and damp than fresh

Velvety: a richer character than smoothness and silkiness, usually a red wine

Vinegary: a wine spoilt by acetic acid, usually a fault

Vinous: a wine that is simply winey, often with little other distinctive character

Viscous: a heavy, thick wine, usually with a fair amount of residual sugar

Volatile: mainly used in reference to excessive acidity on a red wine, apparent on the nose as an initially lively, penetrating fruitiness, but which can quickly lead to the disintegration of the wine; a vinification fault

Watery: lacking in fruit, acid, tannin or any character at all

Weighty: the feel of a wine in the mouth that has body

Well-balanced: a wine in which all components – fruit, acid, sugar, tannin and wood – are in correct proportion to one another, making for a pleasant wine

Woody: negative; too much wood influence.

Yeasty: a biscuity, bready aroma typical in bottle-fermented bubblies or some whites that have spent time on their lees (which includes the dead yeast cells) or in the barrel

Yellow: colour of quality white wine; shades and intensity of yellow can indicate variety or bottle-age

Youthful: the character of a young wine, which is fresh and lively

Zesty: indicates crispness of acid, liveliness of flavour

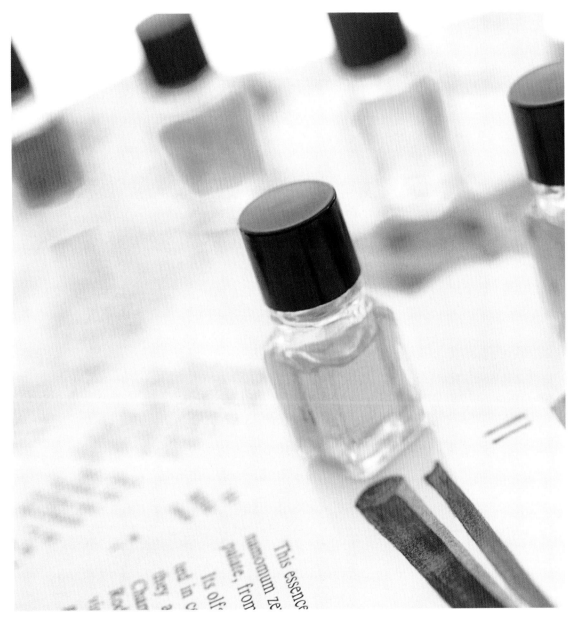

HAMILTON RUSSELL VINEYARDS PROVIDES VISITORS WITH A COLLECTION OF ESSENCES REPLICATED IN WINES AS AN EXERCISE TO SHARPEN YOUR IDENTIFICATION SKILLS.

POURING FOR PLEASURE

THE GLUG-GLUG-GLUG OF WINE BEING poured into a glass is music to a wine lover's ears. Take time to tune those auditory senses, for this simple exercise is a preparation, a period of expectation – and if the anticipation can be prolonged a little by ritual, all the better. For there is ritual aplenty in the serving of wine – whether it be red, white or sparkling – without being too pretentious about it. These are the aspects of wine service that, in a practical and pleasant way, enhance the enjoyment of what is in the glass.

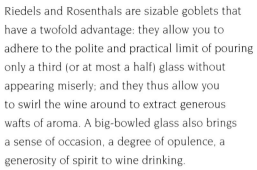

PREVIOUS PAGES: RED WINE MATURES IN FRENCH-OAK BARRELS AT MORGENHOF.

BELOW: MUSIC TO A WINE LOVER'S EARS.

GLASSWARE

Georg Riedel, the youngest in that most estimable Austrian family firm of quality glass manufacturers, may be taking it to extremes: he believes that in directing the flow of wine onto whichever of the four areas of the tongue detects sweet, sour, salt and bitter, the shape of the glass can determine the taste of the wine and the perception of quality. Riedel has proved to even the most sceptical of wine connoisseurs that his is not just sales talk, and his glassware is regarded worldwide as the epitome of fine-wine containers: the most basic retails at around R100 a glass. There are a few other classic ranges, such as Rosenthal, but should your finances not extend to such luxury, do not fear – some of the important elements can be found in less expensive glasses. Size is one such element. The

Riedels and Rosenthals are sizable goblets that have a twofold advantage: they allow you to adhere to the polite and practical limit of pouring only a third (or at most a half) glass without appearing miserly; and they thus allow you to swirl the wine around to extract generous wafts of aroma. A big-bowled glass also brings a sense of occasion, a degree of opulence, a generosity of spirit to wine drinking.

Traditionally, white wine is served in a slightly smaller glass than is red; the relatively greater richness and complexity of red asks for greater play. And two glasses always add to the sparkle of a special dinner-table setting. But if your guests prefer to stick to either white or red or are happy to use the same glass, then bigger is better.

The fineness of the glass is always an important consideration. A delicate glass seems to refine the senses: witness the role of porcelain in the taking of tea. Delicacy is invariably a sign of quality, and this goes for the lip of the glass as well. Support for recycled glass can be accommodated; you just need to look harder to find something delicate.

With fashion favouring the colourful in glassware, wine can land up in anything from dark blue to antique green or orange. Yet it seems a shame to disguise the natural palette of wine's varying shades of gold and red. A pale-green tint can enhance a simple chilled white for informal quaffing, but in dark colours a fine Cape red can be a dead cert for Coke.

Balance is another fundamental. Ever held a top-heavy stemmed glass that threatens to tilt its contents over everything but your taste-buds? A beautifully balanced wine glass adds instant grace to the movements of the imbiber and is less likely to tip over at the merest nudge of the table. So heft and hold that wine glass before you purchase.

Balance is particularly important in a flute, the tall, narrow glass that is the only acceptable container for sparkling wine – not that shallow thing said to have been designed to the shape of Marie Antoinette's breast! Nothing can beat a Champagne flute for simple elegance, though there is also a purely practical reason for its shape: besides

concentrating the bouquet of the wine, much as the slight narrowing towards the top of any wine glass does, it restricts and extends the spiralling streams of little bubbles, thus helping to retain the liquid's precious effervescence that much longer.

As with any wine glass, there is a glass-blower's or manufacturer's art to achieving the correct proportion between bowl, stem and base. Some impossibly long and thin bubbly glasses may look positively ephemeral, but they tip over too easily. Besides which, they barely hold enough liquid for three good draughts, unbearably frustrating for the bubbly lover.

GLASS CARE
Grubby glasses not only look tacky but they affect the taste of the wine too. Do not store your wine glasses upside down or in cardboard containers, as they will soon pick up a musty smell. Rather keep them upright in a closed cabinet, which helps keep dust at bay.

The secret to sparkly clean glasses is hot water, which is the advantage of a dishwasher. If your glasses are very delicate, you may wish to treat them to their own cycle. Keep it short and be sparing with the detergent – this goes for handwashing as well. Don't leave them languishing in the steamy

A GOOD WINE DESERVES FINE, DELICATELY RIMMED, UNEMBELLISHED GLASSWARE. A CLASSIC CHAMPAGNE FLUTE, A DESSERT WINE GLASS AND TWO STANDARDS – THE LARGE FOR RED, THE SMALLER FOR WHITE – PROVIDE FOR MOST EVENTUALITIES.

A GLASS DECANTER
COMES INTO PLAY
WITH AN OLD VINTAGE
THAT MAY THROW A
SEDIMENT, OR A
CRUSTED PORT. IT
IS EVEN A MEANS
OF AERATING A
YOUNGER VINTAGE,
IRONING OUT SOME
LAST REMAINING
ROUGH EDGES.

flavour and complexity as possible. This can result in the forming of sediment – quite harmless – in the bottle. In these rumbunctious rustic youngsters it can be more like sludge stuck to the sides of the bottle, however, compared with the fine, floating particles found in older, bottle-aged vintages. Leaving the bottle to stand for an hour or two will allow the sediment to settle, but decanting will do a better job.

One of the few types of wine that does need decanting is bottle-aged port, particularly the finest vintages, which are best enjoyed after many years in the bottle (during which time a fair amount of sediment accumulates).

If you suspect the presence of sediment in a wine you wish to serve, check the bottle the day before. Hold it against a strong light and, if your suspicions are confirmed, leave the bottle upright to allow the sediment to settle at the bottom. Shortly before serving the wine, tilt both bottle and decanter and try to pour the wine in a slow but steady stream. Consider leaving the last drop of wine behind, thereby avoiding any last-minute deluge of muck landing up in your decanter.

Decanting is a risky business for another reason too: the exposure of a fine, aged red at the peak of its development to the degenerative effects of oxygen. This is why the experts are divided on the subject. Some believe decanting can smooth the rough edges of a youthful or robust red, making it accessible sooner. Detractors maintain that there is an unnecessary loss of flavour and freshness, to which the wine is subjected anyway as it rests in the glass between sips. A blind-tasting test by *Wine* magazine found insufficient evidence of an identifiable difference between freshly opened and decanted wines. Yet, overall, more tasters preferred wines that had not been decanted. Which brings us to breathing.

dishwasher for long, though, as they will quickly pick up that stale, humid dishwasher smell. Piping hot water is also an advantage when it comes to drying; glasses seem to drip-dry quicker with minimal water marks, leaving you to simply buff them up with a clean cloth. Avoid furry cloths: linen is better than brushed cotton.

DECANTING

Decanting red wine may be viewed as a bit of pretension or as just plain old fashioned, but it does have its place. In fact, it may become more fashionable as winemakers return to methods *au naturel* and dispense with fining and filtering in order to retain as much of the wine's natural

BREATHING

Allowing a wine to breathe (either decanting it or simply uncorking it a couple of hours before serving) is commonly held to be beneficial. The theory is that exposing the wine to air induces a slight volatility of aroma, which adds to the bouquet and, by way of the natural oxidisation process, contributes to a form of instant maturation, thereby smoothing and softening the wine.

In the case of uncorking, this is a moot point, for the area of wine exposed to air in a bottle neck is only about 2cm². What the breathing period does allow for, however, is the chance for any slightly stale aroma, usually temporary, to dissipate. It also gives you the chance to taste the wine, confirming its good condition before lumping your guests with something that is past its best or off. Besides, pouring off a wee bit to taste circulates a bit of air in the bottle and leaves a slightly larger surface area in contact with air to assist in that dissipation process.

As with decanting, breathing is a practice confined to relatively more robust and tannic red wines. Whites are usually at their best when fresh out of the bottle, and need to be enjoyed chilled.

SERVING TEMPERATURE

The optimum temperatures at which various styles of wines show to their best advantage are difficult to achieve in your home refrigerator. Most people, through experience, however, have a fair idea how long a white wine takes to 'warm up' after being removed from the fridge.

Even 'room temperature' is not that easy to achieve: in sunny South Africa it can often be much warmer than the average European 18° C. So there's no harm in popping your bottle of red into the fridge for about 20 minutes before opening. A tepid wine is never pleasant, but beware of chilling a wine down to below about 6° C, at which point it not only loses aroma and flavour but actually anaesthetises the tastebuds.

Here is a guide to the optimum temperatures at which wines should be served:

Sweet, semi-sweet white: 8–14° C
Dry, unwooded white: 8–14° C
Wooded white: 8–14° C
Rosé, Blanc de Noir: 8–14° C
Sweet sparkling wine: 5–8° C
Dry sparkling wine: 8–10° C

Light red, Beaujolais: 12–16° C
Full-bodied reds: 16–18° C
Special/Noble Late Harvest: 8–10° C
Muscadel: 8–10° C
Port: 16–18° C

The upper figure is best for tasting – a slightly warmer wine shows more of its aromas and flavours. But a wine should be served as close to the lower figure as possible, as wine warms up quite quickly in the glass.

THE GOOD OLD-FASHIONED ICE-BUCKET STILL DOES THE TRICK OF COOLING DOWN YOUR WINE OR KEEPING IT CHILLED.

a more elegant Pinot Noir or a sweetish Pinotage performing better a degree or two colder than a Cabernet, Merlot or heavyweight blend.

It is never advisable to rush a wine, whether in the making, the drinking... or the bringing it to the suitable temperature for drinking. Life may be too short to drink bad wine, but it should never be too hurried to allow a well-cellared red about half-an-hour at room temperature to take the chill off it, or a white the same time to achieve the required chill in the refrigerator. Ice-water and warm water, freezers and microwave ovens have been put to use, without much detriment to an average wine, but afford something particularly fine the gracious treatment it deserves.

POURING

Dribble- and spillage-free pouring takes a deftness of touch, but there are a few tricks to keep up your sleeve. Hold the bottle around its middle – clutching it around the neck is hardly elegant and makes the canting of the bottle and the amount of liquid it disgorges more difficult to control. Do not rest the bottle on the edge of the glass as you pour; the wine will dribble down the bottle and down the glass as you retract the bottle.

If the wine is particularly fine and of venerable age, but deemed to be hovering on the knife-edge between peak quality and the down-hill slide, apply less of the glug-glug and take the glass in your other hand to facilitate a more gentle pouring, so as not to aerate or disturb the wine excessively.

But if eye-hand motor co-ordination is not your strong-point, there is a nifty little invention that will make your life that much easier, as it has for wine pourers at professional panel and public tastings: a simple little round of silver sheet-foil called a DripStop. Folded like a malleable brandy snap into the neck of the bottle, it is the most amazing aid to drip-free pouring, and is fully re-usable. Find one at your local wine specialist.

The trick to pouring bubbly without having a glass overflowing with foam (and only two fingers of sparkling wine left in the base) is to cant the glass

CLOCKWISE FROM TOP LEFT: WHEN POURING, GRASP THE BOTTLE FIRMLY AROUND ITS MIDDLE, AND DO NOT REST ITS NECK ON THE LIP OF THE GLASS. THE DRIPSTOP FOIL ENSURES A NON-DRIP POUR, WHILE TILTING THE GLASS SLIGHTLY PREVENTS SPLASHING.

Unwooded, dry-white wine is better chilled to disguise the naturally high acidity, while a sweet dessert wine can be too cloying if not sufficiently chilled. Serve a heavy, wooded white such as Chardonnay a little on the warmer side of cold, though, in order to savour its more complex aromas. As with a serious red wine, the higher tannin in the Chardonnay due to wood maturation can also appear bitter if the wine is too cold. But if it is a slightly flabby wine, chilling it will give it fresh appeal. You can be similarly subtle when it comes to red wine, with over and dribble the liquid down the side, slowly righting the glass as it fills. You are not looking for a head here, unlike beer. (By the way, sparkling wine is something you can be more generous with, filling the glass up to at least the two-thirds mark).

PRESERVING THE PRECIOUS REMAINS

There has been a plethora of wine-preservation gadgets marketed in the past decade, for example the suction devices that displace and extract oxygen from a half-full bottle of wine. The one that most appealed was the Vacu-Vin hand pump, which, when used in conjunction with a special rubber stopper, extracted the air from an opened bottle and sealed it. Also used by some was the Wine Saver, a canister that sprayed its contents of inert gas into the bottle; this gas would settle on the surface of the wine, protecting it from contact with the air layer above.

Experimental tastings to test these devices showed that none, in fact, seemed to preserve the wine any better than simply corking the bottle immediately after pouring a couple of glasses and then refrigerating it, or, in the case of red, returning it to the consistently cool temperature in your cellar. At most, wines opened and resealed, in whatever way, only seem to keep for a couple of days.

More full-bodied reds may keep for a day or two longer, but will invariably have changed in some way. They may have lost a little of their richness and assumed a somewhat genteel air – the unmistakable effect of oxidisation.

More delicate whites, such as Gewürztraminer, for example, may not last even a day, compared with pungent and powerful colleagues such as Sauvignon Blanc or Chardonnay. The latter may sometimes appear a little bitter, probably due to loss of fruit and the resultant dominance of the wood. All in all, it is best to make the most of a bottle of vintage red long laid down, and finish it once opened – hardly an onerous task. Besides which, such wine is made to be shared. A fresh and crispy white, on the other hand, does not have much to lose if smartly corked and kept chilled until the next day.

As for bubbly; well, some would swear that if the company, be it one or four, is not going to empty the bottle once cracked, you may as well not pop off the cork to start with. But let this not deter you from a solitary sparkling moment or a glass shared with someone special. Given that a Champagne cork can under no circumstances be replaced once it has mushroomed back into shape – except in the case of a bottle-aged bubbly where it retains its shrivelled stem – an ordinary wine cork will suffice. There is also the Champagne Stopper, a plastic seal that fits over the top of the bottle with two metal wings that clamp down and grip the bottle neck. This can keep a certain amount of fizz in your bubbly for a day or two.

No matter what seal you use, the prerequisite is that you always stopper the bottle and pop it back into the fridge or cellar immediately after pouring.

USEFUL ACCESSORIES

There are a number of accessories available to the wine lover but, with some verging on gadgetry and others pleasing only the aesthete, there are just a few basics needed to enjoy fine wine in the company of friends.

CLOCKWISE FROM TOP LEFT:
A SOLID-STEMMED HELIX MAY
MASH THE CORK; ENSURE THAT
THE CORK IS BROAD ENOUGH
TO FORM A PROPER SEAL;
THE IDEAL SPIRAL HELIX;
USE A NAPKIN TO DRY OFF THE
BOTTLE BEFORE POURING.

There is one accessory that is not only useful but imperative: a corkscrew. But there are corkscrews and corkscrews, and it is not just a matter of aesthetics. Vine branch, bone and pewter handles are all very well, but the secret lies in the screw.

Study the screw (or worm) of a corkscrew with the point facing towards you. When you look down, what is known as the helix will appear hollow, with the spiralling metal forming a tube. The design to avoid has a solid stem with a thread winding around it, like a carpenter's screw. A spiral helix ensures a good grip on the cork, dispersing the

pressure across the width of the cork as it is extracted, especially if the spirals are widely spaced. A solid helix is inclined to mash the cork, to the extent that, at best, you may have a few crumbly bits in your wine or, at worst, a hole in the cork ... which is still in the bottle.

Armed with this basic knowledge, you can pick any of the many practical and beautiful corkscrews out there, be they plastic-handled or antique, winged (the metal ones with arms that tend to snap off after a few years of active service) or attached to your Swiss Army knife (notable in that it sports the proper spiral design, albeit on the short side).

A long screw is an advantage, not only ensuring a firm grip on the cork but catering for the extra-long stoppers some cellars select for their finer reds (expected to spend some time lying horizontal in your cellar). The most common corkscrew is the 'waiter's friend', with a metal arm that hinges on the lip of the bottle against which pressure is exerted to extract the cork. But ease of use is questionable. That attribute is owned by the mechanism that allows you to screw the helix into the cork and simply continue turning until the cork is extracted. This basic principle is incorporated in any number of inexpensive and luxury corkscrews – and most swear by it.

It is also the system on which the various corkscrews in the high-quality ScrewPull range of wine accessories are based, perhaps best known for what is probably the ultimate model of corkscrew. The 'Lever' looks like a medieval instrument of torture but works like a dream. Made of high-quality, durable polycarbon, it consists of two levers with which you clasp the bottle and a third that you pull down to insert the screw and back up to extract the cork. Unclasp the arms and remove the cork from the helix by repeating the 'down-up' motion with the third handle. Simple, but expensive at well over R500.

A foil cutter is a particularly useful item with the advent of non-lead capsules, as anyone who has attempted to slice through and rip off the alternatives such as plastic will know. It also saves on the wear and tear of your precious corkscrew tip as you hack away at the top of the capsule.

A wine cooler or two should be kept on-hand to save trips to the fridge when topping up glasses of white wine. Again, there are all sorts of designs, from the double-sided plastic container to the ice bucket. The former does not keep your wine chilled for very long, while the latter is messy; it makes the label soggy and it usually demands some burrowing to get the bottle back in among the ice cubes. If you prefer the formality and festivity of a shiny ice bucket, use a mixture of ice-cold water and ice-cubes – and a handy 'drying-up' napkin draped across the bucket.

There are variations on the theme, including insulated plastic or Perspex ice buckets with separate compartments or special inserts containing ice or iced water. These work fairly well. But probably the most widespread and effective wine cooler, if used properly, is good old unglazed terracotta. The porous cooler should be thoroughly soaked in iced water (about 30 minutes should do it), emptied and placed on its matching coaster, which should be glazed to prevent damp spots on the table. A touch – so as not to impinge on the aroma of the wine – of chlorine or bleach in the water will prevent fungal growth on the rough surface after prolonged use.

A particularly practical cooling device, though perhaps lacking in aesthetic style, is the Vacu-Vin Rapid Ice, consisting of a flexible sleeve lined with pockets of a liquid that remains malleable despite absorbing extreme cold. Keep it in your freezer and simply slip it over your chilled white on the table. It also successfully chills white wine down from room temperature in about 10 minutes (but rather take the time to slowly cool your best whites).

A Champagne stopper, such as the ScrewPull 'Crown', is always useful – although keeping a jar of good-quality used corks is not to be sneezed at. In fact, any commercial stopper is good, as long as it is a tight fit.

And speaking of sparkling wine, you may wish to invest in a 'Champagne Star', another item in the ScrewPull range, which helps the delicate-of-physique to pull the cork out of a bubbly bottle. It is simply a four-pronged metal clamp.

A silver, filagreed wine coaster is an item of great beauty, but unless you have a waiter in attendance or take the filling of your guests' glasses upon yourself, it ends up not being used.

For the serious wine lover and a host who prides him- or herself on precision, there is the matter of thermometers. Used to determine whether a wine is at the correct temperature for serving, they vary from a flexible, sheet-metal, snap-on model to a reusable adhesive strip. But a practised hand can easily judge whether a wine is at roughly the right temperature for enjoyment.

CLOCKWISE FROM TOP LEFT: A CHAMPAGNE STOPPER SHOULD KEEP YOUR BUBBLY BUBBLY; A FOIL CUTTER MAKES FOR EASY REMOVAL OF CAPSULES; A LINED 'NECKLACE' FOR CATCHING DRIPS; A NIFTY ALTERNATIVE CALLED THE DRIPSTOP.

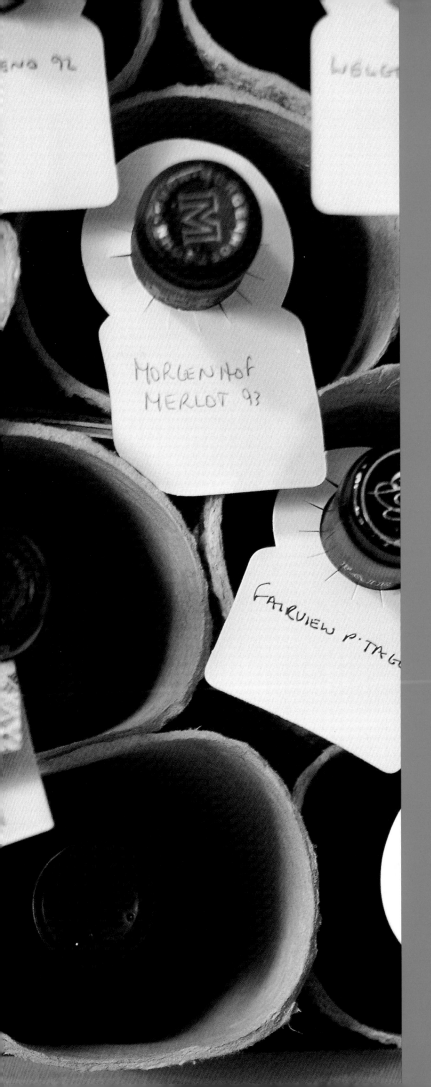

STORING
YOUR TREASURES

HERE IS PRESUMING THAT YOU DO NOT have the wherewithal to go out and design and build your house to incorporate a bona fide new wine cellar. All is not lost. In fact, much is gained, for there is immeasurable pleasure in working with existing spaces, creating something out of a garden shed, a garage, a corner cupboard, a nook here, a cranny there. For your cellar is as personal a space as your bedroom or your bathroom; make it bear your stamp. And beware of architects and interior decorators. They may know about flow and form, line and

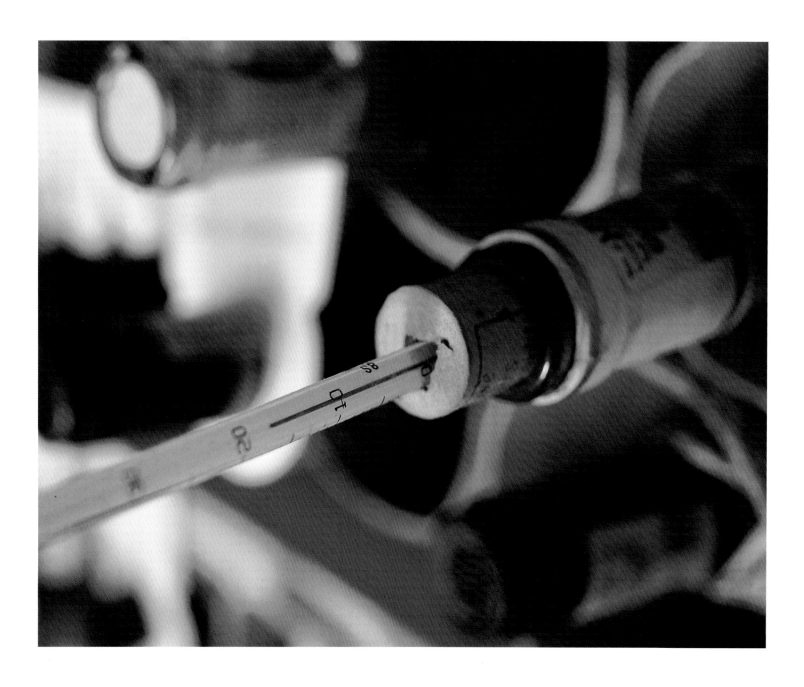

PREVIOUS PAGES: HANG
LABELS ON YOUR WINE BOTTLE-
NECKS FOR QUICK REFERENCE;
CONSTANTLY DISTURBING
THE BOTTLE TO IDENTIFY
THE CONTENTS DOES THE
WINE NO GOOD.

but they will probably not take cognisance of the
effect of those golden summer sunrays on your
choice Chardonnays elegantly displayed against
the north-facing wall of your living room or the
vibration and heat emitted by the dish-washer
next to your built-in rack for vintage reds, in
yellowwood to match the kitchen cupboards.

Before you start thinking about aesthetics,
there are some basic factors to take into
account when reviewing your various wine-
storage options.

TEMPERATURE

The secret to successful wine storage is not so
much the actual temperature but the constancy
thereof, which gives you plenty of lee way between
the optimum cellar temperature of about 12° C
and the fairly average room temperature of between
18°–20° C. The hurdle to overcome is temperature
fluctuation, even in the mild Mediterranean climate
of the Cape – not to speak of the excesses of the
Karoo's dry heat and cold, bone-chilling winters
and the hot, humid summers of the Highveld.

Wines will be equally happy at a constant 13° C as they will be at a constant 19° C. So do not be swayed by the darkness and quiet of a built-in cupboard in a top-floor flat or a loft in an old farmhouse, unless the buildings sport state-of-the art roof insulation – which few do. The fluctuation between day and night temperatures and those of summer and winter will shock you – and your wine even more. Heat and cold affect the chemical reactions of the aroma and flavour compounds of a wine, and radical changes between the two states cause imbalances that damage it.

The lower temperature limit is, nevertheless, recommended for wine storage, as heat affects the development of the wine in the bottle. Wine stored in a constantly warmer environment will mature more quickly, to the extent that, according to the scientific theory on the affect of temperature on chemical reactions, a wine stored at 30° C (although unheard of) will mature twice as fast as one kept at 20° C.

Signs of a wine suffering in a heat-wave include seepage through the cork and leakage between capsule and bottle neck. While the capsule helps minimise exposure of the cork to the drying and damaging effects of air, for example, removing the top of the capsule allows you to keep a check on the condition of the cork. A cork that suddenly starts to protrude slightly, even stretching the top of a capsule (much as a plastic carton of fermenting yoghurt swells its foil seal), is a sure indication of the expansion of the liquid in the bottle due to heat. Drink that wine as soon as possible; in fact, you may already detect some loss of flavour or, in the case of a red, a cooked, jammy taste. It does no harm to feel the sides of your wine bottles every now and then, to detect changes or excesses in temperature. A wall-mounted maximum/minimum thermometer – a nice brass, wood-mounted one to please the eye – will quickly sum up the situation.

By the same token, do not run the risk of freezing a wine. Besides the fact that the expanding liquid will actually push the cork out of the bottle, freezing also affects the chemical reactions of the aroma and flavour compounds, which results in a loss of flavour and imbalances of acids and tannins.

Consider constructing your wine racks in interior spaces and in and against inside walls, as they are less likely to be affected by the vagaries of the climate than are external walls, which are buffeted by chilly winds and baked by the sun. And if you are faced with accommodating an outside wall, better it be south-facing. Concrete, stone or clay-tiled floors also help to keep the environment constantly cool.

LIGHT

Exposure to direct sunlight is a definite no-no. The darker the environment, the better, which is why wines are generally bottled in dark rather than clear glass, especially reds with their longer life expectancy. It also explains why the vintners of the Loire, Champagne and other old European wine-producing regions expended such effort on digging deep underground and into cliff-faces to store their precious liquid.

MOVEMENT

Steer your storage clear of busy areas, particularly if you have freestanding wine racks. Wine does not take kindly to being constantly shaken and, in the case of red wines, peace and quiet allow sediment to settle. The heat and vibration emitted by equipment make the kitchen probably the least suitable room in the house in which to store your wine, though you would not guess it to look at the interiors in many lifestyle magazines. It makes viable storage space only if the rack is part of a brick-and-mortar design, not exposed to the bright light usually required in a kitchen and is reserved for everyday drinking wine.

Freestanding assembled wooden racks and wooden floors do not an ideal combination make, particularly in a high-traffic area, due to

BELOW: CONSTANCY OF
TEMPERATURE IN YOUR CELLAR
IS MORE IMPORTANT THAN
DEGREE, AS LONG AS YOU
SELECT A LEVEL WITHIN A
12°–20° C RANGE.

excessive vibration. Refrain from lining the passage with racks of wine, no matter how impressive such a gallery of liquid art may look.

HUMIDITY

A certain level of humidity – anything between 50 and 70 per cent is regarded as ideal – is advantageous rather than imperative, but it is not easily acquired, unless you have a separate room in which to store your wine. It all has to do with the cork, which can dry out and allow air to flow into the bottle. Keeping the cork moist by storing your bottles horizontally goes a long way towards combating this problem, but beware of going overboard by leaving bottles upside down for any length of time, especially reds, which may throw a sediment. The gunk that can collect on the cork will create problems when pouring.

You may decide to install air-conditioning to keep your cellar temperature down and constant, but watch out: it has a drying effect, anathema to a cork, no matter how the bottle is stored. You may then have to invest in a humidifier, although in a small space a bowl of water does just as well.

Excessive humidity or dampness can cause mould; this may give your cellar a pleasingly authentic look but is probably more trouble than it is worth. It damages the label and you may have a rather smelly, damp cellar on your hands. Some sort of ventilation is usually desirable, for example an airbrick or a fan to keep the air circulating.

RACKING ARRANGEMENTS

Your choice of racks will depend on the size of your collection and the shape of space it takes up – and also your financial position. There is quite a range of racks on the market, made of materials such as metal, wood, clay and hard plastic. Some can be assembled, others come in fixed units of six or 12 and can be stacked, and there are those that call for wall mountings. Some manufacturers are able to install an instant cellar for you.

But there are some useful design factors to bear in mind, whether you are buying your own racks, attempting some DIY or calling in a carpenter or welder to make up units for you.

Adaptability, versatility, call it what you will, but a wine collection has a life of its own: it grows. And with it your tastes, as new discoveries are made and wine styles change. Freestanding units can be moved around, fitted into nooks and crannies and packed vertically and horizontally as space allows or opens up. Moveable units also make rearranging a proper cellar much easier and less traumatic, for you and your wine. Probably the most pleasing wine rack, from both a practical and aesthetic point of view, is the compartmentalised wooden box; this is the modern version of the old case of quarts when milk, cooldrink and beer were bottled in glass instead of cartons and cans, and packed in wooden instead of plastic lug boxes.

Stability is important, so watch out for DIY assemblies that work on a dowel or tongue-and-groove system. They can be wobbly, which limits the height of your stack. If you are having something made up to fit a space or to line a wall, consider having it fixed to the bricks-and-mortar.

Always check what bottle size a wine rack caters for. Bubbly bottles are wide and usually do not fit into the standard pigeon-hole; you may have the same trouble with some imported wines. Bear this in mind when you are having a wine rack made to specification.

Length is also an issue. Ensure that your Cape Noble Late Harvests in their 375ml bottles are catered for. By the same token, extra-long bottles from increasingly fashion-conscious producers can also throw a spanner in the works.

Economy becomes important when you start planning some sort of uniform racking system – at which stage you may safely start referring to your 'collection' (when you start kitting out an entire room you're entitled to use the word 'cellar').

CONVERSION TIPS

A few pointers for the intrepid DIYers who are about to convert that spare room, garden shed or basement area into a cellar. It need not be an expensive exercise, as long as the basic principles are adhered to.

To maintain that sought-after constancy of temperature, insulation is all-important. First check the roof and ceiling. A corrugated-iron roof can be painted with a non-reflective paint and the ceiling can be lined with any of the range of insulation materials out there: simple polystyrene is probably the cheapest. Available in different thicknesses, it can be cut to fit, making it equally useful for sealing and insulating other openings such as windows and doors. An exterior wall that gets a lot of sun can also be lined, although this may not be necessary if the walls are quite thick.

Taking note of the ambient temperature of a room during the various seasons and different times of the day and night before embarking upon any construction work will be time well spent.

The door to your well-insulated cellar can be a weak spot, but you can cover the back of the door with insulation material and fashion some form of temporary seal to cut down on the draughts between door and frame (although this can act as a natural ventilation).

Raw concrete is probably one of the best materials for flooring, as it is cool and absorbent – convenient for spillages and conducive to humidity. It also looks very 'cellarish'. So do not be in a hurry to carpet or do anything else fancy, unless you choose to brick or tile, which are also cool options.

If you are going down into the basement or underground, the ambient temperature and humidity will probably be taken care of by nature. But you may face the problem of seepage or excessive damp, so check your waterproofing. Fixing it is a job for the professionals.

Once the structural changes are in place, the rest is a matter of practicality, common sense and personal taste, taking the rules of successful wine storage into account.

A CUPBOARD PROVIDES PERFECTLY ACCEPTABLE STORAGE SPACE FOR YOUR WINE, AS LONG AS IT IS IN A COOL, QUIET CORNER OF THE HOUSE.

When evaluating the cost-effectiveness of a specific racking system, simply work out the number of bottles you can fit into a square metre. Some very beautiful racks can end up leaving you unnecessarily and frustratingly short of space. After all, in the end it is the wine that counts. And while storing bottles two-deep may help utilise space, it becomes inconvenient if you buy wine across a broad range and in quantities of a 12-bottle case or less.

For the DIYers: if you are making your own shelving, 'bins' created by simple wooden struts and crosspieces are the easiest and most practical. You may wish to consider additional insulation in the form of sheets of the appropriate material as lining for each 'bin'. Also keep the height of each compartment down to about four or five bottles, to minimise the danger of shelves sagging, cracking or breaking under the weight of your wine wealth. And regulate the volume of each 'bin' to your buying and consumption speed: make it manageable, maybe two cases or 30 bottles at the most?

Conducting wine tastings in your cellar sounds more romantic than it often is, unless you are of the more pragmatic school of thought when it comes to storing wine. Bear in mind that the lighting may not be too good. At an air-conditioned 12° C, your guests may suffer some discomfort, while at a constantly maintained 18° to 20° C, you will have to compensate for the additional heat that a few bodies can emit either by turning up the air-conditioner or by leaving the door open – an interesting option on a chilly winter's evening.

RECORD-KEEPING

In the age of computers, keeping track of the comings and goings in your cellar is a little easier than with the former book-keeping system. But it still demands an effort to keep your records updated, not to speak of a certain ability to recall exactly what was removed in the haze of goodwill and vinous fervour that surrounded last night's dinner party or impromptu gathering of friends.

But it is worth it. The set-up need not be complicated. Simply divide your stocks into the categories of your choice, with name, vintage, price, description, amount in stock, date and occasion of consumption being the main information required. Perhaps a small chalkboard or pad and pencil at the door or tacked to the side of a wine rack will help – for a quick hurried scribble as you scurry out with your spur-of-the-moment spoils. Reconciliation can come later, at your leisure, over a glass of wine.

Having a list of your wine stocks saves time and frayed nerves when you need to choose a birthday gift, select a wine for dinner, grab something on your way out to a restaurant or decide which of your older vintages need to be savoured at their prime. It also saves the wine from being disturbed as you pull out bottle after bottle when selecting a wine to open. But, most importantly, it ensures that you do not suffer the disappointment of, during one of your feverish searches, coming upon a venerable old red that has passed its drink-by date because you had forgotten it was there.

An inventory is also an invaluable buying aid, showing what you are short of, what vintages to stock up on, what you paid for specific wines and where you sourced a rarity. And, at the other end of the scale, it can be your personal diary of special times shared with good friends.

RECORD-KEEPING IS IMPORTANT ONCE YOUR CELLAR REACHES CERTAIN PROPORTIONS, IF ONLY NOT TO MISS THAT SPECIAL, PRICY WINE THAT'S LANGUISHING IN A CORNER AND FAST APPROACHING ITS PEAK.

WINE DIRECTORY

◆ Week-day times given indicate normal office hours during which the cellar is open for tastings and

sales (or just sales), but do telephone and check, as times vary

◆ Some cellars charge a tasting fee, sometimes refundable upon any wine purchase

◆ Cellar tours may be by appointment only, so telephone ahead

◆ Wines listed indicate those for which the cellar is most recommended

◆ Telephone numbers marked with an asterisk* are expected to change during 1999

CONSTANTIA

Ambeloui
(Hout Bay)
By appointment
Cap Classique
Tel (021) 790-7386

Buitenverwachting
Monday to Saturday
Sauvignon Blanc,
Chardonnay, Riesling,
Christine red blend
Restaurant, picnic
hampers
Tel (021) 794-5190

Constantia Uitsig
Monday to Saturday
Sauvignon Blanc,
Sémillon,
Chardonnay
Restaurants
Tel (021) 794-1810

Groot Constantia
Monday to Sunday
Sauvignon Blanc,
Chardonnay,
Weisser Riesling,
Gouverneurs Reserve
Cellar tours
Restaurants
Tel (021) 794-5128

Klein Constantia
Monday to Saturday
Sauvignon Blanc,
Riesling, Cabernet
Sauvignon, Shiraz, Vin
de Constance, Noble
Late Harvest
Cellar tours
Tel (021) 794-5188

Steenberg
Monday to Saturday
Sauvignon Blanc,
Sémillon, Merlot
Cellar tours
Restaurant
Tel (021) 713-2211

STELLENBOSCH

Alto
Monday to Saturday
Alto Rouge, Cabernet
Sauvignon
Tel (021) 881-3884

Amani
Tuesday to Saturday
Sauvignon Blanc
Tel (021) 905-1126

Audacia
By appointment
Chardonnay, Merlot
Tel (021) 881-3052

Bergkelder
Monday to Saturday
Stellenryck Sauvignon
Blanc and Cabernet
Sauvignon
Fleur du Cap Noble Late
Harvest, Merlot, Shiraz
Cellar tours
Tel (021) 888-3400

Beyerskloof
Monday to Friday
Beyerskloof (Cabernet
Sauvignon), Pinotage
Tel (021) 882-2135

Blaauwklippen
Monday to Saturday
Zinfandel, Cabernet
Sauvignon, Shiraz
Restaurant
Tel (021) 880-0133

Blue Creek
By appointment
Cabernet Sauvignon
Tel (021) 880-0522/0657

Boschkloof
Monday to Saturday
Chardonnay, Cabernet
Sauvignon
Tel (021) 881-3293

Bottelary
Monday to Saturday
Cabernet Sauvignon
Tel (021) 882-2204 or
881-3870

Bouwland
Monday to Saturday
Cabernet Sauvignon
Merlot blend
Tel (021) 882-2447

Camberley
By appointment
Cabernet Sauvignon
Tel (021) 885-1176

Clos Malverne
Monday to Friday
Pinotage, Cabernet
Sauvignon Shiraz blend,
Auret red blend
Tel (021) 882-2022

Delaire
Monday to Sunday
Chardonnay, Cabernet
Sauvignon Merlot blend
Restaurant
Tel (021) 885-1756

Delheim
Monday to Friday
Chardonnay, Cabernet
Sauvignon, Shiraz,
Spatzendreck Late
Harvest
Tel (021) 882-2033

De Meye
By appointment
Cabernet Sauvignon,
Shiraz blend
Tel (021) 884-4154

De Trafford
By appointment
Cabernet Sauvignon,
Merlot, Vin de Paille
Tel (021) 880-1611

Eersterivier
Monday to Saturday
Muscat d'Alexandrie,
Pinotage, Grand Reserve
red blend
Tel (021) 881-3886

Fort Simon
Monday to Sunday
Chardonnay, Chenin
Blanc, Merlot, Pinotage
Tel (021) 906-0304/2549

Goede Hoop
By appointment
Vintage Rouge, Shiraz
Tel (021) 903-6286

Hartenberg
Monday to Saturday
Weisser Riesling, Shiraz,
Cabernet Sauvignon
Merlot blend, Zinfandel,
Pontac
Tel (021) 882-2541

Hazendal
Monday to Sunday
Chardonnay, Kleine
Hazen Shiraz Cabernet
Sauvignon blend
Cellar tours
Restaurant
Tel (021) 903-5035/4

Jacobsdal
By appointment
Pinotage
Tel (01) 905-1360

JC Le Roux (House of)
Monday to Saturday
Pongrácz Cap Classique,
Chardonnay Cap
Classique, Pinot Noir
Cap Classique
Cellar tours
Restaurant
Tel (021) 882-2590/1/2/3

Jordan
Monday to Saturday
Blanc Fumé,
Chardonnay, Merlot,
Cabernet Sauvignon
blend
Tel (021) 881-3441

Kaapzicht
Monday to Saturday
Pinotage, Cabernet
Sauvignon, Merlot
Tel (021) 906-1620

Kanonkop
Monday to Saturday
Pinotage, Cabernet
Sauvignon, Paul Sauer
Tel (021) 884-4656

Ken Forrester Wines
By appointment
Chenin Blanc
Restaurant
Tel (021) 842-2020 or
882-2363

Klawervlei
Monday to Saturday
Merlot, Chenin Blanc
Reserve
Cellar tours
Tel (021) 882-2746

Klein Gustrouw
By appointment
Cabernet Sauvignon
Merlot blend
Tel (021) 887-4556

Kleine Zalze
Monday to Saturday
Shiraz, Chardonnay, 'Z'
Chenin Blanc Bush Vine
Tel (021) 880-0717

Knorhoek
By appointment
Pinotage, Cabernet
Sauvignon
Tel (021) 882-2114

Koelenhof
Monday to Saturday
Koelenhoffer, Hanepoot
Tel (021) 882-2020/1

Laibach
Monday to Saturday
Chenin Blanc,
Chardonnay, Pinotage,
Cabernet Sauvignon
Cellar tours
Tel (021) 884-4511

Lanzerac
Monday to Saturday
Merlot, Cabernet
Sauvignon
Tel (021) 886-5641

L'Avenir
Monday to Saturday
Chenin Blanc, Pinotage,
Cabernet Sauvignon,
Vin de Meurveur Noble
Late Harvest
Tel (021) 889-5001

Le Bonheur
Monday to Saturday
Sauvignon Blanc, Prima
red blend, Cabernet
Sauvignon
Tel (021) 875-5478

Leef op Hoop
By appointment
Cabernet Sauvignon,
Le Riche Cabernet
Sauvignon Reserve
Tel (021) 887-0789

L'Emigré
Saturday
Azure Sauvignon Blanc,
Muscat d'Alexandrie,
Port
Tel (021) 881-3702

Lievland
Monday to Saturday
Wiesser Riesling,
Lievlander, Shiraz, DVB,
Noble Late Harvest
Cellar tours
Tel (021) 875-5226

Louiesenhof
Monday to Saturday,
Sunday (in season)
Louiesenhof Red
Muscadel, Tawny Port
Tel (021) 889-7309 or
882-2632

Louisvale
Monday to Saturday
Chardonnay, Cabernet
Merlot blend
Tel (021) 882-2422

Meinert
By appointment
Merlot, Cabernet
Merlot blend
Tel (021) 882-2363

Middlevlei
Monday to Thursday,
Saturday
Pinotage, Cabernet
Sauvignon, Shiraz
Tel (021) 883-2565

Mooiplaas
By appointment
Pinotage
Tel (021) 903-6273/4

Morgenhof
Monday to Friday
Saturday and Sunday
(in season)
Chenin Blanc,
Chardonnay, Merlot,
Cabernet Sauvignon,
Noble Late Harvest
Tel (021) 889-5510

Mulderbosch
By appointment
Sauvignon Blanc,
Chardonnay, Steen
op Hout Chenin Blanc,
Faithful Hound red
blend
Tel (021) 882-2488

Muratie
Monday to Saturday
Pinot Noir, Ansela van
de Caab red blend,
Amber
Cellar tours
Tel (021) 882-2330

Neethlingshof
Monday to Sunday
Weisser Riesling,
Sémillon Reserve,
Shiraz, Weisser Riesling
Noble Late Harvest
Cellar tours
Tel (021) 883-8988

Neil Ellis Wines
Monday to Friday
Sauvignon Blanc
(Groenekloof),
Chardonnay (Elgin),
Cabernet Sauvignon
Merlot blend (Neil Ellis
& Inglewood),
Pinot Noir
Tel (021) 887-0649

Overgaauw
Monday to Saturday
Chardonnay, Merlot,
Cabernet Sauvignon,
Tria Corda red blend,
Cape Vintage port
Tel (021) 881-3815

Remhoogte
By appointment
Pinotage, Cabernet
Sauvignon
Tel (021) 889-5005

Rozendal
By appointment
Rozendal red blend
Cellar tours
Restaurant
Tel (021) 883-8737

Rustenberg
Monday to Saturday
Brampton Sauvignon
Blanc, Chardonnay,
Cabernet Sauvignon;
Rustenberg Chardonnay;
Rustenberg red blend,
Rustenberg Peter
Barlow red blend, QF1
botrytised dessert wine
Tel (021) 887-3153

Rust-en-Vrede
Monday to Saturday
Rust-en-Vrede Estate
Wine, Shiraz, Merlot,
Tinta Barocca
Tel (021) 881-3881

Saxenburg
Monday to Saturday,
Sunday (in season)
Private Collection
Pinotage, Shiraz,
Cabernet Sauvignon;
Chardonnay, Gwendolyn
red blend, Grand Vin
Blanc, Grand Vin Rouge
Cellar tours
Restaurant
Tel (021) 903-6113

Signal Hill
By appointment
Cabernet Sauvignon
Tel (021) 880-0908

Simonsig
Monday to Saturday
Kaapse Vonkel Cap
Classique, Sauvignon
Blanc, Chardonnay,
Weisser Riesling,
Pinotage, Tiara red
blend, Frans Malan
Reserve Pinotage
Cabernet, Noble
Late Harvest
Cellar tours
Tel (021) 888-4900

Slaley
By appointment
Shiraz Hunting Family
Reserve, Chardonnay
Hunting Family Reserve
Tel (021) 882-2123

Spier Cellars
Monday to Saturday,
Sunday (in season)
IV Spears Cabernet
Sauvignon, IV Spears
Noble Late Harvest
Cellar tours
Restaurants
Tel (021) 881-3351

**Spier Wine Estate
(Goedgeloof)**
By appointment
Chardonnay
Restaurant
Tel (021) 881-3808

**Stellenbosch Farmers
Winery (SFW)**
Monday to Friday,
Saturday (in season)
Lanzerac Pinotage,
Chateau Libertas,
Zonnebloem Lauréat,
Shiraz, Cabernet
Sauvignon, Special Late
Harvest, Monis VO and
Special Reserve Tawny
ports
Tel (021) 808-7911

**Stellenbosch Wines
Direct**
Monday to Saturday
Twin Oaks Ruby
Cabernet, Dry Red,
Leidersburg Chardonnay
Tel (021) 881-3791

Stellenzicht
By appointment
(also available at
Neethlingshof)
Sauvignon Blanc,
Chardonnay, Sémillon
Reserve, Syrah, Merlot,
Cabernet Sauvignon,
Noble Late Harvest
Tel (021) 880-1103

Stonewall
By appointment
Chenin Blanc, Merlot
Cabernet Sauvignon
blend
Tel (021) 855-3675

Sylvanvale
Monday to Sunday
Pinotage Reserve,
Chenin Blanc 'Laurie's
Vineyard'
Restaurant
Tel (021) 882-2012

Thelema
Monday to Saturday
Sauvignon Blanc,
Chardonnay, Cabernet
Sauvignon, Merlot
Tel (021) 885-1924

Uiterwyk
Monday to Saturday
Sauvignon Blanc,
Pinotage and Pinotage
Top of the Hill, Estate
Cape red blend
Cellar tours
Tel (021) 881-3711

Uitkyk
Monday to Saturday
Sauvignon Blanc,
Chardonnay, Carlonet,
Cabernet Sauvignon
Shiraz blend
Tel (021) 884-4710

Uva Mira
Monday to Friday
Chardonnay
Tel (021) 880-1682

Uitzicht
By appointment
Chenin Blanc
Tel (021) 881-3261

Verdun
Monday to Saturday
Chenin Blanc,
Chardonnay, Interlude
Gamay Noir
Tel (021) 886-5884

Vlottenburg
Monday to Saturday
Rouge, Pinotage, Merlot,
Cabernet Sauvignon
Tel (021) 881-3828

Vredenheim
Monday to Saturday
Pinotage, Dry Red
Cellar tours
Tel (021) 881-3878

Vriesenhof
Monday to Friday
Vriesenhof and
Paradyskloof Pinotage,
Kallista red blend
Cellar tours
Tel (021) 880-0284

Warwick
Monday to Friday,
Saturday (by
appointment)
Cabernet Franc, Merlot,
Cabernet Sauvignon
blend, Trilogy red blend
Tel (021) 884-4410

**Waterford/Kevin
Arnold Wines**
By appointment
Shiraz, Cabernet
Sauvignon
Tel (021) 880-0496

Welmoed
Monday to Sunday
Sauvignon Blancs,
Pinotage, Shiraz
Restaurant
Tel (021) 881-3800

Zevenwacht
Monday to Sunday
Chenin Blanc,
Chardonnay,
Zevernwacht and
Zevenrivieren Shiraz,
Cabernet Sauvignon
Merlot blend
Restaurant
Tel (021) 903-5123

HELDERBERG
Avontuur
Monday to Saturday
Avon Rouge,
Chardonnay, Merlot,
Cabernet Franc
Restaurant
Tel (021) 855-3450

Bredell Wines
Monday to Friday
Bredell's Shiraz, JP
Bredell Cape Vintage
Reserve port, Bredell's
Helderzicht Reserve port
Tel (021) 842-2478

Cordoba
By appointment
Chardonnay, Crescendo
red blend
Tel (021) 855-3744

Dellrust
By appointment
Chenin Blanc, Cinsaut
Tinta Barocca blend
Tel (021) 842-2752

Eikendal
Monday to Sunday
Chardonnay, Merlot,
Cabernet Sauvignon
Reserve, Cap Classique
Cellar tours
Restaurant
Tel (021) 855-1422

Grangehurst
Monday to Friday
Cabernet Sauvignon
Merlot blend, Pinotage,
Hidden Valley Pinotage
Tel (021) 855-3625

Helderberg
Monday to Saturday
Cabernet Sauvignon
Reserve, Chenin Blanc
Reserve
Restaurant
Tel (021) 842-2371

Longridge
Monday to Saturday
Brut Cap Classique,
Chardonnay, Merlot, Bay
Vie Cabernet Pinotage
Tel (021) 855-2004

Meerlust
By appointment
Rubicon, Merlot,
Pinot Noir
Tel (021) 843-3275/3587

Morgenster
By appointment
Morgenster red blend
Tel (021) 852-1738

Mount Rozier
By appointment
Sauvignon Blanc
Tel (021) 858-1130

Onderkloof
By appointment (from
September 1999)
Chenin Blanc, Sauvignon
Blanc, Chardonnay ('99
1st vintage)
Tel (021) 858-1538

Post House
Monday to Saturday
Cabernet Sauvignon
Tel (021) 842-2409

Somerbosch
Monday to Saturday
Cabernet Sauvignon
Tel (021) 855-3616

Vergelegen
Monday to Sunday
Sauvignon Blanc
Reserve, Chardonnay,
Chardonnay Reserve,
Mill Race Red, Merlot,
Sémillon Noble Late
Harvest
Cellar tours
Restaurant
Tel (021) 847-1334

Vergenoegd
Wednesday, Saturday or
by appointment
Reserve red blend,
Cabernet Sauvignon,
Cinsaut Merlot blend,
Cape Vintage port
Tel (021) 843-3248

Yonder Hill
By appointment
Merlot, iNanda red
blend
Tel (021) 855-1008

FRANSCHHOEK
Agusta Wines
Monday to Sunday
Count Agusta
Chardonnay, Count
Agusta Cabernet
Sauvignon, Haute
Provence Chardonnay
Reserve, Haute Provence
Chenin Blanc Reserve
Cellar tours
Restaurant
Tel (021) 876-3195

Ashwood
By appointment
Cape Colours Pinotage
Tel (021) 874-1050

Bellingham
Monday to Saturday
'Spitz' Cabernet Franc,
Cabernet Sauvignon,
Pinotage; Bellingham
Sauvignon Blanc,
Cabernet Sauvignon
Restaurant
Tel (021) 874-1011

Boekenhoutskloof
By appointment
Boekenhoutskloof
Sémillon, Syrah,
Cabernet Sauvignon
Porcupine Ridge Merlot
Tel (021) 876-3320

Boschendal
Monday to Sunday
Boschendal Brut Cap
Classique, Chardonnay,
Merlot, Shiraz Vin d'Or
dessert wine
Restaurant, picnic
hampers
Tel (021) 870-4000

Cabrière
Monday to Saturday
Pierre Jourdan Blanc de
Blanc, Pierre Jourdan
Cuvée Belle Rose, Haute
Cabrière Pinot Noir
Cellar tours
Restaurant
Tel (021) 876-2630

Chamonix
Monday to Sunday
Sauvignon Blanc,
Chardonnay
Restaurant
Tel (021) 876-2494/8

Dieu Donné
Monday to Saturday
Sauvignon Blanc,
Chardonnay
Tel (021) 876-2493

Eikehof
By appointment
Sémillon, Chardonnay,
Cabernet Sauvignon
Tel (021) 876-2469

Elephant Pass
(Oude Kelder)
By appointment
Sauvignon Blanc
Tel (021) 876-3666

Franschhoek Vineyards
Monday to Sunday
Chenin Blanc,
Chardonnay Chenin
Blanc barrel-fermented,
La Cotte Port
Restaurant
Tel (021) 876-2086

La Motte
Monday to Saturday
Blanc Fumé, Shiraz,
Millennium
Tel (021) 876-3119

La Petite Ferme
By appointment
Sauvignon Blanc,
Chardonnay, Shiraz
Restaurant
Tel (021) 876-3016

L'Ormarins
Monday to Saturday
Rhine Riesling, Shiraz,
Cabernet Sauvignon,
Optima, LBV Port
Tel (021) 874-1026/24

Mont Rochelle
Monday to Saturday,
Sunday (in season)
Chardonnay, Cabernet
Sauvignon
Tel (021) 876-3000

Môreson Matin Soleil
Tuesday to Sunday
Premium Chardonnay,
Merlot, Weisser Riesling
Noble Late Harvest
Restaurant
Tel (021) 876-3112/3055

Mouton-Excelsior
By appointment
Le Moutonné Merlot
Tel (021) 426-2684/5

Rickety Bridge
Monday to Sunday
Merlot, Malbec, Shiraz,
Paulinas Reserve red
blend
Tel (021) 876-2129

Stony Brook
Saturday or by
appointment
Sémillon Reserve,
Chardonnay, Shiraz,
Pinotage
Tel (021) 876-2182

TenFiftySix
By appointment
Blanc Fumé, Cabernet
Sauvignon
Tel (021) 551-2284

Von Ortloff
By appointment
Chardonnay, Cabernet
Sauvignon Merlot blend
Cellar tours
Tel (021) 876-3432

PAARL
Ashanti
Monday to Sunday
Pinotage, Peak Chenin
Blanc Chardonnay blend
Tel (021) 862-0789

Backsberg
Monday to Sunday
Chardonnay, Simunye
Sauvignon Blanc,
Cabernet Sauvignon,
Shiraz blend, Klein
Babylonstoren, Malbec
Tel (021) 875-5141

Bernheim
Monday to Friday,
Saturday (by
appointment)
Chenin Blanc
Tel (021) 872-5618

Bodega
Monday to Thursday
Merlot, Cabernet
Sauvignon
Tel (021) 988-2929

Boland
Monday to Saturday
Chenin Blanc, !Um Hap
red blend, Muscadels
Tel (021) 862-6190

Brenthurst
By appointment
Cabernet Sauvigon
Merlot blend
Tel (021) 863-1154 or
424-6602

De Villiers
By appointment
Cabernet Sauvignon,
Merlot
Tel (021) 863-8416

De Zoete Inval
Monday to Saturday
Chloë Cinsaut Cabernet
Sauvignon blend
Tel (021) 863-2375

Diamant
By appointment
Dry Red
Tel (021) 863-1508

Fairview
Monday to Saturday
Chardonnay, Sémillon,
Viognier, Shiraz,
Zinfandel, Malbec,
Gamay
Tel (021) 863-2450

Glen Carlou
Monday to Saturday
Chardonnay, Grande
Classique, Pinot Noir,
Vintage Port
Tel (021) 875-5528

Hoopenburg
Monday to Saturday
Chardonnay, Merlot,
Pinot Noir
Tel (021) 884-4221/2

KWV
Monday to Sunday
Red Muscadel Jerepigo,
Full Tawny Port,
Vintage Port
Restaurant
Cellar tours
(021) 807-3911

Klein Simonsvlei
By appointment
Niel Joubert Sauvignon
Blanc, Chardonnay,
Chenin Blanc
Cellar tours
Tel (021) 875-5419

Laborie
Monday to Saturday
Brut Cap Classique,
Cabernet Sauvignon,
Bin 88 Cabernet Merlot,
Pineau de Laborie
Restaurant
Tel (021) 807-3390

Landskroon
Monday to Saturday
Pinotage, Cabernet
Franc, Port
Restaurant
Tel (021) 863-1039

Nederburg
Monday to Saturday
Nederburg Reserve
Cabernet Sauvignon,
Reserve Chardonnay,
Chardonnay, Baronne,
Paarl Noble Late Harvest
Cellar tours
Lunches by appointment
Tel (021) 862-3104

Nelson
Monday to Saturday
Nelson's Creek
Chardonnay, Cabernet
Sauvignon
Cellar tours
Tel (021) 863-8453

Perdeberg
Monday to Friday
Chardonnay Sauvignon,
Cabernet Merlot
Tel (021) 863-8244

Plaisir de Merle
Monday to Saturday
Merlot, Cabernet
Sauvignon
Cellar tours
Tel (021) 874-1071

R & de R Fredericksburg
Monday to Saturday
Cabernet Merlot
Cellar tours
Tel (021) 874-1648

Rhebokskloof
Monday to Sunday
Chardonnay, Pinotage,
Merlot
Cellar tours
Restaurant
Tel (021) 863-8386

Ruitersvlei
Monday to Saturday
Merlot Reserve,
Cabernet Sauvignon
Reserve, Special Late
Harvest
Restaurant
Tel (021) 863-1517

Savanha (Berg & Brook)
Monday to Saturday
Merlot, Shiraz, Cabernet
Sauvignon
Tel (021) 874-2015

Seidelberg
Monday to Saturday
Seidelberg Cabernet
Merlot; De Leuwen Jagt
Merlot
Restaurant
Tel (021) 863-3495

Simonsvlei
Monday to Saturday
Bush Vine Chenin
Blanc, Hercules Pillar
Chardonnay, Simonsvlei
Shiraz, Pinotage, Premier
White Muscadel
Restaurant
Tel (021) 863-3040

Sonop
By appointment
Cape Soleil Sauvignon
Blanc, Cilmor Cabernet
Franc, African Legend
Shiraz, Kersfontein
Pinotage, Devon View
Cabernet Sauvignon
and Pinotage
Tel (021) 887-2409

Veenwouden
By appointment
Merlot, Vivat Bacchus,
Veenwouden Classic
Tel (021) 872-6806

Villiera
Monday to Saturday
Tradition Cap
Classiques, Sauvignon
Blanc, Bush Vine
Sauvignon Blanc, Rhine
Riesling, Merlot, Cru
Monro red blend, Shiraz
Tel (021) 882-2003

Welgemeend
Wednesday, Saturday
or by appointment
Douelle, Amadé,
Welgemeend Estate
Reserve
Tel (021) 875-5210

Zanddrift
Monday to Friday,
Saturday and Sunday
(by appointment)
Capella Reserve
Chenin Blanc
Tel (021) 863-2076

Zandwijk
Monday to Friday
Kosher wines
Tel (021) 863-2368

WELLINGTON
Bovlei
Monday to Saturday
Pinotage, Cabernet
Sauvignon
Tel (021) 873-1567 or
/864-1283

Cape Wine Cellars
Monday to Saturday
Kleinbosch Pinotage,
Chenin Blanc, Bushvine
Dry Muscat
Tel (021) 873-1101

Claridge
By appointment
Chardonnay, Red
Wellington red blend
Lunches
Tel (021) 864-1241

Jacaranda
Monday to Saturday
Chenin Blanc
Tel (021) 864-1235

Johnsen & Jörgensen
Monday to Friday
Merlot
Tel (021) 864-1237

Linton Park Wines
By appointment
Cabernet Sauvignon,
Capell's Court Cabernet
Sauvignon, Capell's
Court Shiraz
Tel (021) 873-1625

Napier
By appointment
Chardonnay
Tel (021) 864-1231

Oude Wellington
By appointment
Rubignon red blend
Tel (021) 873-2262

Wamakersvallei
Monday to Saturday
Merlot, Cinsaut
Cellar tours
Tel (021) 873-1582

Wellington
Monday to Friday
Pinotage, Cabernet
Sauvignon, Shiraz
Tel (021) 873-1163

TULBAGH
Drostdy
Monday to Saturday
Drostdy-Hof Cape Red,
Merlot, Chardonnay,
Adelpracht Special
Late Harvest
Tel (0236) 30-1086

Kloofzicht
Monday to Sunday
(phone ahead)
Alter Ego
Tel (0236) 30-0658

Lemberg
Monday to Saturday
and by appointment
Hárslevelü
Cellar tours
Tel (0236) 30-0659

Paddagang
Monday to Sunday
Paddajolyt (Cinsaut),
Brulpadda port
Restaurant
Tel (0236) 30-0394

Theuniskraal
By appointment
Sémillon Chardonnay
Tel (0236) 30-0688/9/0

Tulbagh
Monday to Saturday
Seminay Blanc, Merlot
Tel (0236) 30-1001

Twee Jonge Gezellen
Monday to Saturday
Krone Borealis Cap
Classique, Engeltjiepipi
botrytis dessert wine
Cellar tours
Tel (0236) 30-0680

Welvanpas
Monday to Saturday
and by appointment
Chenin Blanc
Chardonnay
Tel (021) 864-1238

DURBANVILLE
Altydgedacht
Monday to Satruday
Chardonnay, Cabernet
Sauvignon, Barbera,
Pinotage
Restaurant
Tel (021) 96-1295

Bloemendal
Monday to Saturday
Sauvignon Blanc, Merlot,
Cap Classique
Restaurant
Tel (021) 96-2682

Diemersdal
Monday to Saturday
Pinotage, Shiraz
Tel (021) 96-3361

Meerendal
Monday to Saturday
Pinotage, Merlot
Tel (021) 975-1655

Nitida
Monday to Saturday
Sauvignon Blanc,
Pinotage, Shiraz
Cellar tours
Tel (021) 96-1467

WALKER BAY
Bartho Eksteen Wines
(The Wine Company)
Monday to Saturday
Sauvignon Blanc
Tel (0283) 2-4029

Beaumont
Monday to Friday,
Saturday (by
appointment)
Chenin Blanc, Pinotage,
Goutte d'Or Natural
Sweet
Tel (02824) 4-9450

Bouchard Finlayson
Monday to Saturday
Chardonnay, Pinot Noir
Tel (0283) 2-3515

Goedvertrouw
By appointment
Chardonnay, Pinot Noir
Tel (02824) 4-9769

Hamilton Russell
Monday to Saturday
HRV Chardonnay, HRV
Pinot Noi, Ashbourne
Chardonnay, Ashbourne
Pinot Noir, Southern
Right Pinotage
Tel (0283) 2-3595

Paul Cluver
Monday to Saturday
Chardonnay, Pinot Noir
Cellar views
Tel (021) 859-0605

Newton Johnson
Monday to Friday
Newton Johnson
Chardonnay, Cape Bay
Pinotage
Tel (0283) 2-3862

WhaleHaven
Monday to Saturday
Chardonnay, Pinot Noir,
Merlot
Tel (0283) 2-1585

Wildekrans
Monday to Saturday
Chenin Blanc Reserve,
Pinotage, Merlot
Cellar tours
Tel (02824) 4-9829

SWARTLAND
Allesverloren
Monday to Saturday
Cabernet Sauvignon,
Tinta Barocca, Port
Tel (022) 461-2320

Darling
Monday to Saturday
Groenekloof Sauvignon
Blanc and Cabernet
Sauvignon, DC Shiraz
Tel (02241) 2276/7/8

Groene Cloof
Monday to Saturday
Pinotage
Tel (02241) 2839

Porterville
Monday to Saturday
Emerald Riesling
Cellar tours
Tel (022) 931-2170

Riebeek
Monday to Friday
Dry Red, Pinotage Tinta
Barocca, Chardonnay
Sémillon
Cellar tours
Tel (022) 448-1213

Spice Route
By appointment
Andrew's Hope Merlot
Cabernet, Chenin Blanc,
Shiraz and Syrah
Reserve, Merlot Reserve,
Cabernet Sauvignon
Merlot Cabernet Franc
red blend
Tel (0224) 7-7139

Swartland
Monday to Saturday
Fernão Pires,
Chardonnay Reserve,
Pinotage Reserve,
Cabernet Sauvignon
Merlot Reserve, Red
Jerepigo
Tel (0224) 2-1134/5/6

Winkelshoek
Monday to Saturday
Grand Cru white blend
Restaurant
Tel (0261) 3-1092

ROBERTSON
Agterkliphoogte
Monday to Friday
Colombard, Ruby
Cabernet
Tel (02351) 6-1103*

Ashton
Monday to Saturday
Red and White
Muscadel, Hanepoot
Tel (0234) 5-1135*

Bon Courage
Monday to Saturday
Gewürztraminer (Off-dry,
Special Late Harvest),
Jacques Bruère Cap
Classique, Chardonnay,
Muscadels
Cellar tours
Tel (02351) 4178*

Bonnievale
Monday to Friday
Colombard, Hanepoot
Jerepigo
Tel (02346) 2795*

Clairvaux
Monday to Saturday
Weisser Riesling,
Golden Jerepigo
Tel (02351) 3842*

De Wetshof
Monday to Saturday
Bon Vallon Chardonnay,
Chardonnay Finesse,
Muscat de Frontignan
Blanc
Cellar tours
Tel (0234) 5-1853/7*

Excelsior
By appointment
Sauvignon Blanc,
Cabernet Sauvignon
Tel (0234) 5-2050

Goedverwacht
By appointment
Colombard, Chardonnay
Sur Lie
Tel (02346) 2845*

Graham Beck
Monday to Saturday
Graham Beck Brut,
Graham Beck Brut Blanc
de Blancs, Chardonnay,
Merlot
Tel (02351) 6-1214

Langverwacht Co-op
Monday to Friday
Colombard
Cellar tours
Tel (0234) 2815*

McGregor
Monday to Saturday
Colombard, Colombard
Chardonnay, Village Red
Tel (02353) 741

Merwespont
Monday to Friday
Cabernet Sauvignon
Tel (02346) 2800*

Mooiuitsig
Monday to Friday
Ouderust White
Muscadel, Ouderust Red
Muscadel Liqueur Wine
Cellar tours
Tel (02346) 2143*

Nordale
Monday to Friday
Colombard, Chardonnay,
Red Muscadel Jerepigo
Cellar tours
Tel (02346) 2050*

Robertson
Monday to Saturday
Colombard Chardonnay,
Rheingold Special Late
Harvest, Cabernet
Sauvignon Reserve,
Wide River Ruby
Cabernet
Cellar tours
Tel (02351) 3059*

Roodezandt
Monday to Saturday
White Muscadel, Red
Muscadel
Cellar tours
Tel (02351) 6-1160*

Rooiberg
Monday to Saturday
Cabernet Sauvignon,
Shiraz, Roodewyn red
blend, Ruby port, Red
Jerepigo
Cellar tours
Tel (02351) 6-1663*

Springfield
Monday to Saturday
Sauvignon Blanc Special
Cuvée, Chardonnay
Méthode Ancienne,
Cabernet Sauvignon
Tel (02351) 3661*

Uitvlucht
Monday to Saturday
Ruby Cabernet, Montagu
Red Muscadel
Tel (0234) 4-1340*

Van Loveren
Monday to Saturday
Chardonnay Reserve,
River Red, Cabernet
Shiraz
Tel (0234) 5-1505*

Van Zylshof
By appointment
Chenin Blanc
Tel (02346) 2940*

Weltevrede
Monday to Saturday
Philip Jonker Brut Cap
Classique, Rhine
Riesling, Chardonnay,
White Muscadel
Cellar tours
Restaurant
Tel (02346) 2141

Zandvliet
Monday to Saturday
Chardonnay, Astonvale
and Kalkveld Shiraz,
Estate Wine Special
Reserve red blend
Tel (0234) 5-1146*

WORCESTER
Aan de Doorns
Monday to Friday
Port
Tel (023) 347-2301

Badsberg
Monday to Friday
Sauvignon Blanc,
Chardonnay, Hanepoot
Tel (023) 349-3021

Bergsig
Monday to Saturday
Pinotage, Sweet
Hanepoot
Tel (023) 355-1603

Botha
Monday to Saturday
Dassie's Reserve
Pinotage, Merlot and
Cabernet, Hanepoot
Jerepigo
Tel (023) 355-1740

Brandvlei
Monday to Friday
Sauvignon Blanc, Ruby
Cabernet Merlot
Tel (023) 349-4215

Deetlefs
By appointment
Chenin Blanc, Sémillon
Tel (023) 349-1260

De Doorns
Monday to Saturday
Sauvignon Blanc
Tel (023) 356-2100

De Wet
Monday to Saturday
Dry Red, Hanepoot, Port
Cellar tours
Tel (023) 349-2710

Du Toitskloof
Monday to Saturday
Cabernet Sauvignon,
Shiraz, Special Late
Harvest, Hanepoot
Jerepigo, Red Muscadel
Tel (023) 349-1601

Goudini
Mounday to Saturday
Umfiki, Ruby Cabernet,
Sweet Hanepoot
Tel (023) 349-1090

Groot Eiland
Monday to Friday
Chardonnay
Tel (023) 349-1140

Louwshoek-Voorsorg
Monday to Friday
Daschbosch Ruby
Cabernet, Nectar
de Provision
Cellar tours
Tel (023) 349-1110

Merwida
Monday to Friday
Ruby Cabernet
Tel (023) 349-1144

Nuy
Monday to Saturday
Rouge de Nuy, Cabernet
Sauvignon, Red and
White Muscadel
Tel (023) 347-0272

Opstal
Monday to Friday,
Saturday (by
appointment)
Carl Everson Reserve
Chardonnay Chenin
Blanc
Tel (023) 349-1066

Overhex
Monday to Friday
Chardonnay, White
Muscadel
Cellar tours
Tel (023) 347-5012

Romansrivier
Monday to Saturday
Ceres Vin Blanc, Ceres
Chardonnay, De Kijker
Pinotage, Cabernet
Sauvignon
Cellar tours
Tel (0236) 31-1070*

Slanghoek
Monday to Friday
Riesling Sémillon,
Special Late Harvest,
Red Jerepigo, Sweet
Hanepoot
Cellar tours
Restaurant
Tel (0231) 349-3026*

Villiersdorp
Monday to Saturday
Overberg Rosé, Overberg
Pinotage, Western Cape
Cabernet Sauvignon
Merlot blend
Cellar tours
Tel (028) 840-4213

Waboomsrivier
Monday to Friday
Ruby Cabernet, Sweet
Hanepoot
Tel (023) 355-1730

KLEIN KAROO
Axe Hill
By appointment
Cape Vintage Port
Tel (021) 780-1051 or
683-2200

Barrydale
Monday to Friday
Cellar tours
Tinta Barocca Ruby
Cabernet blend
Tel (028) 572-1012

Bloupunt
Monday to Saturday
Chardonnay (wooded)
Tel (0234) 4-2385

Boplaas
Monday to Saturday
Cabernet Sauvignon,
Vintage Reserve and
Touriga Nacional ports
Cellar tours
Tel (044) 213-3326

Calitzdorp
Monday to Saturday
Ruby port, Golden
Jerepigo
Cellar tours
Tel (044) 213-3301

Die Krans
Monday to Saturday
Tinta Barocca, White
Muscadel Jerepigo and
Reserve, Cape Ruby,
Cape Vintage and Cape
Vintage Reserve ports
Cellar tours
Tel (04421) 33314/64

Die Poort
Monday to Saturday
Pinotage, white, red and
raisin Jerepigo
Restaurant
Tel (02934) 5-2406

Domein Doornkraal
Monday to Saturday
Merlot Pinotage,
Hanepoot
Cellar tours
Restaurant
Tel (04425) 1-6715

Grundheim
Monday to Saturday
Red Muscadel
Cellar tours
Tel (0443) 22-6927

Kango
Monday to Saturday
White Muscadel, Red
Muscadel
Tel (044) 272-6065

Ladismith
Monday to Friday
Towerkop Ruby Cabernet
Tel (028) 551-1042

Mons Ruber
Monday to Saturday
Muscadel Jerepigo
(Regalis)
Tel (044) 251-6550

Montagu
Monday to Saturday
Muscadel
Cellar tours
Tel (0234) 41125

Withoek
Monday to Friday,
Saturday (school
holidays), Sunday (by
appointment)
Port
Tel (04421) 3-3639

OLIFANTS RIVER
Cederberg
Monday to Saturday
Pinotage, Cabernet
Sauvignon
Tel (027) 482-2825

Goue Vallei
Monday to Saturday
Chianti, Hanepoot
Jerepigo
Restaurant
Tel (022) 2233

Klawer
Monday to Saturday
Chardonnay, Blanc de
Noir, Hanepoot, Sweet
White Muscadel
Cellar tours
Tel (02724) 6-1530

Lutzville
Monday to Saturday
Fleermuisklip Sauvignon
Blanc, Robyn red blend
Cellar tours
Tel (02725) 7-1516

Spruitdrift
Monday to Saturday
Chenin Blanc, Cabernet
Sauvignon Merlot blend
Cellar tours
Tel (0271) 3-3086

Trawal
Monday to Saturday
Travino Pinotage,
Special Late Harvest
Cellar tours
Tel (02724) 6-1616

Vredendal
Monday to Saturday
Dessie Chardonnay,
Maskam Cabaret red
blend, Gôiya G!aan red
blend
Cellar tours
Tel (271) 3-1080

ORANGE RIVER
Douglas
Monday to Friday
Pinotage, Sweet
Hanepoot, Red
Muscadel
Tel (053) 289-1910

Oranjerivier
Monday to Friday,
Saturday (school
holidays)
Pinotage, Muscadels
and Jerepigos
Cellar tours
Tel (054) 332-4651

FREE STATE
Goudveld
Monday to Saturday
Pinot Noir
Tel (057) 352-8650

Hartswater
Monday to Friday,
Saturday
(by appointment)
Hinterland Ruby
Cabernet
Tel (053) 474-0700

Landzicht
Monday to Saturday
Chardonnay, White
Muscadel
Cellar tours
Tel (053) 591-0164

MPUMALANGA
Loopspruit
Monday to Friday,
Saturday and Sunday (by
appointment)
Chardonnay
Cellar tours
Tel (013) 932-4303

OLIFANTS RIVER VALLEY

This hot, dry district runs along the Olifants River. Most of the vineyards are on fertile, alluvial riverbank, red sand and Karoo soils at the northern end of the Cederberg range. The annual rainfall varies from 300mm to 400mm. North lies the Orange River Valley, regarded as a marginal area for fine-wine production, though co-operatives produce large quantities of mostly white wine under irrigation.

1. Cederberg
2. Citrusdal (Goue Vallei)
3. Klawer
4. Lutzville
5. Spruitdrift
6. Trawal
7. Vredendal

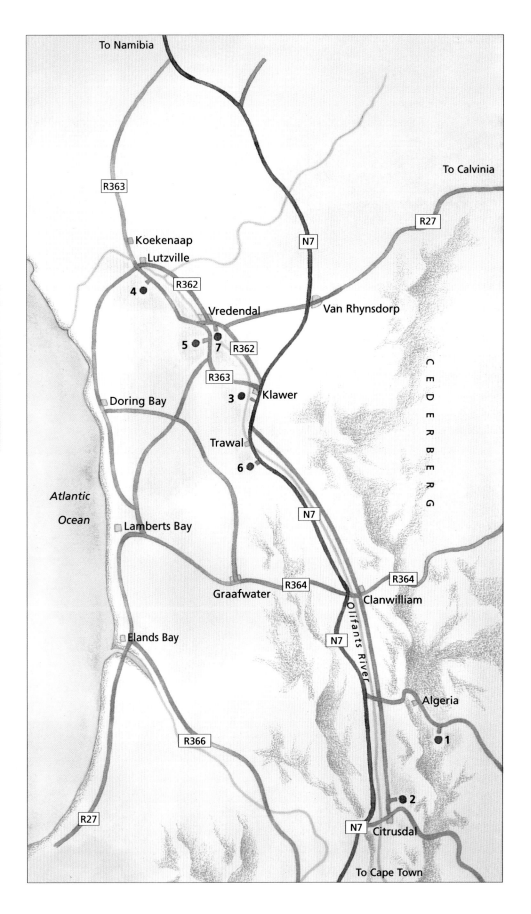

STELLENBOSCH

Although Stellenbosch and environs in the Eerste River Valley can be warm, this large district is influenced by the cool southeast wind off False Bay, which is why it falls within the Coastal Region. Mountains are influential, drawing good winter rainfall (600-800mm annually) and offering deep, well-drained granite soils (mostly Hutton, Clovelly and Tukulu) and sandy Table Mountain sandstone (Longlands, Fernwood and Estcourt). Some of the finest wines are produced along the slopes of the Helderberg, Stellenbosch Mountain, Simonsberg and around the hills of Devon Valley, Papegaaiberg, Stellenboschkloof and Bottelary. And new pockets are still being discovered and cultivated, notably in the cleft between the Stellenbosch and Helderberg mountains and around the base of the Simonsberg peak. The range of terroirs, from alluvial flatland up to slopes of varying aspects and altitudes, makes this what is probably the richest and most diverse viticultural area in the Cape.

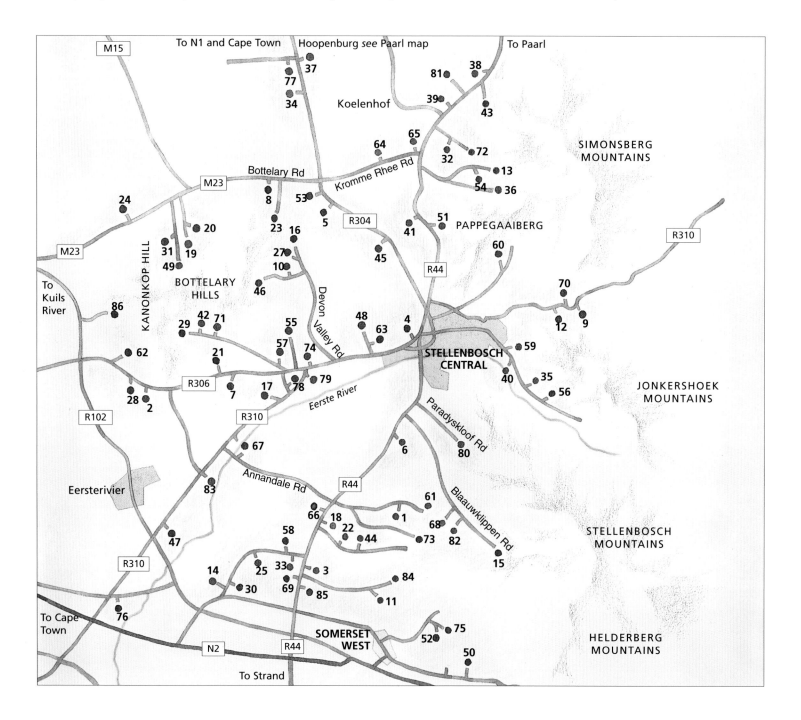

STELLENBOSCH/HELDERBERG

1.	Alto	43.	Lievland
2.	Amani	44.	Longridge
3.	Avontuur	45.	Louiesenhof
4.	Bergkelder	46.	Louisvale
5.	Beyerskloof	47.	Meerlust
6.	Blaauwklippen	48.	Middelvlei
7.	Boschkloof	49.	Mooiplaas
8.	Bottelary	50.	Mont Rozier
9.	Camberley	51.	Morgenhof
10.	Clos Malverne	52.	Morgenster
11.	Cordoba	53.	Mulderbosch
12.	Delaire	54.	Muratie
13.	Delheim	55.	Neethlingshof
14.	Dellrust	56.	Neil Ellis
15.	De Trafford	57.	Overgaauw
16.	Devon Hill	58.	Post House
17.	Eersterivier	59.	Rozendal
18.	Eikendal	60.	Rustenberg
19.	Fort Simon	61.	Rust-en-Vrede
20.	Goede Hoop	62.	Saxenburg
21.	Goedgeloof	63.	SFW
22.	Grangehurst	64.	Simonsig
23.	Hartenberg	65.	Slaley
24.	Hazendal	66.	Somerbosch
25.	Helderberg	67.	Spier
26.	Hoopenburg	68.	Stellenzicht
27.	House of JC le Roux	69.	Stonewall
		70.	Thelema
28.	Jacobsdal	71.	Uiterwyk
29.	Jordan	72.	Uitkyk
30.	JP Bredell	73.	Uva Mira
31.	Kaapzicht	74.	Verdun
32.	Kanonkop	75.	Vergelegen
33.	Ken Forrester/ Scholtzenhof	76.	Vergenoegd
		77.	Villiera
34.	Klawervlei	78.	Vlottenburg
35.	Klein Gustrouw	79.	Vredenheim
36.	Knorhoek	80.	Vriesenhof
37.	Koelenhof	81.	Warwick
38.	La Bonheur	82.	Waterford
39.	Laibach	83.	Welmoed
40.	Lanzerac	84.	West Peak
41.	L'Avenir	85.	Yonder Hill
42.	L'Emigré	86.	Zevenwacht

DURBANVILLE

The Durbanville ward is within the Coastal Region, and is drier than Stellenbosch (300-400mm of annual rain), but the deep, cool, granite soils, with the marked red (sometimes yellow) colour of clay, helps retain water. The vines are cooled by sea breezes from Table Bay and False Bay. The hilly countryside provides slopes of varying aspects and altitudes, allowing for the cultivation of both red and white varieties, which give top-quality fruit.

DURBANVILLE

1. Altydgedacht
2. Bloemendal
3. Diemersdal
4. Meerendal
5. Nitida

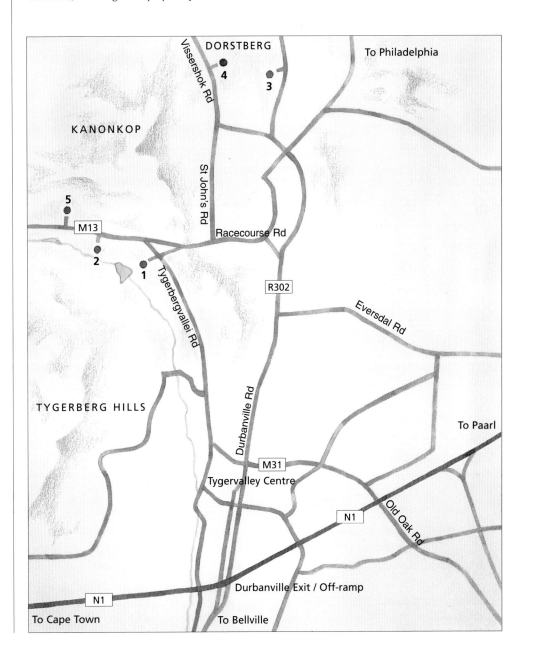

FRANSCHHOEK

At the other, northeastern end of the Paarl district lies the Franschhoek Valley ward, in the curve of the Franschhoek Mountains with the Wemmershoek and Groot Drakenstein ranges on either side. Though the valley is fairly warm, the annual rainfall averages at a generous 900mm. The high-lying slopes of the Franschhoek Mountains are cooled by the summer southeaster wind that comes in over the low Boekenhoutskloof ridge. Soils vary, from good stony, decomposed granite to various red and black alluvial sandy soils along the Franschhoek and Berg rivers at the foot of Dasberg Hill.

1. Agusta
2. Bellingham
3. Boekenhoutskloof
4. Boschendal
5. Cabrière
6. Chamonix
7. Dieu Donné
8. Eikehof
9. Elephant Pass
10. Franschhoek Vineyards
11. Haute Cabrière
12. Jean Daneel Wines
13. L'Ormarins

14. La Motte
15. La Petite Ferme
16. Landau du Val
17. Mont Rochelle
18. Môreson
19. Mouton-Excelsior
20. Plaisir de Merle
21. R & de R Fredericksburg
22. Rickety Bridge
23. Stony Brook
24. TenFiftySix
25. Von Ortloff

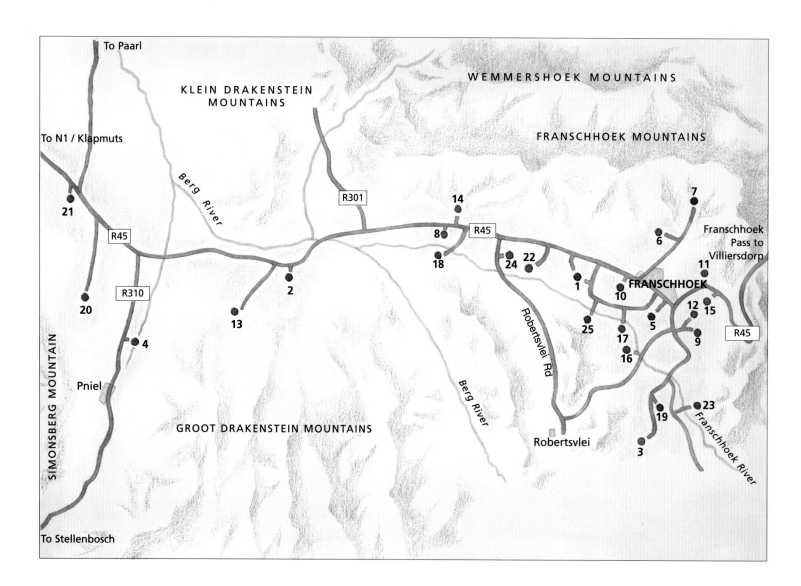

TULBAGH

Surrounded by the towering Groot Winterhoek, Witzenberg and Obiqua mountains, the Tulbagh district is not ideal fine-wine territory with its baking hot summers. Vines are grown with difficulty on the banks of the Little Berg River, with its alluvial sandy, stony soils on a clay substructure. Far more successful are the vineyards up against the mountain slopes – particularly those that are east facing – with their cooler microclimate and better-drained granite soils. But even here, very stony ground with a low pH (which requires the addition of lime to avoid flabby, low-acid wines) makes vineyard preparation hard work. Annual rainfall varies from 450mm to 750mm, and irrigation is required in the dry summer months.

1. Drostdy	5. Theuniskraal
2. Kloofzicht	6. Tulbagh
3. Lemberg	7. Twee Jonge Gezellen
4. Paddagang	

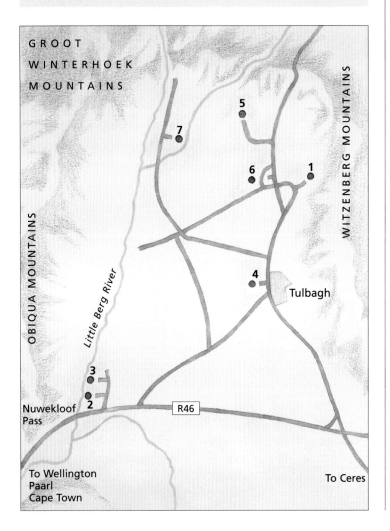

SWARTLAND

The vast, gently undulating hills of the Swartland wheatfields have pockets of hilly land around Malmesbury, Darling and Riebeek West that produce fine wine. Though the Swartland district is hot and the average annual rainfall ranges between 450mm and 600mm, these vineyards are within reach of cooling mists and breezes from the cold Atlantic Ocean between 8km and 15km to the west. Malmesbury shale is the most common soil type, with patches of granite (with red and yellow clay) and sandstone on the hills.

1. Allesverloren	5. Riebeek
2. Darling Cellars	6. Spice Route
3. Groene Cloof	7. Swartland
4. Porterville	8. Winkelshoek

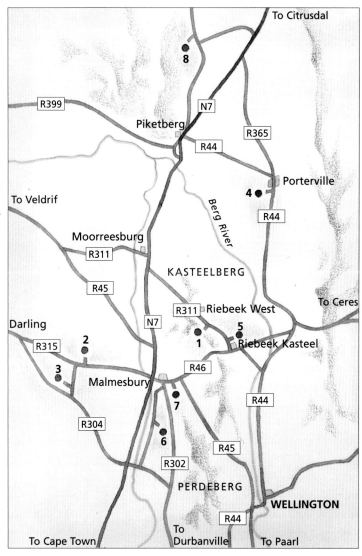

PAARL AND WELLINGTON

Lying further inland from Stellenbosch but still in the Coastal Region, the district of Paarl is slightly hotter with an average annual rainfall of 650mm. The hills around Paarl Mountain (including Agter Paarl) offer respite from the heat, and the deep-drained granite soils with an element of clay ensure that water retention is fair. Along the Berg River, vines are planted in sandy soils derived from Table Mountain sandstone, while shale (Swartland and Glenrosa soils) provides a third suitable viticultural option. North of Paarl lies the ward of Wellington, nestling at the foot of the Hawekwa Mountains and Groenberg. The area is dominated by Glenrosa shale above decomposed granite on the steeper slopes and cool, Oakleaf alluvial soils lower down.

1.	Ashanti	19.	KWV
2.	Backsberg	20.	Laborie
3.	Berg & Brook	21.	Landskroon
4.	Bernheim	22.	Nederburg
5.	Bodega	23.	Nelson
6.	Boland	24.	Perdeberg
7.	Brenthurst	25.	R & de R
8.	De Leuwen Jagt		Fredericksburg
9.	De Meye	26.	Rhebokskloof
10.	De Villiers	27.	Ruitersvlei
11.	De Zoete Inval	28.	Simonsvlei
12.	Diamant	29.	Sonop
13.	Eaglevlei	30.	Veenwouden
14.	Fairview	31.	Villiera
15.	Glen Carlou	32.	Welgemeend
16.	Hoopenburg	33.	Windmeul
17.	Klein Simonsvlei	34.	Zanddrift
18.	Koelenhof	35.	Zandwijk

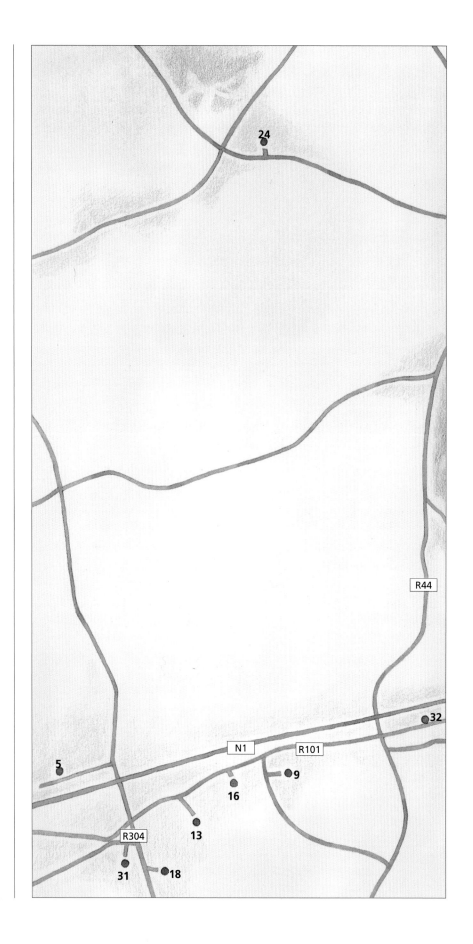

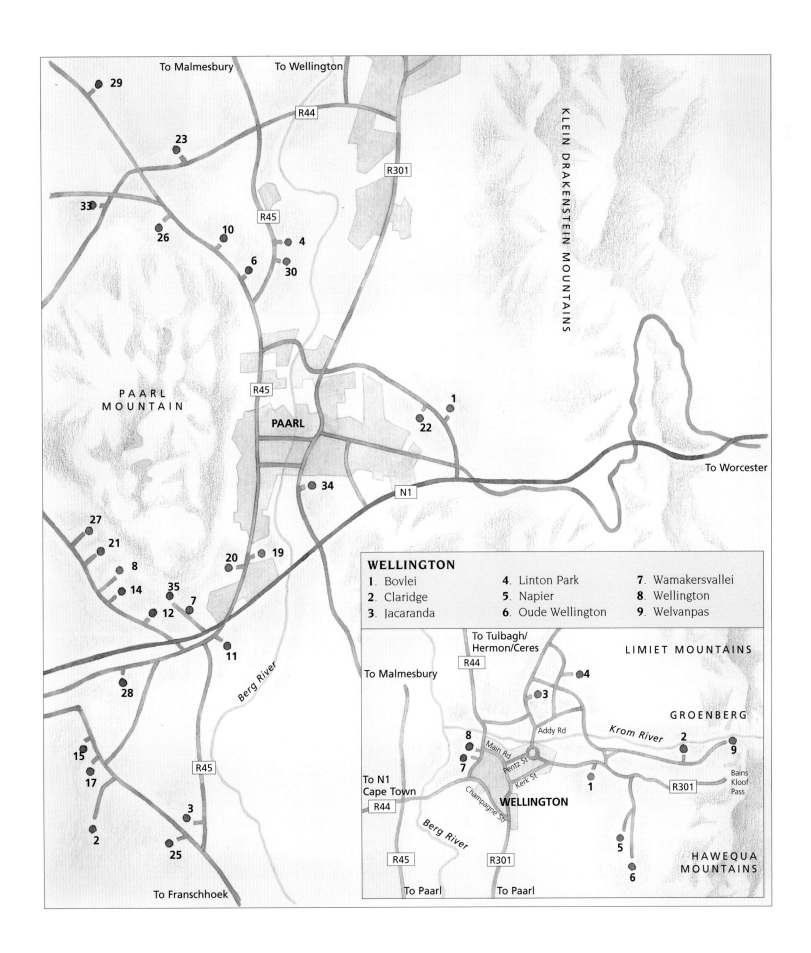

To Malmesbury   To Wellington

29

R44

R301

23

33

R45

26   10   4

6   30

PAARL
MOUNTAIN

R45

1

PAARL

22

34

N1

To Worcester

KLEIN DRAKENSTEIN MOUNTAINS

27

21

8

20   19

14   35

7

12

11

Berg River

28

15

17

R45

3

25

2

To Franschhoek

WELLINGTON

1. Bovlei	**4**. Linton Park	**7**. Wamakersvallei
2. Claridge	**5**. Napier	**8**. Wellington
3. Jacaranda	**6**. Oude Wellington	**9**. Welvanpas

To Tulbagh/
Hermon/Ceres

R44

LIMIET MOUNTAINS

To Malmesbury

4

3

GROENBERG

Krom River

8

Addy Rd

2

9

7

Main Rd

Pentz St

Kerk St

To N1
Cape Town

R44

Champagne Str

WELLINGTON

1

R301

Bains
Kloof
Pass

5

R45

R301

6

HAWEQUA
MOUNTAINS

To Paarl   To Paarl

CONSTANTIA

Also a Coastal Region ward, cool-climate Constantia, caught between the east-facing hills of Constantiaberg and False Bay, offers ideal slow-ripening conditions for optimum quality. The high average annual rainfall of about 1 000mm obviates the need for any irrigation. The hills offer slopes of varying aspects, from the warm, north-facing ones to the cool south- and southeast. Altitudes vary between less than 100m to more than 400m above sea level. Soils are either granite (Huttons or Clovelly with some clay content for good water retention) on the mid-slopes or Table Mountain sandstone higher up. Low-lying areas are sandy sandstone derivatives. Deep and well drained, the soils are relatively fertile, requiring control of the vigorous vine growth to keep yields low for optimum quality.

1. Ambeloui
2. Buitenverwachting
3. Constantia Uitsig
4. Groot Constantia
5. Klein Constantia
6. Steenberg

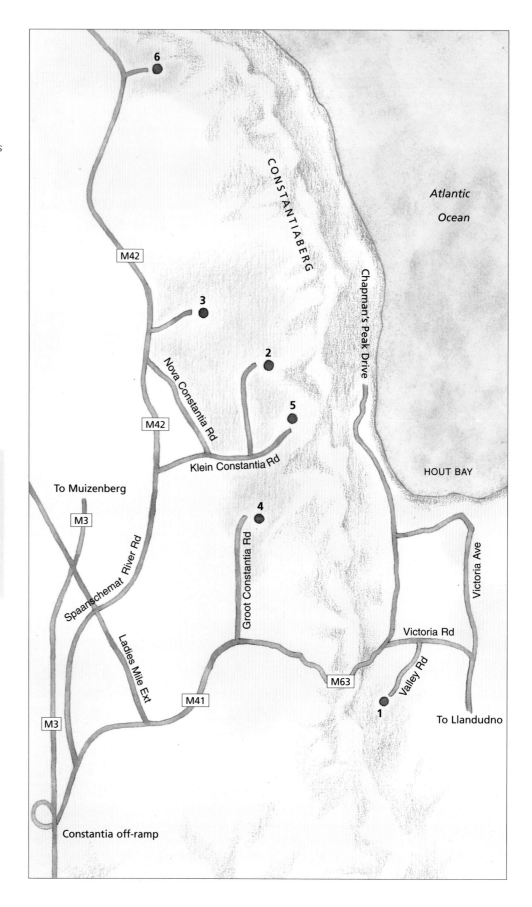

WALKER BAY AND ELGIN

The Walker Bay and Elgin wards are among the newer, cool-climate areas not traditionally planted to vines. But the southerly location of the Walker Bay vineyards near Hermanus, concentrated in the Hemel-en-Aarde Valley between the Raed-na-Gael and Babylonstoren range and up against the Houw Hoek Mountains, has proved to have a prime wine-grape growing climate. Average annual rainfall is 700mm and soils vary from shale to sand and gravel. The high-lying timberland and apple country of Elgin makes for equally fine wine terroir, where soils include Bokkeveld shale and decomposed granite. Snowline vineyards in Villiersdorp between the Aasvoël and Riviersonderend mountains provide similarly suitable sites.

1. Bartho Eksteen
2. Beaumont/Compagnes Drift
3. Bouchard Finlayson
4. Cape Bay
5. Goedvertrouw
6. Hamilton Russell
7. Hermanusrivier
8. Newton Johnson
9. Paul Cluver/De Rust
10. Southern Right
11. WhaleHaven
12. Wildekrans

ROBERTSON AND WORCESTER

Just over the Riviersonderend Mountains lies the Breede River Valley flanked on the opposite side by the Langeberg range. Though a warm, inland area, the Robertson district at the southeastern mouth of the valley benefits from the southeast wind that drives moisture-laden air in from the distant coast. Soils include alluvial sand along the banks of the Breede River and lime-rich, calcareous soil, with a fairly high water-retentive clay content. The valley widens towards the northwest into the hot, flatland of the Worcester district, but here the surrounding mountains – Langeberg, Hex River, Slanghoek and Du Toitskloof – provide unexpectedly varied soil and microclimatic conditions. Soils range from sandy loam to deep riverbank alluvial and calcareous clay, and the average annual rainfall can be as low as 300mm in the east to 1 500mm in the Slanghoek Valley.

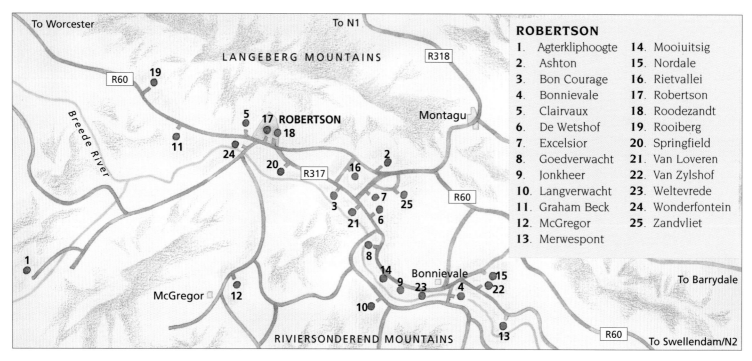

ROBERTSON

1. Agterkliphoogte
2. Ashton
3. Bon Courage
4. Bonnievale
5. Clairvaux
6. De Wetshof
7. Excelsior
8. Goedverwacht
9. Jonkheer
10. Langverwacht
11. Graham Beck
12. McGregor
13. Merwespont
14. Mooiuitsig
15. Nordale
16. Rietvallei
17. Robertson
18. Roodezandt
19. Rooiberg
20. Springfield
21. Van Loveren
22. Van Zylshof
23. Weltevrede
24. Wonderfontein
25. Zandvliet

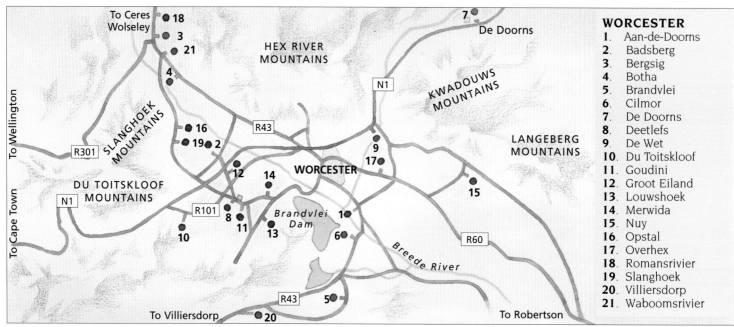

WORCESTER

1. Aan-de-Doorns
2. Badsberg
3. Bergsig
4. Botha
5. Brandvlei
6. Cilmor
7. De Doorns
8. Deetlefs
9. De Wet
10. Du Toitskloof
11. Goudini
12. Groot Eiland
13. Louwshoek
14. Merwida
15. Nuy
16. Opstal
17. Overhex
18. Romansrivier
19. Slanghoek
20. Villiersdorp
21. Waboomsrivier

KLEIN KAROO

This region runs from west to east between the Langeberg and Riviersonderend ranges. It is hot in summer and frosty cold in winter, with an average annual rainfall of less than 300mm. Most vineyards are found in alluvial soils along riverbanks or in deep, clayish shale. The latter, similar to Portugal's Douro Valley, has helped put Calitzdorp on the map for fine port.

KLEIN KAROO

1. Axe Hill
2. Barrydale
3. Bloupunt
4. Boplaas
5. Calitzdorp
6. Cogmans
7. Die Krans
8. Die Poort
9. Domein Doornkraal
10. Grundheim
11. Kango
12. Ladismith
13. Mons Ruber
14. Montagu
15. Rietrivier
16. Ruiterbosch

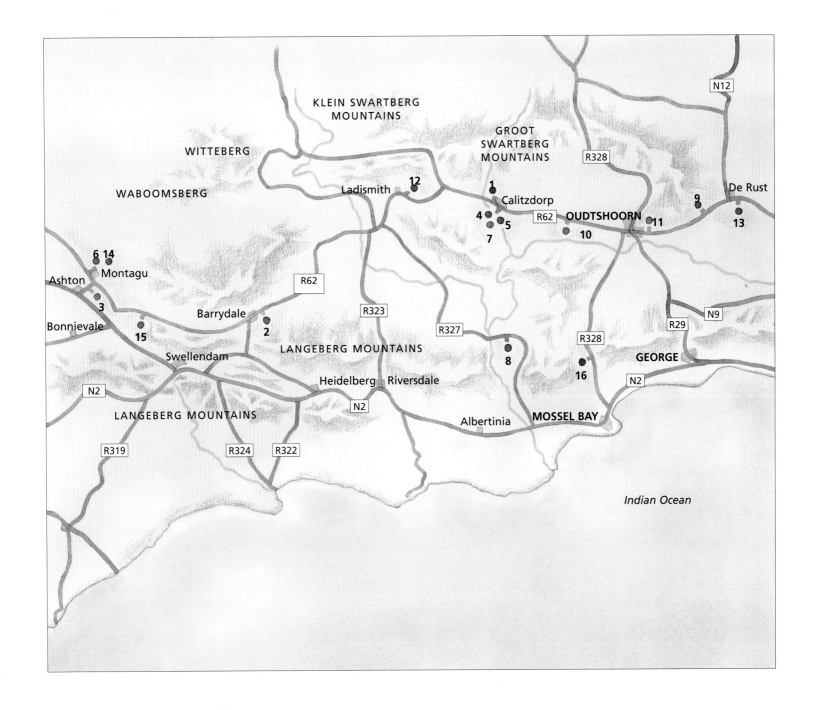

GLOSSARY

alluvial soils: fine-grained soils often found on valley floors, estuaries and beside rivers; usually a fertile mix of sand, silt and mud

ampelographer: a trained vine-plant expert

arrested fermentation: the premature halting of the fermentation process by the vintner, either by adding alcohol (for fortified wines) or cooling the wine down to 6° C or below

Balling: unit of measurement to determine the dissolved compounds in grape juice, thereby indicating the level of grape sugar

barrel toasting: exposing to flame the staves of a barrel in the making; this imparts a certain flavour to the wine matured in that barrel for months or years

base wine: a wine from a single variety, fermented totally dry, which is used as one of the building blocks in assembling a blended sparkling wine

basket press: an old-fashioned round press made of carefully spaced wooden staves. It has a wooden disc that is manually or hydraulically screwed down onto the grapes, allowing the juice to run out between the staves

Bordeaux-style blend: a blended red wine made up from two or more of the varieties common in Bordeaux, France, including Cabernet Sauvignon, Cabernet Franc and Merlot

botrytis: a fungus, *Botrytis cinerea*, which attacks ripe grapes. When harvested and vinified, these grapes are made into very sweet wine.

bottle-ageing: the process by which wine, a living product, changes and develops in the bottle

bush vines: vines left to grow naturally as a bush instead of being trained onto trellis wires

calcareous soils: a limestone-based soil, sometimes mixed with some clay

canopy management: the various practices involved in tending to the vine, from trellising to pruning

canopy: the foliage of the vine

carbonic maceration: fermentation takes place within the whole berries of bunches sealed in a tank with carbon-dioxide, while the normal fermentation of juice squeezed out by the pressure of the top layers of bunches continues

clone: a group of vines that has been propagated from a single mother vine; different clones will come from different mother vines and have different characteristics, without losing the basic character of the variety

cold fermentation: the lowering of the temperature of the juice – which automatically rises as a result of the fermentation process – by running cold water over or through sleeves on the jacket of stainless-steel fermentation tanks and thereby preventing the dissipation of aroma and flavour

crusher: a machine, usually featuring two counter-rotating rollers, that splits the berries, allowing easy penetration by the yeast during fermentation; sometimes combined with a destemmer, which removes the berries from the bunch

downy mildew: a fungal disease that attacks the young leaves which drop off, limiting photosynthesis, delaying fruit ripening and resulting in thin, light wines; particularly common to the Cape with its warm, sometimes humid summers

dry wine: with a residual sugar level of 4g/l or less

Elsenburg: winemaking education and research institute in Stellenbosch

filtering: sending a wine through a filter to remove any particles that may remain, before bottling it (some think this strips the wine of aromatic and flavourful elements)

fining: the use of a product – gelatin, bentonite, casein or egg-white – to remove solid matter (bits of grape flesh or skin, for example) from a fermented wine

fortified wine: wine to which alcohol, usually in the form of grape or brandy spirit, is added

French Huguenots: French Protestants who fled to the Cape from 1688 to escape persecution by the ruling Catholics

goblet vine: a vine pruned into a rounded, bowl shape

Kloppers Commission of Enquiry into Chardonnay: the Presidential commission that in 1986 investigated the unofficial importation of vine cuttings by some grape growers, impatient with the long quarantine period imposed by the Department of Agriculture, and found that what was thought to be Chardonnay was actually a lesser French variety called Auxerrois

Late Harvest: wine made from grapes harvested late in the season, with between 20g/l and 30g/l of residual sugar

lees (or sediment): the dead yeast cells, grapeskins, seeds and flesh, tartrates and fining agent deposits that settle at the bottom of a tank or barrel in which fermentation is occurring.

loamy soils: a good, crumbly soil, combining clay, sand and silt, but sometimes too rich for vines that need some stress to deliver concentrated fruit

maceration: allowing the juice to ferment on the skins

malolactic fermentation: the chemical process that sees the conversion of hard malic acids into softer lactic acids

off-dry wine: with a residual sugar of between 4g/l and 12g/l

phenols/phenolics: chemical compounds that give a grape its colour, tannin and flavour and are influenced by the way the vine develops

phylloxera: an aphid or louse that attacks the vine roots and branches, leaving it prone to lethal infection; originates in the USA and combatted by grafting vines onto phylloxera-resistant American rootstock

port shipper: traditionally and still mainly British-owned firms, based at Vila Nova da Gaia in Oporto, that buy wine from the cellars up the Douro River for the making or further maturation of port in their own cellars before shipping it to England for markets across the globe

potstill brandy: fine brandy that is distilled from grape must in a traditional copper potstill in the style of Cognac

powdery mildew: also called oïdium, proliferating in warm climates under shaded canopies; a cobweb-like fungus that attacks the vine, resulting in poor berry-set, low yields and off-odours in the wine

racking: allowing wine to run off or pumping it off the sediment in the tank or barrel

rebate wine: lesser-quality wine sold off for distilling into brandy, and for which excise issues a tax rebate

reductive winemaking: minimising the exposure of juice and wine to oxygen

residual sugar: the unfermented sugar left in a wine after fermentation (grape sugars are converted into alcohol)

Rupert & de Rothschild: SA billionaire luxury-goods mogul and wine-estate owner Anton Rupert and the late Baron Edmond de Rothschild, proprietor of several French châteaux (including a share in Lafite-Rothschild) invested in a new cellar at Fredericksburg in Paarl in 1998.

screw (continuous) press: a large Archimedes screw with a decreasing pitch for greater pressure to press large quantities of grapes

second fermentation: the fermentation that a Cap Classique or Champagne undergoes in the same bottle in which it is ultimately sold

sediment: a mixture of the gross lees (dead yeast cells and fragments of the grape) and other solid matter that precipitates out of the wine when in tank or barrel; harmless natural deposits including tartrate crystals that settle out in a bottle of wine

semi-sweet wine: a broad term for a wine with a residual sugar of between 12g/l and 30g/l

Shiraz disease: seemingly confined to the Cape and can affect Shiraz, Merlot and Malbec. It is spread by grafting; shoots fail to atrophy into hard wood and the plant loses its leaves very late, showing the gold and red colour typical of leafroll-infected vines; affects berry set and fruit yield

shy-bearing: a vine or variety that produces a small number of bunches on each plant

snowline vineyards: those high up on mountain slopes

sour rot: a combination of bacteria, fungus and yeast that infects ripe berries with a split skin; it thrives in rainy, humid weather

Special Late Harvest: a wine made from full-ripe grapes with a sugar content of not less than 21 Balling and a residual sugar content of between 20g/l and 50g/l

Stellenbosch Farmers Winery SFW): a leading Cape wine and spirit producer/wholesaler

stuck fermentation: when the fermentation process is stopped mid-way by natural occurrences, such as lack of yeast activity or excessively cold temperatures

tank sample: a wine that has not yet undergone final preparation, such as fining and filtering, for bottling

tannins: a group of organic compounds found in the wood, stems, pips and skins of trees, plants and fruits, including the grape and the oak barrels in which wine is fermented or matured; they give an astringency to a wine that can soften with age

terroir: the combination of the soil, climate and geographical site or aspect in which a vine is grown, which determines the character of the wine made (some believe the role of humans should be included in the definition)

vine stock: vine cuttings for propagation

vintage: the year in which the wine was made

viticulture: the science of vine cultivation

Vitis vinifera: the genus (*vitis*) to which the specie of plant the vine (*vinifera*) belongs

white port: made from white grape varieties or from white-fleshed red varieties with minimal or no contact with the skin (from which the colour of a red wine is extracted)

wine routes: the various wine districts that have opened their doors to the public for tastings and sales. In 1971 Frans Malan, Spatz Sperling and Niel Joubert opened the Stellenbosch wine route

wooding: the practice of fermenting and/or maturing a wine in oak barrels

BIBLIOGRAPHY

David Biggs, *Any Port in a Storm*, Ampersand, Kenilworth, 1998

Oz Clarke's Wine Guide, Websters Mitchell Beazley, London, 1995

Decanter (UK) Magazine, Prestige Magazines, London, 1992-1999

Helen Exley, *Wine Quotations*, Exley Publications, Herts, UK, 1994

Phyllis Hands, Dave Hughes *Wines and Brandies of the Cape of Good Hope*, , Stephan Phillips, Somerset West, 1997

Dave Hughes, Phyllis Hands, John Kench, *The Complete Book of South African Wine*, Struik, Cape Town, 1988; *South African Wine*, Struik, Cape Town, 1992

Hugh Johnson, *The Story of Wine*, Mitchell Beazley, London, 1996

Allan Mullins, Myrna Robins, SA *Pocket Guide to Food & Wine*, Tafelberg, Cape Town, 1997

John & Erica Platter, *John Platter's South African Wine Guide*, Stellenbosch, 1982-1997; Creda, Cape Town, 1998-1999

Jancis Robinson, *Vines, Grapes and Wines*, Mitchell Beazley, London, 1994; *The Oxford Companion to Wine*, Oxford University Press, London, 1994.

Joanna Simon, *Discovering Wine*, Mitchell Beazley, London, 1994

Tom Stevenson, *The New Sotheby's Wine Encyclopedia*, Dorling Kindersley, London, 1997

Roger Voss, *Guide to the Wines of the Loire, Alsace, the Rhône*, Mitchell Beazley, London, 1992

Wine (SA) Magazine, Ramsay, Son & Parker, Cape Town, 1993-1999

Wine Magazine's Pocket Guide to Wines & Cellars of South Africa 1999, Ramsay, Son & Parker, Cape Town, 1998

INDEX